AMERICAN LYNCHING

AMERICAN LYNCHING

Ashraf H. A. Rushdy

Yale UNIVERSITY PRESS

NEW HAVEN AND LONDON

Published with assistance from the foundation established in memory of Amasa Stone
Mather of the Class of 1907, Yale College.

Yale University Press books may be purchased in quantity for educational, business,
or promotional use. For information, please e-mail sales.press@yale.edu (U.S. office) or
sales@yaleup.co.uk (U.K. office).

Set in Franklin Gothic and Minion types by IDS Infotech, Ltd.

Printed in the United States of America.

Library of Congress Cataloging-in-Publication Data
Rushdy, Ashraf H. A., 1961–
    American lynching/Ashraf H.A. Rushdy.
        p. cm.
    Includes bibliographical references and index.
    ISBN 978-0-300-18138-8 (Hardcover) ISBN 978-0-300-20587-9 (paperback)
    1. Lynching—United States—History.   2. United States—Race relations—
History.   I. Title.
    HV6457.R867 2012
    364.1'34—dc23

                                                                    2012005835

A catalogue record for this book is available from the British Library.

For my beloved wife, Kidan

CONTENTS

PREFACE: AN AMERICAN ICON ix

ACKNOWLEDGMENTS xv

INTRODUCTION: THE STUDY OF LYNCHING 1

CHAPTER 1
The Rise of Lynching 22

CHAPTER 2
The Race of Lynching 51

CHAPTER 3
The Age of Lynching 69

CHAPTER 4
The Discourse of Lynching 94

CONCLUSION: THE MEANINGS OF LYNCHING 123

EPILOGUE: AMERICAN LYNCHING 154

NOTES 157

BIBLIOGRAPHY 191

INDEX 209

PREFACE

An American Icon

In 1901 Thomas Dixon, Jr., began writing his Klan romances, *The Leopard's Spots* and *The Clansman,* which would become the basis for D. W. Griffith's 1915 movie, *Birth of a Nation.* The movie, which in turn inspired the birth of the new Klan in Georgia, had as one of its key episodes the Klan killing of Gus, a would-be black rapist. This incredibly popular film was viewed by millions and publicly endorsed by then President Woodrow Wilson and at least one Supreme Court justice. It seemed, in the apropos words of one historian, as if "all America had vicariously joined a lynch mob." Also in 1901, Mark Twain wrote an essay as an introduction to a proposed multivolume history of lynching, what he called this "epidemic of bloody insanities"; he titled this brief essay "The United States of Lyncherdom."[1]

Here were two visions of the nation at the turn of the twentieth century—one a glorious celebration of America as a nation redeemed through the reuniting of the South and North, a birth requiring the death of the Negro; the other a tragic jeremiad of America as a nation united only through acts of ritual violence against a reviled caste in the otherwise not "United States." Specific lynchings happened in towns and counties, patterns of lynching could be found in counties and states, but lynching itself was a national practice, and a practice that helped define the boundaries of the nation. The primary reason antilynching advocates wanted to implement a federal antilynching law was that state courts consistently refused to indict or condemn members of lynch mobs, but the antilynching advocates also wanted to make a federal case out of lynching itself, to show it as the shame or crime or sin not of a town or county or state, but of the nation.

Is lynching American, then? If lynching is defined in its broadest sense as a form of collective vigilante justice—the extralegal pursuit of vengeance against an offender of communal moral standards—then we cannot say that lynching is uniquely American. Every human society has practiced some form of lynching. Mobs have murdered for religious reasons, as happened in fifth-century Egypt when a mob of pagans and anti-Arian Christians beat to death George of Cappadocia, the bishop of Alexandria and the titular head of Egypt's Christian community, before parading his body through town and then burning it. Mobs have murdered for political reasons, as happened in 1992 when a mob of Taliban captured deposed Afghanistan leader Muhammad Najibullah, castrated him, beat him to death, and then hanged his body from a traffic warden's observation tower.[2] Indeed, lynching is often described in nineteenth- and twentieth-century political writing as an atavistic activity—the crime of barbarians, the action of the uncivilized—because it is, literally, the form of retributive justice human societies must have employed prior to the organization of institutions of modern nation-states' judicial and police power.

Yet many have held that lynching is, if not uniquely then distinctively, an American activity. "The United States is the native heath of lynching," wrote Lewis Blair in 1894. Even more to the point, he concluded that lynching constituted "a distinguishing feature of American Evangelical Christian civilization." Writing the first academic book-length study of lynching in 1905, James Cutler traced the history of vigilante activity in other continents before calling it a "fact" that "lynching is a criminal practice which is peculiar to the United States." He, like Blair, saw it as constitutive of the national identity when he concluded that "our country's national crime is lynching." Ida B. Wells had maintained this same point in 1895 when she pointed out that "no other civilized nation stands condemned before the world with a series of crimes so peculiarly national."[3] Indeed, not only did many intellectuals believe lynching to be a distinctively American crime, but some went so far as to suggest that even within America it was uniquely the work of "free-born American citizens," not naturalized Americans, or even "foreigners" or "political anarchists."[4]

In the first half of the twentieth century, antilynching advocates would continue to insist, as did the National Association for the Advancement of Colored People (NAACP) in 1919, that "the United States has for long been the only advanced nation whose government has tolerated lynching." In 1924 the NAACP referred to lynching as the "Great American Specialty," and in 1934 placed a caption under the picture of a hanged lynch victim: "This is what happens in America—*and no other place on earth!*"[5]

Why, then, do some American intellectuals believe lynching to be a uniquely American phenomenon, something akin to another form of

American exceptionalism? Partly, this is a result of political rhetoric in the antilynching campaign. When Wells and Cutler and the NAACP noted that lynching occurs only in the United States, this information is meant to shame the citizens who countenance the practice or at least do not agitate for the passage of legislation that punishes those who do it. But there is something more than political rhetoric at work here. Lynching is in some senses distinctively American. A history of the practice in America would demonstrate the ways Americans have thought of lynching as an expression of ideals they hold sacred—ranging from Puritan religious ideals of communal lustration to Revolutionary political ideals of popular sovereignty. The contexts in which lynchings occurred in America—on the frontier, in corrupt cities, as a way of controlling labor and community mores—are just that, contexts.

The truly meaningful place to locate what is distinctively American about lynching is in the political traditions Americans have formulated and the political myths they have held. In the case of lynching, that requires us to return to the earliest institutions of American life and see how they shaped the central ideology of lynching: the belief in the right of a group of people to punish by virtue of their own volition. That belief, I argue, developed out of the two first institutions to be established, almost simultaneously, on American soil. The first institution, the House of Burgesses, defined the terms of freedom, while the second, slavery, created and refined through laws passed by the House of Burgesses, defined its opposite. As we will see in this book, lynching arose precisely out of an ideology of the sense of what rights accrued to someone possessing democratic freedom (which evolved into the argument for popular sovereignty), and that that sense of those rights was directly and formally a product of the earliest and most essential mandates of a slave society. It is, then, in the earliest American institutions that we can find the origins of the political traditions that would come to define and be used to defend American lynching.

Let me clarify first the terms of the argument I am making here, and then the implications of that argument.

In stating the lynching is distinctively American because of the political myths and the political traditions that developed in the earliest American institutions—the House of Burgesses, which governed the transfer of property; and slave laws, which governed property itself—I am not claiming a directly causal connection between those original institutions in the first colonies founded in Virginia and the later lynchings that spread like a miasma across the nation. Lynchers in the eighteenth and nineteenth centuries did not understand or explain their actions by referring to those earlier statutes, nor did they necessarily believe them to be the source of the sanction on which they acted. Instead, I am claiming that the imperatives that drove the House of Burgesses to pass formative laws that defined the terms of freedom and enslavement, and identified the appropriate bearers of those forms of existence, produced both a formal set of legal statutes and an informal suite of ideological and intellectual rationales concerning the place of collective violence in the service of controlling freedom and slavery that, in turn, created, informed, and influenced the very cultural mores that lynchers acted on and justified. Slave laws, then, did not *cause* lynchings, but they did directly produce the very cultural values that inspired and gave lynching its impetus in America.

What is implied in that argument, then, is that lynching is not an aberration in American history, which some antilynching advocates hopefully suggested, but a result of the fundamental contradictions that faced the nation at its origins. That is what makes lynching distinctively American—that the earliest American legislators solved a set of intractable problems by legislating bills that promoted an act of collective violence, directed in certain ways at specific groups of people, that was originally, and later, meant to exhibit a particular kind of social power and exercise a particular kind of social control. What is *not* implied in this argument is that lynching is therefore uniformly practiced wherever the institution of slavery was established, or that it was absent where slavery was prohibited. What it means, rather, is that those laws created at the origins of the founding of the first states, in what would become the United States, produced a set of values and practices that would migrate with the westward expansion. The relative absence of lynchings in slaveholding Northern states and the occurrence of lynching in nonslaveholding western states is explained, then, by the extent to which the mores and established precedents that emerged from those original slave laws took hold of the imagination of the residents of those states, and to what extent they developed or relied on other forms of social control.

Finally, it should also be noted that what inspired the resistance to lynching was equally a product of those American cultural values that emerged at the origins of the nation. Antilynching advocates—both those who wished for the victory of law and order over anarchy, and those who wished the end of racial terrorism against African Americans—were inspired and moved by the same complex of cultural mores that valorized freedom as the defining feature of American life (the freedom from fear, in this case, to use the formulations that Franklin Delano Roosevelt employed). The crusaders and campaigns fighting for the end of lynching were also distinctively American in the same sense.

This book is a modest attempt to understand how lynching arose and evolved in America. In the Introduction, I discuss the problems involved in defining lynching as a practice, and then offer a working definition that is flexible and capacious without being diffuse. A major point in this chapter is that we need definitions that allow us to see the continuities in the evolution of lynching without losing sight of the specificities of the kinds of lynchings that arose at different historical moments. In the three chapters that follow, I describe the major contours in the history of American lynching, from its Revolutionary-era origins to its most recent recrudescence in the late twentieth century. In Chapter Four, I delineate what I am calling the "discourse of lynching," that is, the cultural narrative about lynching that emerged in the last two decades of the nineteenth century and became hegemonic thereafter. Finally, in the Conclusion, I attempt to discern just what deeper meaning we can find in the history and practice of lynching. I draw on two ways of understanding the *meaning* of lynching: first, to understand the practice as an expression of the particular motivations of those people who employ violence to effect and mask their ends; and, second, to understand it as an expression of those political ideas that emerged with the origins of the nation itself.

Part of our concern in this study is to examine the rationales and justifications that lynchers and their apologists produced, to tease out what these defenses of lynching reveal about American political discourse of all kinds. The most recent manifestation of that discourse has been African American public figures who have described their political ordeals as a "high-tech lynching" (Supreme Court Justice Clarence Thomas in 1991 at his Senate confirmation hearing) or the media coverage of a legal indictment for perjury as exhibiting an "unethical, illegal lynch mob mentality" (Detroit Mayor Kwame Kilpatrick in the 2008 State of the City Address). The rhetoric here is meant to evoke the image of lynching with which most Americans in the early twenty-first century are familiar—the vicious violence against a lone black man by a white mob. In these cases, then, the term "lynching" operates as shorthand for a particular historical experience, which also conveniently erases certain stubborn facts at odds with the evoked scenario—such as the African American woman law professor reluctantly bringing forth charges of sexual harassment, or the African American woman county prosecutor issuing the indictments.

But while we can rightly deplore the opportunistic rhetoric these politicians have employed to evade their responsibilities, we can also appreciate what changes in the society their claims of being lynched are meant to mark. These black politicians are tapping into a post–civil rights discourse that America is a nation of law, and that now, unlike the era of spectacle lynchings, people in a democratic society would not idly watch a lynching but would intervene in some way. What these claims suggest is that we do live in a different world, one in which the claim of being lynched is supposed to inspire widespread opposition, not celebration, one in which lynchings can be employed as metaphor because they are purportedly no longer employed as a material practice.[6]

At the same, time, we are also forced to recognize the ways that lynching as both metaphor and reality continues to haunt the republic. As we shall see later, America continues to witness actual lynchings, as it did in the 1998 lynching of James Byrd in Jasper, Texas. In more regular ways, there are frequent metaphorical employments of lynching as a way of terrorizing black Americans. In just the past few years, for instance, nooses were found in a Long Island town's police locker room after an African American man was named deputy chief, on a Columbia University black professor's office door, and in several incidents connected to the events around the so-called Jena 6 in Louisiana. Even then President George W. Bush, whose record of support for capital punishment is beyond reproach, recognized that in these cases the "noose is not a symbol of prairie justice, but of gross injustice," and that the lynchings for which the noose was a metaphor constituted a "shameful chapter in American history."[7] In the chapters that follow, I hope to demonstrate the extent to which the practice of lynching in American history is not only shameful but central, and how this practice is not merely a chapter but a theme running through the whole book.

ACKNOWLEDGMENTS

I would like to begin by thanking two people who read the complete manuscript carefully and thoughtfully and made extremely helpful suggestions for revisions. With uncommon attention and rigorous intelligence, Nathan Connolly and Jeff Kerr-Ritchie showed me where arguments could be more focused and where ideas could be more developed. I am indeed fortunate in having such conscientious and generous readers.

Of the people who have read parts of the manuscript, and who have provided me with key ideas, important references, and invaluable guidance along the way, I would like especially to thank Noreen O'Connor-Abel and Rochelle Gurstein, two expert and gifted readers who have made this book better for their commentary.

I would like to thank Laura Davulis at Yale University Press for her original interest in the manuscript, and for making this book possible. It has been a genuine pleasure working with her. I would also like to thank Jeffrey Schier for his intelligence and rigor in copyediting this book.

I, like every other author, could not do the work I do without the help and kindness of librarians. I have been particularly lucky in having some wonderful research librarians at the Olin Library at Wesleyan University, at the Sterling Library at Yale University, and at the National Humanities Center. In particular, I would like to thank Dianne Kelly and Erhard Konerding at Wesleyan for their gracious and considerate help throughout, and Katherine Wolfe for her dogged and successful pursuit of a critical text at just the moment I needed it.

I have been extraordinarily fortunate in having colleagues at Wesleyan who have been thoughtful and generous with their time and conversation. There are too many to name individually, but I would be remiss if I did not name Khachig Tölölyan, who has, over the course of twenty years, been a constant source of friendship and wisdom.

My family, extended all over the world, has made it possible for me to do the work I do in innumerable ways, large and small. My father and mother have been an endless source of support and love and encouragement. Everything I have done is a small tribute to their commitment, to their compassion, and to their example. I would like especially to thank my brother Amgad, who has been a role model and a devoted supporter for all my life; he has made more things possible than I can thank him for. My sisters Janice and Senait have been steadfast believers in me and my work, and I thank them from the bottom of my heart. My niece Anna and my nephew Alex have watched me working on this book for most of their lives, and I am glad now to be less distracted during our family visits. In addition I would like to thank my aunts and uncles, especially Tante Nabila in Canada, Tante Ensuf and Amo Enayat in Egypt, and all of my Detroit family. My family in New Jersey, Nevolia Ogletree and Kassahun Checole, always asked me about my project and listened with genuine care when I was able to share, and showed incredible understanding when I wasn't. I am glad to present this to all of my family as a testament of their faith in me.

My sons, Zidane and Aziz, have lived with this book their entire lives without knowing it. I hope that when they are old enough to read it they realize why Poppy spent so much time reading and in front of the 'puter. During the writing of some of these chapters, they provided me with a much-needed reprieve; their joyous faces were always an antidote to the accounts I was reading of injustice and hatred. Many is the day when I happily turned from these accounts to relish the pleasure and joy they bring to every day, and to enjoy their infectious enthusiasm for all of life.

Finally, I end where I begin this book with my most profound and yet inexpressible gratitude to the person to whom it is dedicated—my wife, Kidan. She has been a constant and profound source of emotional and intellectual support in every way. She bore with loving patience the ebbs and flows of my writing; and, more importantly, she provided guidance and grounding and care. For all that she has done to allow me write this book, and for the much greater things she has done that have nothing to do with this book, I cherish her and dedicate this book to her.

AMERICAN LYNCHING

INTRODUCTION

The Study of Lynching

There is a crucial scene toward the end of Owen Wister's 1902 *The Virginian* that ties together and leads to the resolution of both the political and romance plots of the novel. Judge Henry, a former federal judge and now a Wyoming cattle rancher, engages in a debate with Molly Wood in order to justify the acts and career of the eponymous hero of the novel, the lover of Molly and the hired gunslinger from Virginia whose job is to kill cattle rustlers in Wyoming. As Judge Henry considers the task before him, he realizes that his defense cannot resort to "mere platitudes and humdrum formulas" because the stakes—the course of "true love" between Molly and the Virginian—are too high. In the end, the Judge, and love, prevail. He ably defends his politics, and Molly becomes resolved to what the man who will shortly become her husband does for a living.

What the Virginian does, what the judge defends, and what Molly accepts, is lynching. The judge justifies lynching in terms that had become long familiar by the 1880s and 1890s. Lynching, he argues, is ultimately a sign of the sovereignty of the people. Although laws are most often made and upheld by elected and appointed officials, it is the "people" who elect those officials and therefore remain the final arbiter of justice. Indeed, "far from being a *defiance* of the law," lynching, the judge concludes, is rather "an *assertion* of it—the fundamental assertion of self-governing men, upon whom our whole social-fabric is based." For the judge, popular sovereignty is the principle, lynching the practice. The other part of his defense is less robust, since he confronts a thicket of contradictions in defining the key terms of his "principle," notably identifying the "people." The reason the people have to lynch, he argues, is that the "courts, or rather the juries, into whose hand we have put the law, are not dealing the law." In other words, some "people" have to pursue justice outside the courts because other "people" fail to do it in the courts. The "people" is a convenient fiction here, as elsewhere, as we will see in the course of this book.

The marriage plot in *The Virginian* is ingenious in having a *federal* judge defend extralegal justice in order to encourage the marriage of Molly Woods, who is repeatedly called the "New England girl," to the "Virginian"—all now living in the West. Lynching, then, is both an emblem of popular sovereignty and the democratic principle that unites all parts of the United States (North, South, West). The defense of lynching makes possible the romance of the nation redeemed, as much as it leads to the marriage of the couple in question. We saw, in the Preface, that this dynamic was popular at the turn of the twentieth century, and that Thomas Dixon's Klan romances essentially followed the same formula. The crucial difference is that Wister condemns the kind of lynching Dixon celebrates. Indeed, the judge is most insistent on this point, repeatedly asserting that he sees "no likeness in principle whatever between burning Southern negroes in public and hanging Wyoming horse-thieves in private." The lynching of black Americans proves that the South is "semi-barbarous," while the lynching of horse thieves proves that "Wyoming is determined to become civilized."[1]

The distinction Wister makes in his novel in 1902 is the same one that the historian Hubert Howe Bancroft had earlier made in his 1887 book, *Popular Tribunals*. In defending vigilante groups, especially the San Francisco Vigilance Committees of 1851 and 1856, Bancroft had to distinguish between Southern and Western lynchers—the former "a turbulent, disorderly rabble, hot with passion, breaking the law for vile purposes," the latter a "convention of virtuous, intelligent, and responsible citizens with coolness and deliberation arresting momentarily the operations of law for the salvation of society."[2] Like Wister after him, Bancroft upholds the principle of popular sovereignty—that the people have a fundamental right to lynch—while attempting to make distinctions about what kinds of lynchings are acceptable manifestations of that principle, and what kinds are aberrations.

Three things are worth noting about the strategies Wister and Bancroft adopt in defending lynching. First, they are intent on seeing lynching as a manifestation of larger social, almost philosophical, issues—in this case, the rights of the "people" to express themselves immediately, unencumbered by the social apparatus of police and courts that they have established through intermediaries. Second, they see lynching as a phase in the evolution of a social order, a stage in the march of history from primitive societies practicing rudimentary revenge to modern societies with mature mechanisms of administering justice. Sometimes it becomes necessary to resort to lynching because of corruptions in those modern mechanisms, but lynching is nonetheless presented as a practice that will necessarily be replaced by a more "civilized" means of dispensing justice. Finally, they are both confounded by a problem of definition. They have to distinguish between two practices—to defend one and abhor the other—that share sufficient common properties as to be designated by the same name: lynching.

Bancroft and Wister provide a paradigmatic case of the problems faced by the contemporary students of lynching. We can identify the three questions they ask as fundamental to the study of lynching. First, in their defense of lynching, they ask the question of the relationship of lynching to a given set of enduring political principles—in this case, the people's rights under democracy to extralegal expression of their disapprobation of an identified victim. Second, in their suggestion of the place that lynching occupies as a common practice in the transition from barbarity to civilization (to use Wister's terms), they ask the question of the historical evolution of lynching in relationship to the other practices of the society. Finally, in confronting the difficulty of affirming that some lynchings are acceptable while others are not, they confront the question of definition, of how to distinguish what is an appropriate manifestation of the principle (democracy) at the appropriate historical moment (frontier or corrupt society) from what is an inappropriate act of gratuitous mob violence both historically and politically out of place. The questions, then, are essentially questions of the relationship of lynching to the political order of democracy, the relationship of lynching to the evolving historical state of the society, and the relationship of lynching to other forms of collective violence.

It should be noted that there are fundamental contradictions in the different answers Bancroft and Wister (and a host of others who preceded or followed them) have given to these questions. Most important, there is no way to reconcile the principle of the first issue (lynching is an example of democratic rights) with the assumption of the second (that lynching must fade as more mature societies develop more organized modes of dispensing justice). There can, at best, be an uneasy coexistence between a state that believes its police and judicial apparatus is fulfilling the responsibilities of protecting the people and meting out justice, and an unyielding principle that allows the people to police, judge, and execute on their own imperative. The principle (popular sovereignty) is inherently at odds with the model of historical evolution (maturing society). These are the kinds of pressing questions, and dilemmas, that make lynching an appropriate subject of study for those of us who wish better to understand the nature of all social action, all practices that produce and reproduce a society.

In the end, we will follow Wister's and Bancroft's example and attempt to understand both the larger social issues involved in lynching and the place of lynching in a historical trajectory, but we must first deal with the dilemma of definition that is as perplexing now as it was a century ago. We can proceed by first identifying some of the vexing problems that make it difficult to define lynching. These problems, I think, fall into two large categories—problems in general and problems of application. I will first identify some of those problems in general, and then, working with one of the most widely accepted definitions of lynching, explicate some of the problems in application. I will end by proposing how we might encompass, if not solve, the problem of definition, by pursuing a strategy of having two different kinds of definitions.

The problem Bancroft and Wister faced in defending lynching at the end of the nineteenth century is similar to the one a contemporary student confronts in defining lynching at the dawn of the twenty-first. There are different kinds of lynching, different sorts of acts, some of which are called lynchings and others not, driven by different motives, employing different strategies, and occurring in different historical contexts. For Wister and Bancroft, the problem was how to distinguish what they applauded as an act of popular sovereignty from what they deplored as an act of people's savagery. For the contemporary student of lynching, the problem is how to determine what precisely are the constitutive features of a lynching that make it a lynching, so that we can discern patterns and meanings in that particular kind of violence. How, in other words, can we define "lynching," given the multiplicity of acts, practices, and events that are called by that name or sometimes denied that name?

More and more, scholars of the history of lynching are recognizing that the "first question" they must address in any study of the phenomenon is, "What constitutes a lynching?"[3] And the more they do that, they more they recognize the complexities and difficulties in that task. Some are now suggesting that it is so fundamental a problem that it might require more than just additional rigor in identifying the characteristic features of the events that are understood as, or have been called, lynchings. At least one urges us to come up with a new term. Jackie Goldsby has recently argued that "the history of lynching poses too great a burden for one word to carry," and suggests that "to produce a history of lynching attentive to its constitution and operations through language, we need to invent a new name for the violence." And another decides that the current term is effectively inoperative. The leading scholar of the evolution of the word "lynching" in American history, Christopher Waldrep, has come to the conclusion that "the word 'lynching' cannot be defined."[4]

Given the range of events that the word "lynching" has been used to designate, the political agendas behind the definition of the term, and the other myriad problems in trying to come to a working definition, it is perhaps tempting to embrace the ambiguity in the term and claim it as what W. B. Gallie would call an "essentially contested concept," or agreeing with Waldrep that it simply cannot be defined. Before doing that, however, it might prove instructive to see how various definitions of lynching have limited our understanding of the practice and how they might be modified so that they do not. In other words, much of what we understand about the history and dynamics of lynching depends on how we define lynchings. For that reason, we cannot afford to be complacent with what appears a dominant, though largely undeclared, definition. For, in the end, whether we have an explicit or implicit definition, we are usually working with some model in mind, and it is preferable for that model to be transparent rather than opaque.

One way to encompass the problem is to provide two kinds of definitions, what I will call *capacious* and *specific*. The capacious definition distinguishes lynching from other kinds of social violence, murder, dueling, rioting, and so on. A capacious definition requires us to identify the rudimentary elements that make an event a lynching and distinguish it from another sort of act. The second kind of definition—the specific—distinguishes one sort of lynching from another, usually but not always based on the historical moment in which we find those lynchings. The capacious definition allows us to appreciate the historical continuity in the practice, while the specific permits us to see the historical particularities of the practice at different moments in the past. The combination of capacious and specific definitions, I believe, will allow us to see both the large-scale evolution and the distinct species of lynching in American history. I will suggest a working capacious definition at the end of this chapter. First, though, in order to see if that solution is the proper one, we need to see what the terms of the problem are.

For some readers, I imagine, the idea that "lynching" is an ambiguous term and difficult to define might seem unbelievable, and they might well look askance at a chapter devoted entirely to defining lynching— what Gore Vidal called "the kind of thing that gives mindless pedantry a bad name."[5] How, after all, can a practice that has such iconic properties be ambiguous? How can a term so easily employed in political rhetoric not be obvious?

That has partly been the problem—that "lynching" is a term more evocative than descriptive. For this reason, at this moment in our history a noose can be an effective material symbol of the practice, and a black male politician's reference to being a lynching victim is immediately resonant. It is likely that now most Americans think of African American men as the primary victims of lynching, and hanging as the primary mode. Billie Holliday's classic anthem captures this connection in one powerful couplet: "Black body swinging in the Southern breeze/Strange fruit hanging from the poplar trees."[6] Yet it is worth noting that this has not always been the case. In a foundational study of lynching less than two decades ago, a prominent historian in the early 1990s noted that for "many modern-day white Americans, lynch mobs conjure up images of cowboys, cattle rustlers, and a generally wholesome tradition of frontier justice"—what former President George W. Bush referred to as "prairie justice."[7] We can call this the problem of popular understanding, or the problem of fashion. The term "lynching" has, at different times in the nineteenth and twentieth centuries, connoted quite different historical acts among the population. This, as we saw, was the problem that confronted Wister and Bancroft.

A second problem is that this same term has been used to designate acts that demonstrate a wide range of diverse motives, strategies, technologies, and meanings. The term has been variously used to describe forms of corporal but not lethal punishment (whipping, tarring and feathering) as well as fatal punishment; the same term is used to define acts of rough justice in frontier societies lacking the apparatus of state judiciaries as well as acts of direct defiance of those state judiciaries in more established societies; it defines acts of vigilante justice or racial terrorism by long-standing vigilance committees, by terrorist groups, or by ad hoc mobs. It is a term, in other words, burdened by having to denote a remarkable range of acts of extralegal violence for varying purposes, by different kinds of agents, and through diverse means.

A third problem is that "lynching" is a politically encumbered term. During the Progressive era, politicians like Senators Ben Tillman and Rebecca Lattimer Felton and Governor Cole Blease defended lynching as a form of Southern chivalry, because lynching was an act that, for them, implied popular sovereignty and Southern honor.[8] Later, however, when the term came to imply the failure and not the apogee of a democratic civilization, politicians challenged the use of the term when it was applied to their constituencies in an effort to avoid the stigma attached to it. During the 1920s, governors from at least six states wrote to Monroe Nathan Work, the collector of data for the famed Tuskegee Institute lynching reports, requesting that he reclassify what was recorded as a lynching in their state.[9] Politicians would continue to contest the application of the term to their counties and states. In 1955 the governor of Mississippi insisted to the media and to the National Association for the Advancement of Colored People (NAACP) that Emmett Till was murdered, not lynched.[10]

Those opposed to lynching were also attuned to the politics of the term. Three major institutions of civil society—the Association of Southern Women for the Prevention of Lynching (ASWPL), the NAACP, and Tuskegee Institute—debated among themselves what could or could not be counted as a lynching. The NAACP accused the ASWPL of prematurely attempting to record a "lynch-free year" as a sign of its success, while the ASWPL and Tuskegee accused the NAACP of being more interested in propaganda than accuracy. The definition each agency used, whether inclusive or stringent, served a particular political end.[11]

These three problems—of diverse phenomena, diverse implications, and diverse political resonance—are representative of the kinds of difficulties facing those who want a tidy definition. These problems, I hasten to add, are neither insuperable nor particularly prohibitive. They are simply the type of problem one confronts when dealing with a given phenomenon that changes, in practice and meaning, over time. One is tempted to say that it would be the occupational hazard of the historian, were it not the occupation. The other type of problem, the problem of application, is more difficult because these consist of acts that limit the range of the subject in significant and, I argue, detrimental ways.

In order to address these types of problems, we can turn to one of the most influential historical definitions of lynching that in many ways has guided the contemporary study of the subject. James Cutler formulated that definition in the first book-length academic study of lynching in 1905. Cutler defined lynching as "an illegal and summary execution at the hands of a mob, or a number of persons, who have in some degree the public opinion of the community behind them." He emphasized the last point by claiming "it is not too much to say that popular justification is the *sine qua non* of lynching." By "popular justification" Cutler meant "public approval, or supposed favorable public sentiment, behind a lynching."[12] As Waldrep points out, this first definition emphasizing community support has "long been a touchstone" for twentieth-century reformers. Indeed, Waldrep in his 2002 book-length academic study of lynching uses something like the Cutler definition in his working definition of what constitutes a lynching—"an act of violence sanctioned, endorsed, or carried out by the neighborhood or community outside the law."[13]

There are deep problems with this definition—as a definition for the history of lynching, that is, as opposed to a specific type or era of lynching. The Cutler definition, published in 1905, draws on the types of lynching ascendant in the Progressive era—the large-scale lynchings that arose during the 1890s and began to diminish in frequency by the 1930s. These are the most iconic lynchings—attended by thousands of people, involving ritual acts of torture and dismemberment, and covered graphically in the newspapers. Because of the mass attendance and the news coverage, there does seem to be evidence of "favorable public sentiment." But these are only one type of lynching—the spectacle lynching of the

Progressive era—and by no means the only type. In fact, they were not even the most common type during that time. Lynchings during, before, and after had different dynamics and different degrees of community support, which cannot then be the sine qua non of lynchings.

Moreover, lynchers, for a century and a half, from the American Revolution to the interwar period, have claimed rather than enjoyed popular support. Edmund Morgan has brilliantly demonstrated that claims of "popular sovereignty"—on which claims of community support rest—are political fictions whose necessary characteristic is precisely "the impossibility of empirical demonstration."[14] The "proof" in such a case, then, is essentially the testimony of the lynchers and their apologists—that is, the channels for propagating and controlling information sympathetic to lynchers: newspaper coverage, editorials, sermons, and other informal testimonials from community members.

The main problem with this definition, then, is that it is too restrictive because it is premised on the idea that only one sort of lynching tableau is authentic, that only one dynamic constitutes a genuine lynching. Let us now trace some of the problems of application that have emerged in particular from historians' use of the restrictive Cutler definition. Because contemporary scholars so often implicitly assume, as did Cutler, that the Progressive era lynching was the authentic thing, they discount other kinds of collective violence as not being lynchings. We can see the problems with using a restrictive definition most clearly by looking at how historians treat the collective violence of the period before the Progressive era—particularly the years of Reconstruction.[15]

First, historians tend to find in Reconstruction either rudimentary or faux lynchings dissimilar in motive and level of popular support to the later spectacle lynchings. Waldrep, for instance, claims that contemporaries did not call the admittedly "brutal racial violence" of Reconstruction "lynchings" because "white societal support for the killings was not yet solid or beyond dispute." The term most often used during Reconstruction, he notes, is "outrage," a term, he suggests, that "implies a crime against the community" rather than "a killing carried out by the community."[16]

We can see here the way that the Cutler definition, with its tenet of societal support as the sine qua non of lynching, has overdetermined this historical interpretation in some crucial ways. First, it requires us to make a distinction between two words ("outrage" and "lynching") that much contemporary evidence shows to be specious. I am not in a position to say whether "lynching" or "outrage" was the more popular term, and I will defer to Waldrep, who notes that the term "outrage" appeared in headlines throughout the nation, and that it was a term preferred by many contemporaries to describe Reconstruction violence. I wonder, though, about the ways that the term "outrage" registered for those who used it. Consider the example of Albion Tourgée, the Union army veteran appointed to a judgeship in North Carolina during Reconstruction, someone particularly attentive to language as both a novelist for whom words were his stock in trade and a federal judge who understood the nuances of the terms describing extralegal violence during his tenure on the bench. Waldrep contends that the words used in "Tourgée's prose do not cry lynching; instead they shriek 'murder,' 'assassination,' and 'outrage.'"[17]

In his 1879 novel on Reconstruction, Tourgée does indeed offer a catalogue of violent activities under "the fearful category of 'outrages.'" But "outrage" for Tourgée does not at all imply the absence of communal support for violence. Indeed, at one point, he writes: "Many openly approved the course of the mob; others faintly condemned; and no one took any steps to prevent the consummation of the outrage threatened."[18] Even if "outrage" were the ascendant term for lynchings during Reconstruction, it did not, I think, imply the absence of widespread support, just as the term "lynching" did not imply the presence of it. (Again, recall that the support of the masses is a rhetorical strategy used to manipulate and not describe the phenomenon it names.)

In the end, "outrage" does not seem to suggest the difference from "lynching" that Waldrep insists on, as we can find a great deal of overlap in these terms, as Reconstruction writers used them. Consider the coverage of the crimes associated with Kinston, North Carolina, where five men were taken from jail and lynched (one white, four black), and then a white man was killed after firing into a group of black men he thought were assaulting a white woman near his house in Duplin County. When the *New York Herald* first reported the story, on January

30, 1869, the writer made a distinction between the two crimes, calling the multiple murder of the jailed men a "lynching" and the killing of the lone white man in his home an "outrage" (making the distinction in both the headline and the story). When two Ohio newspapers picked up the story, they reprinted the article verbatim but changed the headline. The *Cleveland Plain-Dealer* referred to the "Lynching and Outrages," making some distinction, while the *Cincinnati Daily Enquirer* elided all distinction when it referred to "The Recent Lynching Outrage." These words were often interchangeable, and editors did not hesitate to alter them as they saw fit. Indeed, when the *New York Herald* returned to this story nine months later, in an effort to connect those Kinston crimes to the Klan, it simply conflated the two crimes it had previously distinguished and explicitly referred to "lynching" as just one kind of "outrage" against law and order: "Among the most noted of these outrages was the lynching of a white man and five negroes who had been forcibly taken from Kinston jail."[19]

In many other cases, the two terms are used during Reconstruction journalism as they would come to be in the decades following 1880, with "outrage" reserved to describe the attempted rape that "lynching" is intended to punish. A representative article from the *Cleveland Plain-Dealer,* for example, tells us of the "outrage" against Alice Thompson, and the subsequent "lynching" of Charles Brown and Jacob Berryman. Likewise, the *Indianapolis Sentinel* reported that Eliza Chamberlain was "most fiendishly outraged" and that the culprit just caught was facing "threats of lynching." The *Baltimore Sun* seems to have used this terminology consistently through Reconstruction. In 1868, the newspaper called Isaac Moore's attempted assault on Ms. Oldfield an "outrage," and his subsequent hanging a "lynching." In 1877, it reported that George Jackson had "outraged" a little girl and subsequently suffered at the hands of a "lynching party."[20]

That verbal distinction, then, does not appear to hold. What is more important, though, is that the dependence on the restrictive Cutler definition also leads to a teleological reading of history, in which acts that look like lynchings before the 1880s are cast as "not yet" lynchings because they have not exhibited the trait Cutler defined as categorical, and which some historians use to make a categorical distinction between historical eras. Consider this example of that kind of teleological reading of history: the problem the historian who wants to validate the Cutler definition confronts is that Reconstruction-era violence *looks* like a Progressive-era lynching. The solution is not to question the definition, but rather to argue that the earlier mob (in Reconstruction) actively *anticipated* the definition and modified its actions accordingly. Waldrep, for instance, suggests that the Klan "designed their killings to resemble lynchings, hoping to win community support by making it look like they already had it." A mob of Klansmen, then, performs an action of hanging and shooting a person in much the same way that a mob during the Progressive era would do, but the difference is that the former replicates "the look of a lynching" in order to *pretend* it has "community support" while the latter has it.[21]

This insistence on reading the past as if its trajectory were inevitable, and the fact that earlier actors imitated later ones in anticipation, reveal something about how a restrictive definition can mislead us. It also reveals something about what some historians feel to be the stakes in denying the historical continuities in a practice when that continuity conflicts with their ready sense of established historical epochs. Waldrep, for example, goes into some detail about the importance of making the distinction between Reconstruction and the period following the 1880s, by again insisting on the Cutler criterion: "Understanding why racial violence in the Reconstruction era was not called lynching helps explain the difference between Reconstruction and the lynching era. . . . Once the white population seized power and rallied itself into a racial bloc, then, and only then, could they kill confident that they had the support of what they defined as the community. And they understood a community-sanctioned killing to be a lynching." Waldrep concludes that "to describe the Klan as guilty of lynching not only ignores an important part of Reconstruction history, but it also assumes that all white Southerners opposed Reconstruction or that they all accepted the Klan's definition of community."[22]

The historical record, however, shows that journalists regularly referred to Reconstruction and Klan violence as "lynching," without implying that the term indicated community support of the act. A representative 1868 article introducing the newly formed Klan to its readers in the *New-Hampshire Patriot and State Gazette* repeatedly described the Klan as lynching African Americans, purportedly to punish criminals and likely to derail racial political equality. The reporter for the *New-Hampshire Patriot and State Gazette,* writing in the midst of Reconstruction, does not make that kind of assumption when he uses the term "lynching" to describe Klan activity: "It is probable that the leaders of the 'Ku-Klux Klan' have an object far beyond that of lynching criminals who escape justice through the sympathy of governors or the connivance of courts and juries."[23] And the writer for the *New York Herald,* as we saw before, referred to Klan violence as both an "outrage" and a "lynching." Neither paper accepted the Klan's definition of community (and, indeed, community does not seem to matter at all to them, because they see lynching in quite different terms).

I have gone on at some length in exploring how the Cutler definition can cause tunnel vision in even the most astute historians because it is important for us to see how a restrictive definition can produce only a particular kind of historical interpretation, closing off some avenues of research that can prove incomparably fruitful. Let me be clear. I am by no means suggesting that we dispense with, or are disserved by, definitions that are particular rather than general—definitions, that is, that attempt to identify the key elements that make lynching during a specific historical moment distinctive. As I said above, I think the best way of proceeding in our attempt to understand the history of lynching is by having both specific and capacious definitions. Such a restrictive one as Cutler's, however, works better as a specific one for the era in which he wrote (the late nineteenth century) than as a capacious one for the entire trajectory of lynching in the American past.

There are good reasons that Waldrep wants to keep separate what he calls the "era of lynching"—those roughly five decades after 1880—from earlier epochs in American history. I will explore in detail in Chapter Three some of the reasons that this era is indeed distinctive and exceptional. It is worth spending a little time here, though, examining some of the challenges that other historians have faced—and that I will face—in making those distinctions. Here I want to look at a popular and seemingly compelling reason historians distinguish between Reconstruction violence and the lynchings of the 1890s, and then to examine what I think is one of the primary, unspoken reasons behind the dating of the era of lynching.

Historians of lynching have been loath to see the continuity from Reconstruction lynchings to spectacle lynchings because they believe that the lynchings of the earlier period are more politically motivated than those of the later. Fitzhugh Brundage, for instance, notes that while the "extralegal justice of Reconstruction presaged the epidemic of violence of the late nineteenth and early twentieth centuries, it also differed significantly. Much of Reconstruction violence was a direct attack on Republican state governments and ruling political parties. Lynch mobs later in the century, in contrast, rarely had such overtly political motives."[24] Brundage is quite correct that the later lynchings were rarely justified with any kind of overtly political statements, and that they were not apparently motivated by the same kind of narrowly defined political impetus as the violence of Reconstruction.

Nonetheless, we must also search through the rhetorical apologia for lynching during both epochs in order to detect the ways that these statements hid their politics within more popularly accepted justifications. Tourgée again helps us here. When he writes about extralegal violence against African Americans during Reconstruction, he notes that the violence was indeed *political*. It was an expression, he writes, of "an ineradicable sentiment of hostility to the negro *as a political integer.*" Yet, Tourgée also exposes the ways that these attacks are justified through subterfuge. When black people were whipped by the Klan, he tells us that the "reason *given* was that they had been *sassy:* the true reason is believed to be that they were acquiring property, and becoming independent." Using a specific case, Tourgée continues to make the case of how the justification for lynching differed significantly between Reconstruction mobs and Klan groups: "James Leroy was hanged by the Ku-Klux on Tuesday night, his tongue being first cut out, and put in his pocket. He was *accused* of having slandered a white woman. The truth is, he was an independent colored man."[25]

By demonstrating the indirection of the accusations, by showing that the reasons for lynchings during Reconstruction were as masked as the Klan night riders who executed them, Tourgée raises an important consideration. Might not the justifications given during the 1890s likewise hide the true reasons white mobs lynched black people? Let me be perfectly clear. There is a much more compelling record of lynchings from the 1880s to the 1930s that shows that there were more direct criminal allegations that led to lynchings. At least partly this is a result of the fact that there are substantial records for the later period that do not exist for the earlier. But it is also worth considering the degree to which these later lynchings were motivated by political concerns—both the specific concerns with black accumulation of wealth or electoral power, or the general concern of the threats to white supremacy. Without necessarily denying that there are more clearly defined "political" motives in the extralegal violence of Reconstruction than in that during the Progressive era, we can still note that in both form and stated motive the lynchings of Reconstruction are nonetheless lynchings.[26] James Leroy may have suffered what would be called an "outrage" for the political crime of being independent, but he was tortured, mutilated, and hanged for the alleged reason of being too free with a white woman in precisely the same way, and for the same allegations, as would thousands of African Americans during the half century following the end of Reconstruction. In other words, James Leroy was lynched.

Let me turn now to what I think is an implicit—and good—reason that historians insist on distinguishing the "age of lynching," and the reason it is most frequently said to commence in about 1880. In 1882, the *Chicago Tribune* began to publish an annual report that tabulated lynchings, offering data on lynching by provenance, alleged crime, and race. In subsequent years, the Tuskegee Institute followed suit, as did later the NAACP. It is that body of data that has proven invaluable for all later historians of lynching. And it is not surprising that a majority of books on lynching begin their survey of a given state or region in the early 1880s.

Indeed, the statistical data can cast a veritable spell on the student of lynching since there are so many variables and so much data to be manipulated. Lynchings can be classified and tracked by state, by region, by date, by season, by mode of murder, by alleged crime, by provenance of the victim (taken from a jail cell or not), and by race. These statistics also provide a seemingly concrete set of data that reveal patterns, which can then be used to expose causes (tied to seasonal or labor rhythms, for instance). In addition, these statistics are often used to argue for large-scale historical patterns of declining mob violence as signs of progress in race relations or policing. I do not deny that the data are important, and constitute a significant historical source, but without invoking Mark

Twain's gradation of deceit—lies, damned lies, and then statistics—we can nonetheless note the numerous ways they are flawed. At the core of the flawed data is the primary problem of definition, of determining what is or is not a lynching.

There are two particularly pressing problems in the statistical data we have available. The first is that it is limited to the years after 1880, which in itself is not so much of a problem. What is problematic is that historians of lynching who draw on that data tend to discount or actively dismiss any lynching that occurred prior to that year, with the assumption that only events that fit the implicit definition used by those agencies collecting that data are genuine lynchings.

The second problem is that within the years covered by the data, those agencies also did not count certain kinds of collective violence as lynchings. Consider, for instance, the case of an unnamed black man tortured to death, his fingers and toes amputated for souvenirs for the white mob spurred on by rumors of rampant black rapists. The fact that he was killed by a mob, employing the rationale conventionally used by lynchers during this era, and suffered the degrading rituals of mob violence common to spectacle lynchings would suggest that he was lynched. But because he was killed during the 1906 Atlanta race riot, he is not classified as such in the usual sources of statistical information on lynchings. Neither are the more than two dozen other African American victims of the Atlanta mob nor the numberless victims of other race riots in American history.[27]

What does it mean, then, when what looks by all accounts like a traditional lynching by any of the accepted definitions is discounted because it occurred in an urban space during a spree of mob violence or, as we saw in the case of Reconstruction, occurred prior to the conventional date at which lynchings began to be tabulated as lynchings? First, it means that the body of data (the routinely offered numbers from the Tuskegee, *Chicago Tribune*, and NAACP surveys) that is the source of so much of the scholarship on Progressive-era lynchings is quite limited and misrepresentative—limited by virtue of the dates of its compilation (from the 1880s to the 1940s) and misrepresentative to the extent that it does not account for victims of so-called race riots (which are more often white massacres of black victims). That in turn means that much of the interpretation of lynchings, insofar as they are derived from the supposed patterns of lynching by demography and chronology, are likewise limited and subject to some skepticism. The suggestion that lynching became a crime against black people in the year when the data show more black than white people being lynched (1886) can be disproved by taking account of the lynching of African Americans during slavery and Reconstruction. The suggestion of who was the "typical" victim of a lynching or what constituted the dynamic of the typical lynch mob is likewise inaccurate to the extent that it ignores those earlier periods or dismisses later acts of collective violence as something other than lynchings.[28]

These, then, constitute some of the most important problems in the study of lynching. They can be described as intellectual problems and technical problems. The intellectual problems are those found in Wister and Bancroft at the beginning of this chapter—the problem of comprehending the philosophical defense of lynching as a quasi-democratic code, the problem of appreciating the historical vision of those who situate lynching as a practice that waxes and wanes in relation to the evolution of other mechanisms for ensuring justice. It is that subject, that intellectual problem, which we will be spending the rest of the book attempting to understand and explicate. The technical problems are those concerning the data and definitions of lynching. It is that subject, and a possible solution to it, that we will spend the rest of this chapter attempting to limn.

We have seen, then, that the definitions historically and still used by scholars of lynchings are problematic to the extent that they exclude events that should be included, and they do so because they draw on the most iconic lynching scenario—the Progressive-era spectacle lynching—and then define any earlier, later, or other form of collective violence as something else. What might allow us to get around this problem is to try and develop a series of flexible definitions attuned to the changing dynamics of collective extralegal violence. For the subject of our study to be most meaningful, to open up for us the deepest significance of vigilante mob violence, we need to be able to discern both the *specificity* and the *continuity* of lynching in America. We need, in other words, to ask what acts of extralegal mob violence in any given era meant, and the meaning of the trajectory of these diverse acts in different historical epochs. For us to be better able to do that, we need definitions that are both capacious and specific.

The advantage of a capacious definition is that we can better appreciate the continuity of the phenomenon. For instance, we would be able to see in what ways mob violence at different times is a protest against the state's monopoly on punishment, or a resistance to the state itself. With a capacious definition, we can more clearly see the common impetus that motivated acts otherwise as different as, say, the hanging of James Stuart by the 1851 San Francisco Vigilance Committee and the immolation of Jesse Washington by a mob of fifteen thousand in Waco, Texas, in 1916. They were both challenges to the state by differently organized groups (the Vigilance Committee had offices and officers, the Waco mob was a seemingly ad hoc affair) that acted on the pretext that the state was unable to punish the alleged crime effectively and, in the explicit words of the Committee and the implicit beliefs of the mob, that "we, the people, are superior to law."[29]

The advantage of specific definitions, on the other hand, is that they allow us to appreciate the significant differences in motives, forms, and practices in acts of collective violence at a given time. What is important here is not necessarily the principle the actors share (resistance to the state) but the more immediate and more pressing ways they pursue that resistance. We can better sense the difference between the hanging of Stuart and the immolation of Washington by attending to the differences between the organized forms pursued by the Vigilance Committee and the relatively disorganized collective violence of the mob in Waco, say, or the difference between a nativist sensibility in the West in the 1850s and a white supremacist one in the South in the 1910s.

Having the combination of a capacious definition and a set of specific historical definitions will allow us to discern the continuity in the *longue durée* and also to appreciate the distinctiveness of a particular set of acts performed by groups of people with variegated motives in different periods in American history. The focus on continuity does come with some costs, though, and it is only fair we acknowledge them here. The 1780s, the 1830s, the 1880s, the 1930s, and the 1990s—to select decades to which we give some extended attention in what follows—are obviously very different historical moments that contain their own specific conflicts, and their own particular political, economic, and social contexts. I attempt to address those differences where I can, especially in identifying the kinds of lynchings that evolve from one age to the next, but, to some extent, I honestly do not offer much extended analysis of those contextual differences. The reason has to do with focus. Given what I think is the prevalent trend in the current state of scholarship on lynching—that is, that it emphasizes discontinuity—I think it more important now to focus on the ways that the practice retained identifiable features over the course of more than two centuries. It is only by doing that, I believe, that we can address what I think is a deep flaw in the scholarship, namely, that it does not give much or proper attention to lynching during the periods of slavery and Reconstruction and, more generally, that it does not adequately recognize just what is continuous in the practice.[30]

Throughout the first three chapters and in the Conclusion, I will be identifying the various historically specific definitions of what constituted a lynching during several different epochs in American history. We can end this chapter by discussing briefly the rudimentary capacious definition that has guided the research and writing of this study.

That definition attempts to identify the minimal number of maximally shared characteristics that distinguish lynchings from other forms of social violence. So that it can be most representative, it draws on both legal precedents and earlier definitions produced by civil society groups, in other words, by both governmental and nongovernmental agencies that had a stake in offering differently inflected broad definitions.

The government law that I most draw on—and the one that provided a model for most later ones—is what historians recognize as the "first legal definition" of lynching in the 1896 law passed by the Ohio legislature: "That any collection of individuals, assembled for any unlawful purpose, intending to do damage or injury to any one or pretending to exercise correctional power over other persons by violence, and without authority of law, shall for the purpose of this act be regarded as a 'mob,' and any act of violence exercised by them upon the body of any person shall constitute a 'lynching.'"[31]

The civil society definition that has most guided the capacious definition I use comes from the 1940 summit of antilynching advocates called in the wake of the acrimonious debates among Tuskegee, ASWPL, and the NAACP. The summit defined "lynching" by noting four necessary conditions: "There must be legal evidence that a person has been killed, and that he met his death illegally at the hands of a group acting under the pretext of service to justice, race, or tradition."[32] It should be noted that two of the agencies that attended and approved the definition at the summit—the NAACP and the ASWPL—ended up contesting it later, the NAACP because it did not cover enough and the ASWPL because it covered too much and, in their words, could be used "to convert into a lynching the death of every Negro at the hands of white persons."[33] That disagreement and dissent does not invalidate the definition; I think it tells us something important about the political agendas of the groups, and the political climate of their times.

Drawing on these two definitions, among others, and attempting to identify those characteristics that most evidently distinguished lynchings over the past two and a half centuries of American life, I offer the following working capacious definition: *a lynching is an act of extralegal collective violence by a group alleging pursuit of summary justice.*

Let me note what questions are assumed—or begged—in each clause of this definition (again, striving for transparency and acknowledging the premises instead of hiding them). Let me begin with the three key words at the heart of the definition, "extralegal collective violence": 1) what constitutes "extralegal" depends on our accepting the "legal" status of the state (a status that at various times is more or less obviously apparent and/or contested); 2) what is "collective" or a "group" or a "mob" is open to interpretation: state legal codes define a "mob" either with ambiguity—"any number" (Alabama, Indiana), "a collection of people assembled for unlawful purpose" (Nebraska, Ohio, Virginia)—or by designating a number ranging from "three or more persons" (Pennsylvania) to "twelve or more persons who are riotously or tumultuously assembled" (Massachusetts);[34] 3) what type of "violence" rises to the level of lynching differs at different times (from corporal to lethal).

The clause that identifies motive—"alleging pursuit of summary justice"—is, I believe, a useful corrective to the Ohio law and summit definition's insistence on pretense ("pretending to exercise correctional power" and "under the pretext of service to justice, race, or tradition"). It employs the language lynchers use ("summary justice"), which strikes me as more accurate of what these mobs do—they not only correct, that is, punish, but they also police and judge in other ways. Additionally, they do not pursue "justice" as the summit definition has it, but only a particular form of justice ("summary") that they cast as more efficient and effective than formal or state-sanctioned justice. Finally, it is important to emphasize what mobs allege in order to compare that with what they do. Lynchers almost always claim to pursue "summary justice"— justice, that is, not restrained or averted by the state's legal apparatus— but that claim (that allegation) is often at odds with what manifestly appears to be a mob's actions in exercising social control of a victimized group, sometimes represented in the punishment of a particular individual and other times in the mob violence performed against a specified population.

The final point I wish to make about this definition concerns the term "act." I have already noted above that these acts, at different times, meant different levels of physical violence—from shaming rituals to murder. In addition, it is important to recognize that "acts" are not isolated events unconnected to other kinds of acts. They constitute a continuum with other forms of extralegal policing of social groups— both earlier in the nation's history and in the moment of that particular mob's formation. For that reason, some riots can be lynchings or can contain lynchings as part of the actions of the riot. Riots that involve what a historian of rioting in America calls "actions of communal regulation" (so-called race riots and other pogroms) differ from lynchings only in that they have multiple victims and occur in more widespread terrain. They often start with lynchings and develop into riots.[35] These kinds of riots would be counted as lynchings. Other forms of rioting, around particular political issues or during elections, would not fit within this definition.

The questions assumed or begged by this definition are not unimportant, but they are less important for this book than having a definition that permits us to class together different acts that share enough common properties as to reveal something meaningful about the persistence, depth, and trajectory of this particular form of American violence. With that capacious definition guiding us, then, we can now turn to the specific forms that lynchings took over the course of two and a half centuries. We can begin by turning to the beginnings of that particular kind of violence that came to be named "lynching."

1

The Rise of Lynching

At the National Convention of Colored Men held in Syracuse, New York, in early October 1864, the Reverend H. H. Garnet reminded his listeners of a particularly notorious act of mob violence done the previous July during the New York City draft riots. After an African American man was hanged from a tree, a member of the largely Irish-American mob took "a sharp knife, cut out pieces of the quivering flesh, and offered it to the greedy, blood-thirsty mob, saying, 'Who wants some nigger meat?'" Reflecting on the uniformly kind treatment he had received while he traveled in Ireland, "from Belfast to Cork, and from Dublin to the Giant's Causeway," Garnet wondered what could have happened "that men crossing the ocean only should change as much as they." He himself concluded that the reason for the change from generous Irish to race-baiting Irish-Americans was "the debasing influence of unprincipled American politicians."[1]

Garnet's question invites some serious reflection about the processes through which mostly European immigrants became inculcated into a peculiarly American form of racial violence. The work of more than "unprincipled American politicians," although they can certainly shoulder their share of the blame, that process has its own beginnings in the very origins of the American republic itself. The story of how violence came to be "a determinant of both the form and the substance of American life," as Richard Maxwell Brown phrases it, is arguably the concurrent story of how a people came to define themselves as

Americans, and, especially, of how they came to define themselves through the practice of systemic forms of violence against people they defined as not Americans.[2] One part of that complicated story begins for us during the Revolutionary War, when Americans were fighting to define an identity as American as the independence they had already declared.

"WITH THE JOINT CONSENT OF NEAR THREE HUNDRED MEN": REVOLUTIONARY WAR, 1780–1782

Although scholars throughout the nineteenth and early twentieth century offered several competing stories and myths of the European, biblical, and ancient origins of vigilante, extralegal justice, there is fairly widespread consensus that the origins of the term "lynch law" to define the practice of vigilante violence are to be found in the Revolutionary War.[3]

They are more specifically to be found in the actions of the militia of Bedford County, Virginia. During the summer of 1780, the militia captured what it described as "insurgent" Tories. They whipped two of these enemy combatants and hanged a third, all without a trial or military tribunal of any kind. One member of the militia, Colonel William Campbell, justified the hanging of the "insurgent" Tory by insisting that it was done "I believe with the joint consent of near three hundred men."[4] The leader of the Bedford County militia was a man named Colonel Charles Lynch.

The Governor of Virginia, Thomas Jefferson, wrote a tactful letter to Lynch to commend him for what he had done, although Jefferson, realizing just what precedent had been set by Lynch's actions, suggested that in the future Colonel Lynch ought to take any prisoners he captured and deliver them to the Commonwealth rather than deal with them in his own way. "The method of seizing them at once which you have adopted is much the best," Jefferson noted. "You have only to take care that they be regularly tried after," he continued, suggesting that Lynch consult the attorney for the Commonwealth in Bedford County about how to proceed in those trials.[5] For Jefferson, what Campbell claimed was the "joint consent" of the people was apparently not the kind of force or authority he wanted to replace the courts and legal system of the Commonwealth of Virginia.

Charles Lynch, however, ignored Jefferson's advice and continued to pursue his own course. He and his militia continued to resort to extrajudicial forms of examination and punishment in what he called "trying torys &c &c." Indeed, two years after his first efforts at extrajudicial punishment of those he captured, he began to use the phrase "Lynchs Law" to describe the rough justice he dispensed to those he deemed enemies of the state. Those placed under that rubric included people who traded illegally in slaves and, in one particularly notable instance, Welsh lead miners who ran afoul of Lynch and whom he suppressed violently.[6]

Historians of lynching have rightly called Charles Lynch "the first lyncher," that is, the first American who employed the particular practice of summary justice under the name of "Lynch law," the phrase that would later become "lynching." The term "Lynch law," then, entered the local parlance in the James River region of Virginia shortly after Lynch coined it in 1782. It began quickly to spread throughout the rest of the Southern states, as one poetic example demonstrates. A wag writing in an Augusta, Georgia, newspaper in 1794 commented nostalgically: "Lynch's Law, ought still to be in vogue, / It will rid the town of every cursed rogue."[7] The term appeared as far west as Indiana by the 1820s. Nonetheless, it is important to note that the term neither replaced other terms for popular or vigilante justice, nor appeared too frequently in print prior to the 1830s.[8]

In the Revolutionary-era origin of lynching, we can find the matrix of a variety of the themes and tensions that would manifest themselves in its later development. One of the foremost contemporary scholars of lynching, Christopher Waldrep, has made a compelling case for seeing two competing notions of lynching during the Revolutionary War: one in which militia officers exceed their assigned authority, and the other in which ordinary people act entirely outside of the law. Charles Lynch's actions demonstrate the tension between those two notions. On the one hand, the militia campaign clearly bespeaks the case of officers who do exceed their authority and who are at least tepidly warned by the governor of having done so; while on the other, Lynch also presents himself as a "frontier hero seeking justice outside of law," and seeks "good over procedural values and institutional constraints."[9]

Waldrep also notes the "ethnic dimension of the violence" in this earliest employment of "Lynchs Law," citing as evidence a letter from the wife of one of the Welsh miners, in which she notes that "there is a misunderstanding between Colo Lynch and the Welsh in General." In addition to being a minority population, the Welsh were also the laborers in a lead mine that was in the midst of a boom. Charles Lynch himself wrote that he had "received accounts of a fine prospect of ore, and the Greatest Quantity raisd now Lying on hand that we have Ever had at any one time."[10] His brusque and violent actions aimed at controlling this ethnic minority population of laborers necessary to harvesting an economic staple, and in a time of perceived political crisis, also set the stage for later lynchings in American history.

We see, then, in the earliest practitioners of lynching many of the elements that would continue to define the motives and practices of later lynchers, including the use of summary justice to suppress minority ethnic populations. Even more, though, we can find what I would argue are the two rudimentary claims of the first American lynchers, which we should summarize even in a somewhat schematic way since these two claims tell us much about how American lynch mobs would continue to justify their actions for the next century and a half.

First, there is the claim that the lynchers employed what they described as "frontier justice" because they deemed the courts and other institutions of the law to be either unavailable or unreliable. In the case of the Bedford militia, they felt particularly justified in their summary procedures because they were operating in a state of war. The proper institutions of the society, in this case the courts, were not absent per se but undergoing revolutionary changes. It is perhaps for this reason that Governor Jefferson was not as emphatic as he would have been under conditions of peace in alerting Colonel Lynch to this breach of protocol and justice. It is also perhaps for this reason that the Virginia legislature would indemnify Lynch and his fellow militia members in a 1782 Act that tactfully praised them for suppressing the "conspiracy" by "timely and effectual measures" that while "not . . . strictly warranted by law" were nonetheless "justifiable from the imminence of the danger." This Act of Indemnity left the Bedford militia members "exonerated of and from all pains, penalties, prosecutions, actions, suits, and damages." Should they ever be indicted or prosecuted for their extralegal violence, they "may plead in bar, or the general issue, and give this act in evidence."[11] Ironically, then, the lawmakers of the state placed beyond the reach of the law the first American lynchers, the first under that name to usurp the role of courts and executioners.

Second, there is the claim of popular sovereignty—essentially the argument that the people constituted the original and primal force of governance, and could therefore consent or not consent to the making and enforcing of the law by their representatives. Here, we can note how important it was that the Bedford militia borrowed from the vocabulary of democratic revolution in order to sanction their extralegal acts. Colonel Campbell's claim that the militia acted with the "joint consent" of the people suggests that their actions were not just those of military officers but of representatives of those whose "consent" they enjoyed. The colonel cannily used a key term that would be difficult to impeach. The governor who urged them to employ trials in the future had four years earlier penned a declaration stating the "right of the people" to be governed by their "consent." This was the American language of the revolution, but it was also the language of earlier dissenters. The anti-monarchists in England and the Puritans in colonial Massachusetts had likewise employed precisely the same concept, as when John Winthrop, for instance, claimed the power of the "consent of a certaine companie of people."[12] Here was a situation of colonial revolutionaries struggling against monarchists, who implicitly believe "consent" to be immaterial in the matter of governance (a monarch does not require consent), fighting for their right to identify whose "consent" matters and constitutes the force to justify any action. The term "consent," then, in this context, was shorthand for the idea of popular sovereignty.

Nobody has done a better job of demonstrating the subterfuge involved in the concept of popular sovereignty than Edmund Morgan. In a remarkable study, he exposes how the elites in colonial and revolutionary America invented the idea of "the people" as a serviceable political fiction that would enable those elites to make claims about the popular sovereignty they enjoyed and in whose name they acted. What they used the claim of popular sovereignty for, ironically, is to advocate and demand deference from their underlings, rather than insurgence. There was nothing "popular" about their sovereignty. Later, the concept would continue to serve this same oppressive function as the yeomanry employed it to counsel deference in matters of politics and power from paupers and the property-less.[13] It was only later that the myth of popular sovereignty would become a weapon in the hands of the enfranchised masses. That largely happened, as we shall see below, around the time that the term "lynching" entered American print culture during the Jackson presidency.[14]

Once that happened, the "people" became a term lynchers of all sorts used to justify the act of murder by a select, self-appointed group. In the 1850s, defenders of the Vigilance Committee in California described the masses pursuing vigilante justice as "not a mob, but the *people,* in the highest sense of the term."[15] Half a century later, Tom Watson, still the populist though no longer a Populist, vehemently defended the lynchers of Leo Frank by postulating that the "people" may delegate but never surrender to their "agents" the power of governance. "When the Sheriff kills," Watson argued, "it is not his act; *it is the act of the People,* performed through their statutory law." When the sheriff fails to act in accordance with what the people want, the lynching that follows is just as legal because its sanction comes from the ultimate source of all law. "The Voice of the People Is the Voice of God," ran the headline for Watson's article.[16]

These, in sum, were the two primary claims made by the first people to practice lynching under the name of "Lynch Law." Their first justification involved the claim that the institutions upholding the law were either absent, insufficient, or corrupt. The people needed to protect themselves and their property through their own means. This claim would become the one most often used by those who inhabited the "frontier"—in the West or in their minds. The second justification involved the claim of popular sovereignty, that is, that the "people" constituted the final arbiters and appeal for their representatives, and therefore could act on the powers they granted to their elected or appointed officials. This claim had previously, and would thereafter, be employed by those who believed that formal legal systems—with rights and procedures to protect individual liberties—in no way reflected the more important informal system of communal values and mores. When the community enforced its own values by punishing those who violated widely accepted norms by meting out what it felt to be appropriately harsh penalties, it claimed to be dispensing a form of justice that was not corrupted or derailed by an excessive dependence on formal constraints meant to protect individuals from the power of the state. Here, it argued, was substantial justice unfettered, upholding genuine communal values.

While we are making a mild distinction between these two claims, they do belong to the same system of values and in discussions of lynching were more often conflated than distinguished. The reason for us to make the distinction at all is that it demonstrates the different strands of prolynching rhetoric and reveals the differing emphases placed by some on situation (frontier) and by others on democratic values (popular sovereignty). The notable difference, as I suggested in the Introduction, is that the frontier argument rests on the supposition that the situation will inevitably change—lynchers perform justice that one day will be performed by more civilized and established systems— while the popular sovereignty argument rests on an attitude of perpetual confrontation to those established systems. Representative politics for the popular sovereignty argument is not simply a formal system with annual or biennial elections; it is a system in which "consent" can be given by a fraction of the population to self-proclaimed executors of the public will in ad hoc acts of directed collective violence.

THE RISE OF LYNCHING IN THE 1830s

At the end of the Revolutionary War, the terms "lynching" and "Lynch law" had not yet assumed the meanings they would later assume— extralegal murder by a mob intent on upholding communal values, including white supremacy. Indeed, although Lynch law could prove fatal, as it did for the Tory hanged by the Bedford militia, it could also manifest itself in nonlethal ways, as it did for the other two men the Bedford militia had whipped. The term was used to describe a range of shaming rituals, such as whipping and tarring and feathering, as well as execution-style mob activity. One of the very first newspapers to define the term for a reading public noted somewhat vaguely that lynching was "a mode of punishment provided for such as become obnoxious in a manner which the law cannot reach."[17] That paper was the *Vicksburg Register,* and the acts of violence it was reporting proved to be a crucial turning point in the development of American lynching.

On July 4, 1835, in Vicksburg, Mississippi, a fight threatened to break out between an officer of the corps of Vicksburg volunteers and a gambler named Cabler at the Independence Day barbecue. The fight was momentarily averted when Cabler departed, but he soon returned to the barbecue to continue where he had left off—this time, though, armed with a large knife, a dagger, and a loaded pistol. The crowd disarmed and punished him. A reporter covering the story wrote that a "crowd of respectable citizens" marched Cabler out into the woods, tied him to a tree, and then proceeded first to whip and then tar and feather him. Once his punishment was finished, the crowd told Cabler to leave Vicksburg within forty-eight hours. After the crowd completed the work of punishing Cabler, they began to fear that his peers would exact revenge on the town.

That night the citizens held a meeting in the courthouse and drafted a notice that gave twenty-four hours for all gamblers to leave town. Most of Vicksburg's gamblers took the notice seriously, and quickly and peaceably left town the next day. Some, however, did not. The day following, a mob of Vicksburg citizens and members of a military corps burst into a suspected gambling house to roust out those who had failed to leave. The gamblers inside the house fired on the mob and killed one of the citizens. The now-enraged mob renewed its attack on the house and captured five residents. The mob then executed these five by hanging them from the town scaffold.[18]

Interestingly, it is the first act of violence—the whipping and tarring and feathering of Cabler—that the *Vicksburg Register* used to define "lynching," not the later hanging of the five gamblers without the benefit of trial. Two things are worth noting about the happenings in Vicksburg and their place in the evolution of lynching in America. First, the term "Lynch law" was now being used to describe a particular kind of civilian mob activity. The earlier case we had examined of Charles Lynch in 1780 concerned the actions of a militia. General Andrew Jackson in 1818 established what one historian calls a "model for lynchers" in his having hanged two Indian chiefs and two English subjects while he was attempting to conquer and annex the Spanish colony of Florida.[19] A year later, an early newspaper reference to Lynch law praised "this summary mode of dispersing justice" as it described the order issued by a military general who would proclaim martial law in the event of discovering offenders who purchased stolen cotton.[20] Although members of the Vicksburg volunteer corps were directly involved in the 1835 episode, it was largely the citizens of Vicksburg who formed the mob; and it was largely civilian actions that newspapers described in their attempt to fix the meaning of lynching.

Second, the meaning of lynching was still very much in flux, especially as to its severity. We noted that the Vicksburg newspaper called only the whipping and tarring and feathering of Cabler a "lynching," not the hanging of the five gamblers, although its definition certainly fit both cases. Two months later, the Lynch Club of Charleston, South Carolina, clarified the term in a letter it published in order to distinguish its mode of proceeding from that of imitators "unfriendly to the *Lynch Club*." The Lynch Club correspondent noted that the Club's practice is to submit a personal letter only to the "most dissolute and abandoned," telling them to leave town. Any person who does not go away as ordered "will be Lynched; and if any member of the Club, in the enforcement of the order of the club, be wounded, or severely injured, the person offending shall forthwith be hung up as a public example."[21] The "lynching," then, by an organization that used the term in its name, was a less severe action than killing, a punishment to be inflicted only on those who violently resisted their "lynching."

When newspapers in other states began to publish accounts of what happened in Vicksburg, the word "lynching" entered the American lexicon in a powerful way, and it was generally used to describe the hangings rather than the whipping. Several newspapers attempted to offer definitions of what struck them all as a relatively new phenomenon. The *Louisiana Advertiser* made gestures at defining the term, referring to "this summary execution, or Lynch law as it is called," in a story that had used the headline "Lynch Law—Five Gamblers Hung Without Trial." Other newspapers reprinting the *Louisiana Advertiser* story offered either different headlines—"Frightful Affair" in the *Portsmouth Journal of Literature and Politics*—or added explanatory subtitles using more widely known terms for acts of unsanctioned violence—"Outrage at Vicksburg" in the *Connecticut Courant*. Some made the term a localism—"Lynch Law, as it is called at the West" in the *New-Hampshire Sentinel*—while others combined more familiar terms with the region in which the violence occurred, as the *New Bedford Mercury* did in its article headlined "Southern Atrocities."[22]

The few months after July 1835 proved to be a period of extreme flux in the emergence of the term "lynching." Newspapers responded to the Vicksburg episode by either finding examples of lynching in their own states or tracing the origins of the term "Lynch law." In the first case, they often simply confounded their readers by misusing the term. Sometimes what appeared to be the cataclysmic appearance of a new phenomenon turned out to be merely a new way to denominate any kind of lawlessness. After declaring that "Judge Lynch has extended his jurisdiction into the land of steady habits," the *Portsmouth Journal of Literature and Politics* described two acts of property vandalism against the Old Town House in Norwalk and the African Church in Hartford, Connecticut.[23] Likewise, a writer in a New Hampshire newspaper who "did not even dream that Judge Lynch would so soon arrive in 'the Granite State'" told the story of how a lecturer at the Anti-Slavery Society in Northfield had his lecture interrupted by a mob and was arrested for vagrancy by the sheriff.[24]

The origins stories the newspapers published proved to be almost as confounding as their misuse of the term. The most popular accounts found someone named Lynch who was chosen as an arbiter in a case, usually of theft, most often horse theft, and who ordered a punishment of whipping, typically of thirty-nine lashes. The editor of the *Boston Commercial Gazette,* for instance, claimed that the practice was named for John Lynch, a native of North Carolina who was named as an interim judge by Daniel Boone in the territory of what would become the state of Kentucky, and ordered thirty-nine lashes for the thief of Boone's horse. The *Philadelphia Enquirer* noted that term originated in Georgia and the standing order of Lynch was: "Take that fellow, and tie him to a tree, and give him forty lashes, save one,—then start him—and tell him never to show his face here again on pain of the same punishment."[25]

Some newspapers even offered competing origins stories. Immediately after the Vicksburg lynchings, the *New Bedford Mercury,* tracing the origins of a term that it described as having "recently become almost as general as it is proverbial," gave the story of a Washington County, Pennsylvania, farmer named Van Swearingen whose neighbor, a farmer named Lynch, acted as judge in a dispute over the theft of a calf and ordered the punishment of three hundred lashes and expulsion within twenty-four hours. A year later, the *New Bedford*

Mercury offered a different origins story, quoting the *Southern Literary Messenger*, which dated the origin to 1780 and Colonel William Lynch's "infliction of summary justice by private and unauthorized individuals" on horse thieves in the area.[26]

The Vicksburg lynching, then, set off a concerted media effort to define and trace the etymological and social origins of what seemed a new American practice. Having been made popular in the press in 1835, the term "lynching" shortly thereafter entered government documents as early as 1837, in a memorial written by the citizens of Philadelphia (the site of a race riot in 1835), in which they feared the "wild advances of anarchy" evident in the "various outbreakings, riots, lynchings, and lawless proceedings that have taken place within these past few years."[27]

The strong desire newspapers exhibited in finding lynchings where there were merely other forms of lawlessness, and the impetus editors acted on to find an origin for the new term, are evidence of newly discerned patterns of violence in America. When newspapers made claims such as "riots and mobs have become so fashionable [and] we have heard much of 'Judge Lynch,' 'Lynch's Law' &c. &c. in connection with them," they were not exaggerating. When they expressed fears that lynching ("this popular code") would "soon super[s]ede all other laws, and the necessity of any further legislation," they were articulating a fear that Jacksonian democratic mores, or what they termed "mobocracy," was threatening the social order in a way that no other form of popular or foreign insurgency had hitherto done.[28] The year 1835 saw at least 147 riots, 109 of which occurred in the summer. Eight lives were lost in the sixty-eight riots in the North, while sixty-three lives were lost in the seventy-nine riots in the South. It was, as historian David Grimsted notes, the year of "violent indecision," a year of "maximum mob mayhem, in numbers and variety of riot never before or since surpassed in the United States."[29] Unsurpassed it may have been, but it was not anomalous, since 1834 had been almost as riotous a year.[30] And the years following would likewise witness continuing popular violence. In an appendix to a book published in 1840, the British émigré Thomas Brothers looked back in horror as he compiled a list of "Miscellaneous Murders, Riots, and Other Outrages, in 1834, 1835, 1836, 1837, and 1838."[31]

The violence was directed primarily, but not exclusively, at three groups: the Irish, African Americans, and abolitionists. Many of the mob riots and lynchings of these years were attempts to purge, punish, and terrorize those who were aliens, by virtue of immigrant status, race, or political affiliation. The violence sometimes seemed direction-less—1835 saw the first attempted presidential assassination in America, as a madman attempted to murder Andrew Jackson. Yet it was also seen as politically useful by those whose sworn obligation was to stem it. Jackson's secretary of state, John Forsyth, for instance, suggested to Vice President Martin Van Buren that he arrange for more Northern "mob discipline" against the abolitionists.[32] Also in 1835, Congressman James Henry Hammond attempted to publish a letter stating that abolitionists "can be silenced in but one way. *Terror and Death.*" The newspaper editor who chose not to publish the letter might have been concerned less with Hammond's reputation than with the possible antiabolitionist riots those fiery words could well inspire. There were thirty-five such riots against abolitionists in 1835.[33]

This mob violence against abolitionists was the popular equivalent to the "gag rule" that would take effect in Congress in 1836, essentially silencing abolitionist sentiment in government. The postmaster general, Amos Kendall, rendered the mails equally antagonistic to abolitionists' freedom of speech, advising postmasters to obey the law only when it suited them. Contemporary commentators discerned and identified the connection between government acts and mob activity. A diarist wrote that the "notorious Amos Kendall . . . embodies all the essence of the abominable doctrine on which the Vicksburgh and Baltimore riots were founded; viz, that the people are to be governed by the law just so long as it pleases them." A more public denunciation in a Kentucky news-paper referred to the postmaster general's "Post Office Lynch Law."[34]

The mob violence of these years was also sadistic. In the Philadelphia riot, for example, there was at least one castration and one rape. In the Southern riots, the brutality of the violence reached levels of torture that would rival Progressive-era spectacle lynchings. Victims, including slaves, were burned alive, skinned alive, and beheaded. About one quarter of the episodes of mob violence in the South routinely included such brutality.[35] That brutality was quite often aimed at slaves as well as at those who advocated the abolition of slavery. After Virgil Stewart published his sensational account of John Murrell's purportedly fomenting slave rebellion in 1835, an insurrection panic in Mississippi, within fifteen miles of where Stewart was living, led to the mob murder of ten whites and thirty slaves. That same year, in Madison County, Mississippi, a citizen mob put five slaves to death without benefit of trial, and the next year saw a slave burned until he was half dead and then beheaded. The year after that, in Red River, Louisiana, three free and nine enslaved African Americans were lynched.[36]

Nothing better exemplifies the direction and practice of lynching during these years than the connected cases of Francis McIntosh, a free black man, and Elijah Lovejoy, a white abolitionist and editor of an anti-slavery newspaper. In April 1836 McIntosh was taken from his Saint Louis jail cell and burned to death by a mob. The presiding judge of the impaneled grand jury investigating the lynching, who proved himself to be the appropriately named Judge Luke Lawless, counseled the jury not to indict anybody if the murder proved to be the act not of the "few" (individuals) but of the "many" (the multitude), whose acts in that case, as an expression of communal sentiment, would be beyond the jury's jurisdiction and "beyond the reach of human law." Lawless concluded this sanction for lynching by noting that McIntosh was evidently influenced by abolitionists and proceeded to read from the antislavery *St. Louis Observer*. Inspired by the judge's words, and in response to the editor Lovejoy's critique of Lawless, a mob destroyed the printing press of the antislavery newspaper. Lovejoy left Saint Louis and reestablished his newspaper in the town of Alton, across the river in Illinois. A year later, a mob killed Lovejoy as he was protecting his printing press from attack for the fourth time in a year.[37]

About six months after the mob murder of Lovejoy in Illinois, a young lawyer from the state reflected on the previous three years' violence, from Vicksburg to Alton, and saw that accounts of "outrages by mobs" were becoming a staple of the daily news, and that these "ravages of mob law" were gaining momentum. In Mississippi, the mob went from hanging "gamblers to negroes, from negroes to white citizens, and from these to strangers; till, dead men were seen literally dangling from the boughs of trees upon every road side; and in numbers almost sufficient, to rival the native Spanish moss of the country, as a drapery of the forest." In Saint Louis and Alton, he continued, the mob was able with impunity to "burn churches, ravage and rob provision stores, throw printing presses into rivers, shoot editors, and hang and burn obnoxious persons at pleasure." Such a situation, he thought, was a dire threat to the American "political edifice of liberty and equal rights." When there is a virtual war between "good men, men who love tranquility, who desire to abide by the laws, and enjoy their benefits," and other men who are "lawless in spirit," "lawless in practice," when there is an "increasing disregard for law," and a "growing disposition to substitute the wild and furious passions" of the mob for the "sober judgment of Courts"—under such conditions, the lawyer perorated, "this Government cannot last."[38] Fearful more for his country than for his profession, this Springfield lawyer would win election to Congress as a Whig in 1846 and to the White House as a Republican in 1860. The crisis Abraham Lincoln faced there was no longer a virtual war between law and lawlessness.

To return to Vicksburg and sum up, then, we can see that the specific form of mob activity that inspired the rest of the nation to define a term that thereafter assumed a prominent place in the American lexicon of violence also inaugurated what would become the standard rhetoric of lynching advocacy. Briefly, we can discern four important themes that the *Vicksburg Register* raised and used to defend the community in the aftermath of the lynching.

The first two themes are the ones we have seen inaugurated or, better, refined into a rudimentary form by the Bedford militia during the Revolutionary War. One is the claim of the need for "frontier justice," that is, the claim that the institutions and apparatus of the court are inefficient. In the case in Vicksburg, the residents of the town felt that the law was simply unable to deal with the gamblers. Taking up first the case of Cabler, who returned to the barbecue armed and ready, the Vicksburg reporter notes that Cabler needed to be punished *before* he committed any crime. If he had been taken to court at that moment, it would have proved impossible to indict him. Indeed, continues the reporter, "to proceed against him at law would have been mere mockery, inasmuch as, not having had the opportunity of consummating his design, no adequate punishment could have been inflicted on him."[39] This was likewise the case with the rest of the gamblers in the city. The law simply required too high a standard of evidence and proof. "The laws, however severe in their provision," he wrote, "have never been sufficient to correct a vice which must be established by positive proof, and cannot, like others, be shown from circumstantial testimony." The citizens of Vicksburg took the law into their own hands, then, because the laws on the books, and the ways they were upheld by the police and in the courts, were inadequate to the needs of protecting the city from those who faced its residents with guns and impunity.

The second claim, also echoing the Bedford militia, and indeed all the vigilante groups—such as those calling themselves "regulators"—that had anticipated the militia, was the claim of popular sovereignty, that is, the claim that those who whipped, tarred and feathered, and hanged their enemies enjoyed the full support of the people in whose name they performed those actions. They had a mandate, and, as the reporter put it, it was the mandate of an agitated and like-minded community. The action received the "unanimous" support of the citizens of Vicksburg, not one of whom had "been heard to utter a syllable of censure against either the act or the manner in which it was performed."[40]

The third and fourth themes address another question altogether, what I think we can call the issue of citizenship in this community, that is, defining those who are and those who emphatically are not. Lynchers almost uniformly have a Manichaean sensibility not only about what crimes deserve immediate and unmediated punishment, but also about who commits the crimes deserving of lynchings. In the earliest cases of Charles Lynch and Andrew Jackson, the people lynched are literally outsiders, enemies of the state. In later cases, they would be outsiders in a variety of different ways—during Reconstruction, people who did not belong in the region or in the voting polls; and during the Progressive-era racial spectacle lynchings, people who were not from the community, people who were "not from around here" or "strange Negroes," in the politest forms of that formulation.

The *Vicksburg Register* referred to them simply as "Professional Gamblers, destitute of all sense of moral obligations—unconnected with society by any of its ordinary ties," men who "have made Vicksburg their place of rendezvous," not their residence, not their home, not their community. In the same act of ridding their town of unwanted transients in a communal ritual, the community defines itself, first against those aliens it lynches, and then, in the aftermath, against those who would harshly judge the community's act of violence.

Consider the way the reporter assumed a classical defensive posture: "It is not expected that this act will pass without censure from most who had not an opportunity of knowing and feeling the dire necessity out of which it originated." These are classical examples of the kind of rhetorical appeal that helps to define citizenship in a community, and it does it in two connected ways. First of all, it creates the illusion of community by stating the terms by which one belongs or not. If you know and feel that dire necessity, you belong; if you do not, if you have doubts about what might seem rash actions in a moment of crisis, you do not belong. To live in Vicksburg, to be a member of that community, is to know the "dire necessity" and implicitly to have given consent for the resolution to it. Second, it makes local experience the test of community. Anyone who does not live here, or who fails to recognize the situation as the kind of crisis it is represented as being, is, by dint of that failure, an outsider. To know is to approve, and only those who live in that locale, and approve, can know and judge appropriately. It is a circular and vicious logic, as many schemes for identifying belonging are.

Finally, the newspaper makes its most resonant appeal by drawing on the most ancient form of belonging to a larger community—that is, the community of men. The men in Vicksburg, the newspaper reported, "had borne with their enormities, until to have suffered them any longer would . . . have proved us destitute of every manly sentiment."[41] This was a case not simply of crime and punishment, but of honor, masculine honor—the right to protect hearth, home, and family. The failure to appreciate that imperative, it is implied, requires and can receive no answer.

Here, then, is what the case of Vicksburg added to the earlier discourse of lynching. Those who defended the lynching used the earlier claims we saw employed by the Bedford militia and others—that lynching was an act of popular sovereignty and an act of frontier justice. The Vicksburg apologists added two important claims—that of community and that of manhood.

Lynchers act with "manly sentiment" because they recognize the danger posed to the community by transients and outsiders; and they are simply the only ones who can understand and appreciate the danger they avenged or averted. To be a member of a lynch mob or, what becomes effectively the same thing, to defend a lynch mob, is to be a member of the community that performed it, to be a man who either did or would have performed it, and to be singularly impervious to those who would criticize that mob because they are "outsiders." In 1835, the "outsiders" were defined as those not living in Vicksburg; a half-century later, it would become those not living in the South.

In those decades, the sense of what constituted a community and a locality expanded, partly a result of a regional division that would result in a civil war, and partly a result of a revolution in communications and transportations systems that would help produce a sense of expanded and divided communities. As well, that half-century witnessed a considerable expansion of America itself, as waves of settler societies conquered newer and newer places that required, for them, varying levels of collective mob violence to establish and protect what they thought of as their frontiers.

"VIGILANCE WITH ORDER, OR A MOB WITH ANARCHY?": AMERICAN FRONTIERS

America's mythical "Frontier experience," writes Richard Slotkin, in reality constitutes six or seven major frontier expansions, starting with the seventeenth-century transoceanic crossing and the establishment of settlements on the eastern seaboard of North America, then progressing to the Alleghenies, the trans-Allegheny frontier and then the Mississippi Valley frontier. During the nineteenth century, that expansion extended to the Mexican frontier, included the Oregon and California acquisitions, and then concluded with the development of the Great Plains as an "internal" frontier by the 1880s. Many forces were at work in stimulating these successive expansions, including "geometrically multiplied populations, coupled with advances in the technology of transportation and the development of newer, more efficient modes of economic and political organization." Each of these large-scale frontiers, and each of the more local frontiers within them, contained its own dynamic and were marked by particular sets of conflicts (of social classes, economic interests, and slave and free-soil partisans).[42] Yet, despite the particulars of each frontier, we might discern a general pattern that helps us define the frontier experience of collective violence.

This pattern is not universal but widespread, in which in the first stage collective violence is exercised against those accused of crimes against property in the early days of settlement, while the territory still lacks legal and judicial apparatus. In the second stage, the more mature society, having established and instituted legal and judicial apparatus, punishes primarily crimes of homicide or especially heinous crimes of other sorts, sometimes in the absence of the legal apparatus, often despite its presence. The third stage is marked by the development of a vigilante violence that emerges to become a tool for capitalists who use it as they establish dominance in particular economies. Richard Maxwell Brown has called this stage the "Western Civil War of Incorporation," in which agents of "the conservative, consolidating authority of modern capitalistic forces," that is, barons of oil, steel, and cattle, employ vigilantes, hired gunfighters, to intimidate and eliminate local small-scale rivals.[43] Finally, in the fourth and final stage lynching becomes a weapon of terrorism used to control the mobility of particular groups that are defined along ethnic, racial, or class lines. These stages are somewhat sequential, but there is overlap, and particularly since the second stage often continues well into the twentieth century. Lynching, then, in frontier societies is not an unchanging ritual but a practice adapted for and rationalized through new ideologies.

In Colorado, for instance, where the first lynching in that state was recorded in 1859, two years before Colorado was made a U.S. territory, lynchers in the 1860s did their work in the open daylight, lynchers in the 1870s wore masks and conducted more nocturnal lynchings, and lynchers after the 1880s reserved their lethal work only for those accused of committing horrible crimes or those who were not white. The public justifications offered for lynching likewise followed a similar pattern. During the early pioneer era, the press and politicians claimed that lynchings were necessary to protect a community because lawmen were corrupt, judges inept, and jails flimsy. Later, they would claim that lynchings were cost-effective in saving the counties the tax dollars necessary to mount a legal case and stage an execution.[44] What began in Colorado as a relatively organized means of protecting material property by the extralegal "People's Court" eventually became an orgiastic means of protecting the far more important property of whiteness, as people of Chinese, Italian, Mexican, and African descent were lynched in the 1880s.[45]

Wyoming presents another paradigmatic case of the evolution of collective violence on an American frontier. During the early territorial period of the 1860s, vigilante committees constituted the forces of law and order in a lawless frontier, policing and punishing crimes of property at first, and then predominantly homicide in the next two decades. By the 1880s, as was common in other frontier societies, the Wyoming press felt called on to defend vigilante activity, which it did, sometimes by noting the inadequacy of legal apparatus on the frontier, as a mob of Wyoming lynchers did when it attached a note to the corpse of its victim that read: "Process of law is a trifle slow,/So this is the way we have to go." It was signed "PEOPLES VERDICT." In other cases, though, prolynching advocates asserted the superiority of an informal justice system.

The editor of the *Ft. Collins Express* made the case by describing an anemic and ineffective system in the East, where, he writes, "foul and brutal murderers are saved from the gallows by the interposition of the law, trial after trial, and oftentimes acquittal being had upon flimsy technicalities." Murderers in the "east" are coddled, he continued, and prison life "brightened by the visits of fair women bringing bouquets and delicacies." The "people of the west," on the other hand, "will not stand any such nonsense," and will perform the righteous and manly execution demanded by "an indignant and outraged populace."[46]

The next evolution in Wyoming's lynching history involves that period of vigilante violence against local ranchers (which I will discuss in greater detail below). The final stage in Wyoming involves the lynching of racial minorities in the state during the first two decades of the twentieth century, when, as Michael J. Pfeifer notes, "lynching became a tool for white Wyomingites to assert racial hierarchy in industrializing and urbanizing settings."[47] As in Colorado, lynching was likewise transformed in Wyoming from a form of frontier policing to a form of terrorism, first of those local ranchers who stood in the way of industrialization and then of specified racial groups.

The experience in Texas differs somewhat from that of Colorado and Wyoming in that Texas's frontier was created from a war against two racial groups, Mexicans and Indians, a war that vigilantes and mobs continued through expulsions and lynchings. In the 1850s, shortly after the Texas Revolution, white mobs lynched Mexicans for alleged crimes against property, or for providing lower-cost goods, as happened during the summer of 1857 when white mobs killed about seventy-five Mexicans accused of bringing goods from Mexico to San Antonio. White mobs likewise lynched Indians with impunity. In one instance in 1858, a white mob sought out and then fired into a group of sleeping

Indians (peaceful Caddos and Anadarkos), killing seven, three of whom were women. Four months later, another mob entered the Brazos Indian reservation and scalped and murdered an eighty-year-old Waco. These crimes were clearly meant to provoke the Native Americans into responding, which they did, and created conditions where federal agency officials were not able to protect the Indians from the vigilante acts of the white Texans. The event at Brazos eventually led to the removal of the reservation to Oklahoma.

Seen as a continuation of the war effort, these episodes of vigilante violence, lynching, and "Indian fighting" reveal how white colonizers were motivated by material desires (land, exploitative economic practices) while also clearing the way for white supremacy and manifest destiny. A frontier created by those motivations was also generated for another form of white supremacist economic exploitation. "Texas," Stephen F. Austin had earlier proclaimed, "shall be effectually, and fully, Americanized," which meant, as he concluded, "Texas must be a slave country." Once it became a slave country, rebellious slaves, or enslaved people accused of being rebellious, became the third primary target of white mobs.[48]

These were the rudimentary events that created what historian William D. Carrigan refers to as Texas's "lynching culture." The sponta-neous formation of "volunteer Indian fighters" provided a model for the formation of lynch mobs, the rhetoric of "Indian fighting" fed the discourse justifying collective violence against minorities, and the commemoration of Texas's Indian fighting heroes romanticized a tradi-tion of extralegal violence. Given how integral was this particular legend—what Slotkin refers to as "the mythologized view of American-history-as-Indian-war"—it is not surprising that the first whites to be lynched in central Texas were those who did not act sufficiently like white men. In 1860, a mob that had just lynched four Indian horse thieves pursued and lynched what the leader of the mob described as "white horse thieves." The adjective was meant to suggest precisely the failure of their being "white." Another white lynch victim of the mob had in fact joined an Indian tribe and participated in the murder of two white fami-lies. Here was a case of the dangers of those settlers who "go native"—who, in the words of the Texas lynchers, became "white Indians."[49]

Other whites were also lynched in 1860 because they did not under-stand what it meant to be white in what Austin called an "Americanized slave country." Lynched for fomenting slave rebellion, these whites "went native" in another way, delighting, as one disgusted Texan, Gideon Lincecum, put it, "in the odor of the Negro" (confusing the organs of olfaction and propagation, he counseled castration for such whites). The long, hot summers of 1859 and 1860 produced a wave of lynchings throughout Texas as each rumor of slave rebellion plots led to the hanging of suspected whites and more frequent burning of suspected black slaves. Vigilance committees were struck and performed the work of translating vague rumors into exacted retribution. One in Denton County, for example, created a Central Committee of Safety that appointed subcommittees in each neighborhood to guard against and discover what they called persons "known to be of the blackest and most incendiary character" (an appropriate description for a committee primarily interested in slave rebels and arsonists). Anywhere from seventy-five to several hundred slaves and reputed abolitionists were hanged, including such notables as the Reverend Anthony Bewley, an ordained elder of the Methodist Episcopal Church. This spirit of lawlessness connected to fears of slave insurrections eventually culminated in the "Great Hanging" of Gainesville, in which at least forty-two white Unionists were hanged by an impromptu extralegal court in 1862.[50] Texas's frontier days, then, began and ended with the mob killing of Mexicans, Native Americans, and African Americans; and when it extended to the killing of whites, mobs chose to lynch those whites who acted like or sympathized with those oppressed groups.

Let us now reconsider the third stage in many of these frontier societies, which, as I mentioned above, involved vigilante violence used by capitalist forces to conquer small-scale rivals or quell conditions unfavorable to their incorporation. Before examining historical examples, it is worthwhile first to address the question of vigilante movements as a form of lynching. Many who write about vigilance committees or vigilante movements more generally insist on making a distinction between this particular form of extralegal collective violence and the more traditionally understood lynch mobs.[51] As we saw in the Introduction, the judge in Owen Wister's *The Virginian* begins his defense of lynching by insisting that there was "no likeness in principle whatever between burning Southern negroes in public and hanging Wyoming horse-thieves in private." Indeed, the "burning [is] a proof that the South is semi-barbarous, and the hanging a proof that Wyoming is determined to become civilized."[52] Nobody devoted more energy or more pages to making that distinction than did Hubert Howe Bancroft in his two-volume, 1500-page *Popular Tribunals*, published in 1887.

For Bancroft, the shift of the American frontier from Arkansas and Missouri to California led to the shift from lynching to vigilance, and it was then, he concluded, "that the popular tribunal assumed respectability." The vigilance committee is to a mob "as revolution is to rebellion," the former "based upon principle and the other upon passion." An "unorganized rabble," the mob is bent on "revenge." An "organization officered" by efficient members and "acting under fixed rules of its own making," the vigilance committee pursues "justice." There were further distinctions between "intelligent and high-minded vigilance organizations" and "blood-drunken orgies of frontier lynch-law executions." "The mob was mobile, they were firm; the mob was passionate, they were cool; the mob hanged first and tried afterward, they executed justice only after the most solemn judgment." The only common feature between a mob and a vigilance committee seems to be that they both "regarded not, at all times, the letter of the law." He concludes in the second volume as he had introduced the first by insisting on the indisputable differences between "a turbulent, disorderly rabble, hot with passion, breaking the law for vile purposes, and a convention of virtuous, intelligent, and responsible citizens with coolness and deliberation arresting momentarily the operations of law for the salvation of society." As he quotes one of those virtuous, intelligent citizens at the formation of the 1856 San Francisco Vigilance Committee, the choice in that group's mind was indeed between "vigilance with order, or a mob with anarchy."[53]

There are three ways to respond to Bancroft's arguments. One can do as he accuses the "law and order" zealots of doing, by insisting that the shared illegality of the mob and vigilance committee is what supremely matters. As I suggested in the Introduction, that is not an insignificant point, although it raises what for Bancroft and for law and order zealots would be the more troubling idea of a state potentially based on almost as arbitrary a claim of coercive power as that of the mob and committee.

A second strategy is to delineate the ways in which vigilance committees are not so noble-minded and disinterested in their pursuit of nothing but justice, as he suggests. Consider the Vigilance Committee of Thirteen, formed in 1835 by 160 citizens in the town of Livingston, Mississippi. Provoked by a panic about a rumored slave insurrection, the mob and then the Committee lynched about thirty slaves and several white çitizens. Mississippi newspapers justified the work of the mob/Committee by reprinting Thomas Jefferson's statements on the rights of popular sovereignty. But how "popular" were the members of this Committee, and how much was their interest in the sovereignty of their fellow citizens? It turns out that the Committee was quite unrepresentative, with twelve of the thirteen members having vested economic interests in its work (being mid- to large-scale slave owners). And how disinterested in the pursuit of justice was the Committee when the two people who first proposed its formation, Dr. Joseph Pugh, and Dr. M. D. Mitchell (who also was the first chair), had much to gain when the Committee hanged three and exiled one more of their "medical competitors"?[54]

Or consider the Montana Vigilantes, for instance, a group inspired by the San Francisco Vigilance Committee and created by at least one former member of the Committee. They lynched individuals, like Sheriff Henry Plummer, who might or might not have been as guilty as they were charged to be. During a lynching spree in which they killed twenty-two people in just over one month, and a total of fifty-seven by the end of their seven-year existence, the Montana Vigilantes lynched one man who stole a small item from his cabinmate while he was drunk (and offered to return it if his life were spared), another who was injured, another whose victim was not yet dead (and who recovered in the end), another who had been pardoned by a legally constituted court, and another who happened to be a critic of the Vigilantes. Nor were these "decent, orderly" executions. The lynching of José Pizanthia, who was guilty of being a "rough," was gruesome, as he was killed with a howitzer and then his body was hanged, riddled with bullets, and immolated, and his cabin was burned down as well. Finally, it is clear that the Vigilantes were not a particularly deliberative group. On one occasion, after they voted on the punishment of two victims, one of the Vigilantes who had misgivings and wished to leave was persuaded at gunpoint to stay and participate. The inspiration and model of the Montana Vigilantes, the San Francisco Vigilance Committee, was not so gruesome, or murderous, but it certainly acted on the vested interests of its members. Even the apologists for the San Francisco Vigilance Committee noted that it banished mostly Australians in 1851 and mostly "Irish, and other foreigners of low birth" in 1856. This xenophobic sensibility—running off "vast numbers of scruffy young men, some of them guilty of nothing more than having a foreign accent"—does not fall into the category of disinterested, dispassionate activity, or justice of any sort.[55]

A third way to challenge Bancroft is to dispute his representation of lynch mobs, whose formation, at least at times, was not nearly as spontaneous an event as he suggests. Frequently, mobs displayed "thorough organization," as one historian notes, referring to an Adams County, Iowa, lynch mob in 1887, in which each member of the mob "was called by a number and no names were spoken during the proceedings." There was no passion, and much deliberation, evident in another Iowa mob in 1840 that voted on the punishment of its victim—"white beans were cast by those in favor of hanging and red beans by those in favor of whipping"—and even moved that the vote be made unanimous after the bean counters found in favor of whipping (forty-two to thirty-eight). The same deliberation was shown by a Coffey County, Kansas, mob that voted on the death sentence by walking either to the right or to the left side of a building. It may not be equivalent to the polling of a jury, but it is not much different—and, in tabulation, seems considerably more accurate—than the San Francisco Vigilance Committee's practice of announcing its verdict, telling the people it would execute the sentence within an hour, and *then* asking them to register their approval or disapproval with a voice vote.[56]

More measured students of vigilance movements have exhibited greater caution in distinguishing a vigilante movement from a conventionally understood lynch mob. Unlike an ephemeral lynch mob, which is traditionally assumed to arise from and violently redress a particular alleged crime, vigilante movements are characterized by their "regular (though illegal) organization" and their "existence for a definite (often short) period of time." We have seen that organization in some cases differs in degree, not kind, and it is worth noting, as we will demonstrate in Chapter Three, how agents of both the state and civil society were involved in the formation of lynch mobs in a way that suggests much more regular organization than is usually ascribed to them. Mobs frequently had the appearance of spontaneity because the forces that led to their formation—including the press, pulpit, and police—have been insufficiently appreciated as an enduring organizational impetus to these mobs. Without necessarily disputing that vigilance committees may be distinguished by their more enduring forms and organizational structure, we would just conclude that there is ample evidence suggesting that mobs too have elements of organization that make the distinction less than stark.[57]

The most famous of the vigilante movements, and one that inspired several others in the settlement of the "internal" frontier of the Great Plains, was the San Francisco Vigilance Committee (formed in 1851, reconstituted in 1856). The main periods of activity for the Committee were between June and September of 1851, and May and August of 1856. During those two stretches, the Committee hanged eight men charged with crimes and banished about sixty more. The 1851 Committee was formed primarily to punish criminals whose offenses were against property and person. In its constitution, the 1851 Committee stated its purpose as to ensure that "no thief, burglar, incendiary or assassin, shall escape punishment, either by the quibbles of the law, the insecurity of prisons, the carelessness or corruption of the police, or a laxity of those who pretend to administer justice." The 1856 Committee was formed primarily to punish political graft and election fraud. The 1856 Committee revised its constitution to make itself responsible for "the protection of the ballot-box, the lives, liberty, and property of the citizens and residents of San Francisco." The 1856 Committee continued to meet until November 1859, but it punished no one after August 1856, when it held its grand review and parade. The Committee also formed a political party, the People's Party, in August 1856, a week before its final parade.[58]

Bancroft, easily the most enthusiastic of the Committee's historians, did not shy away from claiming a great deal for the two groups. He called the 1851 Committee "the most perfect and powerful organization hitherto established in any country for the guarding of the public weal." And the 1856 Committee received even greater accolades as "the largest,

most powerful, and efficient popular tribunal known in history."
Modern historians have found less to celebrate and more to critique in
these agencies. They acknowledge the importance of the two, especially
the 1856 Committee, as "pivotal in the history of American vigilantism"
because it combined the practices of the old vigilante movements
(hanging, banishing) with the new ethnic victims (especially Irish-
Catholic immigrants). As well, historians noted that the San Francisco
organizations constituted a shift from "rural frontier disorder" to a
concern with the problems of a "new urban America." Finally, one
historian also notes that the groups established an important historical
precedent by helping to legitimize "the crowd in the street shortly before
the Civil War began," although it is clear that the unruly street crowd or
mob had a much longer history, as shown by the historians of American
mobbing.[59]

The San Francisco Vigilance Committee does indeed mark an
important historical shift in the practice of extralegal policing of urban
spaces, in directing extralegal violence against a specified ethnic
minority, and, especially, in inspiring a series of imitators, numerous
vigilante groups that spread throughout California and the newly established rural frontiers east of California. The point we would wish to
stress, however, is that the shift between the 1851 and the 1856 Vigilance
Committee also constitutes a significant shift in the evolution of
American lynching in frontier societies. More specifically, the
1856 Committee represents that third phase I noted above—the use of
collective extralegal violence for capitalist incorporation.

While Bancroft celebrated the diversity of the 1856 Committee
membership, claiming the "body was composed of all classes and
conditions of men," representing every "nationality, every political and
religious sentiment, every trade, profession, and occupation"—in a
word, all the classes of all "the white-skinned races"—a study of the
actual makeup of the Committee demonstrates that most American
members were originally from the Northeast, most European members
also from the North Atlantic basin. The members were primarily
merchants, tradesmen, and craftsmen, and their apprentices. Few were
laborers, few Irish were allowed to join, and gamblers were not allowed
to apply. As Richard Maxwell Brown points out, the "mercantile
complexion" of the Committee reveals a great deal about its terms of

operation. The Committee, made up of merchants deeply dependent on credit from eastern businessmen, had to showcase San Francisco's "municipal and financial stability" to their creditors. In order to demonstrate that "conservative, right-thinking men had definitely gained control" of the city, the Committee essentially attempted to overthrow the political machine of David C. Broderick, sentencing his Irish "bully boys" to expulsion, and banishing twenty-eight of Broderick's chief lieutenants. As another historian puts it, the Committee, "under the guise of moral purification, purified the city largely of Democrats." In the end, then, the Committee that inaugurated itself under the motto "No Creed. No Party. No Sectional Issues" formed a political party to replace the one it destroyed, and followed a creed that was essentially fiscal conservatism. The "people" served by the People's Party turned out to be businessmen who were well served by the tax cuts and dramatically lowered municipal expenses (and services) that the People's Party delivered.[60] The tribunal was no more popular than the party was for the people; it was in reality a mercantile putsch disguised as a vigilante movement.

In Wyoming, to give one final example of how vigilante movements served the interests of what Brown calls "the conservative, consolidating authority of modern capitalistic forces," in the 1880s cattle barons began employing hired guns to intimidate and kill their much smaller rival farmers. In the most famous case, the so-called Johnson County War, a battle raged between the big absentee ranchers in the Wyoming Stock-Growers' Association and the small local ranchers of Johnson County. The Association employed cowboys to intimidate the smaller ranchers, while it pursued a legal strategy to create anti-rustling legislation. The Johnson County ranchers responded by forming political alliances with grangers and populists (and Democrats) to challenge control of the Association-friendly Republican state government. In turn, the Association undertook a full-scale war by hiring what one newspaper called "Texas gunslingers," who lynched those accused of cattle rustling and those who were recognized leaders of the Johnson County ranchers. The defense of the mob violence followed the standard lines established at least a century earlier. As a character in Owen Wister's 1902 novel of the Johnson County War puts it, "in Wyoming the law has been letting our cattle-thieves go for two years," and lynching was necessary until "civilization can reach us." But the "civilization" of which he speaks is already there in the form of established legal apparatus. It is not the existence of that system but its functioning that he points to as the reason lynching is necessary: "The courts, or rather the juries, into whose hands we have put the law, are not dealing the law." As we mentioned earlier, the speaker of these words, aptly Judge Henry, is a cattle baron, and the person he is trying to persuade of the necessity of lynching is Molly Woods, referred to as "the New England girl." The argument for lynching is cast as a manly western phenomenon unappreciated and misunderstood by an effete or feminized East, echoing the *Ft. Collins Express* editor.[61] Even a "Judge" can recognize real justice in the hands of the "people" as more important than formal justice in the hands of easterners or western jury members insufficiently aware of the needs of the Association.

Lynching, then, as we can see, constituted an elemental force in American frontiers, from their earliest settlement (against the original residents or wayward settlers) to their transformation through industrialization and incorporation. In different frontiers, we find somewhat different stages of collective violence developing, but there do seem to be at least the lineaments of a common pattern in the use of lynching, first by those who wanted to punish criminals, then by those who wanted to expand capitalist enterprise by eliminating small-scale competitors, and finally by those who wanted to control or banish minority populations. We can see how the lynchers on the American frontiers of the nineteenth century took the rationales of eighteenth-century lynchers and developed them in such a way as to serve their evolving needs for the claiming of new lands, the controlling of particular populations, and the domination of certain economies. Lynching, then, was a strategy for settling new territory (or clearing out places like San Francisco), for acting on the imperatives of what they considered manly honor, and for expressing their belief in what they continued to call popular sovereignty. Lynching also became during these years a strategy for establishing capitalism and white supremacy—and, a word they would not use, a form of terrorism.

The story of lynching in the first century of the American nation—from Charles Lynch's extralegal execution of a British Tory in 1780 to the multiple lynchings by Wyoming cattle barons, masked Colorado mobs, and white supremacists throughout the country in the 1880s—reveals the ways that mobs of Americans, formed in militias, communities, and settlements, acted to punish and terrorize those who struck them as "outsiders," those who did not share their values, their politics, and their color. These lynchers and their defenders developed both ritual forms of corporal and then lethal violence while simultaneously advancing a set of justifications for exercising extralegal authority. New political entities were evoked as much more relevant communities. Communities, it turns out, could be defined only by those within them, and they were empowered by those within them to punish individuals who violated their codes and challenged their values. Violence, when exercised by a "collective," became an expression of communal values (something that Judge Lawless felt was beyond the reach of the law). The formation and mobilization of the justifications for mob violence—the rationale, or what we can call the discourse of lynching—that developed during the first century of lynching provided the rudimentary elements of what would become the mature discourse of lynching that would arise in the second century of American lynching, starting in the 1880s.

Before turning to that era, though, we need to return to where we began this chapter, at the eve of the Civil War. That unnamed African American mentioned by Reverend Garnet, hanged from a tree during the New York draft riots and whose body was then desecrated for the amusement and political consecration of a mob newly fed on "nigger meat" and antiblack sensibility, appears to be an early victim in the next stage of white supremacy and of the evolution of lynching in America—that is, the era when lynching was exercised increasingly and then almost exclusively against black Americans. For most historians, that era begins in the 1880s (particularly 1886). From that perspective, this victim was just that, an "early" victim of a crime that would later evolve to target and terrorize those like him. In the next chapter, we will challenge that view and look not at the prehistory of racial lynching but rather at its formative history—the use of collective mob violence against people of African descent in antebellum America, Civil War America, and Reconstruction America

2

The Race of Lynching

Popular representations of lynching assume that there are two distinct activities that fall under that rubric—one involving the hanging of cattle rustlers on frontiers, and the other the torture and brutal mob killing of African Americans. In the terms George W. Bush used in 2008, the former would be "prairie justice," the latter "gross injustice." Both, in popular representations, are products of post-Reconstruction America, the "age of lynching," as it were. And, in particular, the lynching of African Americans, the "gross injustice" of racial lynching, is most emphatically seen as a phenomenon that begins in the 1880s. We have seen already lynching's long history, dating from the Revolutionary era; it did not begin in 1880, when statistics pertaining to lynching began to be collected. Yet, even those who want to trace the continuities from that early history to the age of lynching do so in misleading ways. Sometimes a historian will make a tacit nod to the continuity, as does Paul A. Gilje, for instance, when he notes that during "Reconstruction thousands of African Americans were killed, and thousands more died at the hands of Judge Lynch after 1877." Or sometimes a writer will argue polemically that the racial lynchings of the Progressive era constitute a "recrudescence" that "dates from the period of Reconstruction," as does James Weldon Johnson, for example.[1] In either case, though, there seems to be a clean break between the collective mob violence before and after the Civil War and/or Reconstruction.

This insistence that there is a discernible discontinuity in the summary justice inflicted on black Americans is understandable, since the racial lynchings occurring in the fifty years following Reconstruction did indeed strike many as a novelty and a nadir in American brutality. As President Theodore Roosevelt noted in 1911, while lynch-law "is itself a dreadful thing," the "manifestations that accompany it when the cause is due to race hatred are peculiarly horrible."[2] But this insistence on discontinuity is also deeply problematic. First, it masks rather than reveals how racial lynching is an evolving practice, with evolving strategies, motives, and forms. Moreover, it prevents us from understanding either the relationship of racial lynching to other kinds of vigilante actions on the broad spectrum of extralegal violence, or the place racial lynching occupies among a panoply of social control strategies used to limit African American mobility (and life) in different historical periods. The story of the rise of racial lynching, then, the story of how lynching became an American practice used to control, terrorize, and subjugate a people, who in turn resisted it and the political imperatives of white supremacy behind it, is a story that begins in the era of American enslavement.

"AS IF SUCH ACCIDENT NEVER HAPPENED": LYNCHING AND SLAVERY

It is popularly believed that African Americans were infrequently the victims of antebellum mob violence. In 1941, Wilbur Cash speculated that less than 10 percent of the more than three hundred people hanged or burned by mobs between 1840 and 1860 were of African descent, a figure and ratio offered without source but accepted uncritically by some modern historians of slavery.[3] Despite the absence of hard evidence, the reasoning behind this speculation is sound. The majority of African Americans were enslaved, and the mob killing of a slave, unlike the mob killing of a free person, had dire legal implications, since the slave was property and his or her master had standing in court. In addition, it would have been redundant to lynch black people since slavery acted as the primary form of social control of African Americans prior to the Civil War, and there were virtually no constraints on the severity of punishment a master could inflict on his slaves. The kind of lynching that was a form of racial terrorism is truly a postbellum phenomenon, and in many ways it replaced slavery and supplemented disfranchisement, economic disempowerment, and Jim Crow segregation as a primary strategy of social control over African Americans. The popular belief about the infrequency of slave lynchings is largely correct, then, although much anecdotal evidence renders Cash's estimate wholly too low.

There are three noteworthy points we can make about the lynching of enslaved and free African Americans prior to Reconstruction. First, the alleged crimes for which slaves were indeed lynched—murder of a master, rape, and plotting an insurrection—tell us a great deal about the sorts of fears that beset a panicked slave society. This was a society that feared being unable to ensure the safety of its propertied class, protect its womanhood, and maintain a hegemonic society founded on the idea that slaves were happy or at least willing participants in their enslavement. Second, the exaggerated brutality that attended the lynching of slaves proves that the kind of spectacle lynchings that involved horrific violence was not strictly a product of the 1890s, as many scholars suggest, although the spectacle lynchings of the 1890s do constitute a special development for reasons I will discuss in the next chapter. Finally, the state laws regulating the conduct and punishment of slaves provide, I believe, a potent source for promoting a widespread popular belief in the efficacy and essential fairness of racial lynching as a practice (I will discuss this point in the Conclusion).

A charge of a flagrant crime of a slave against his master could lead to mob violence, as happened as early as 1707 in New York, when a slave was lynched by a mob after he apparently killed his master's family, or 1797 in Scriven County, Georgia, when another was accused of killing his master, or in De Soto County, Mississippi, in 1852, when a group of slaves were accused of the same crime.[4] Although we do not have accurate statistics about lynchings prior to the 1880s, anecdotal evidence drawn from newspapers and scholarship on slavery generally reveal that slaves seem to have been lynched more frequently as slavery itself was imperiled, either by fears of a slave rebellion or by the reality of the Civil War. Historian Clarence Mohr has noted that black Georgians "fell victim to the fury of enraged mobs" during the Civil War with remarkable regularity. During a three-month stretch in 1862, seven slaves were lynched by mobs in three counties.[5] In the wake of John Brown's attempted raid on Harper's Ferry, white Southerners responded more keenly to any perceived insurrectionary rumors and exacted vigilante violence against any alleged plotters.[6] In the summer of 1860, for instance, at least fifty people were lynched in Texas in the wake of a series of fires that were rumored to be an abolitionist plot.[7] Two years later, a self-appointed citizens court in Gainesville, Texas, hanged forty-two Unionists, as Confederate Texans elsewhere followed suit and lynched what one contemporary claimed were over two hundred Unionists.[8]

Although there does seem to be more widespread lynching in the wake of Harper's Ferry and with the onset of the Civil War, rumors and acts of slave insurrections had elicited similar orgies of violence earlier in the century. In 1835, in Madison County, Mississippi, a self-appointed "Committee of Safety" conducted impromptu trials of abolitionists and slaves before hanging them; from the reports, it is difficult to determine the number of slaves killed, but it ranges from a very conservative estimate of fifteen to a more plausible fifty. The local *Clinton Gazette* reported that the slave conspiracy "embraced the whole slave region from Maryland to Louisiana, and contemplated the total destruction of the white population of all the slave states, and the absolute conquest and dominion of the country."[9] Given the frequency and magnitude of fears of such extensive slave revolts, and given that not every county forming a committee of safety was also compelled to produce some record of its proceedings but that many counties did often form random mobs committed only to wreaking havoc, it becomes almost impossible to say how many slaves were killed by vengeful whites in the aftermath of the dozens of attempted slave rebellions in the Old South.

While we know that somewhere around thirty-five slaves were executed by the state for their involvement in the slave rebellion of Gabriel Prosser in Richmond, Virginia, in 1800, and twenty-five more in Sancho Booker's in Halifax, Virginia, in 1802, we do not have adequate records of those who suffered at the hands of mobs who chose to supplement the state's work.[10] The states of Virginia and North Carolina executed somewhere between forty to fifty African Americans in the wake of Nat Turner's rebellion in Southampton County in 1831. The rest of the more than 200 slaves and free blacks killed were presumably lynched by mobs who "had gone on a rampage, shooting and axing every Negro they could find," making a trip to Southampton in order to "kill somebody else's niggers" with impunity, as one contemporary put it.[11] In the wake of the Stono rebellion in South Carolina in 1739, roving mobs, according to one contemporary source, immediately "kill'd twenty odd more" suspected slave rebels and then later captured another forty who were immediately executed, "some shot, some hang'd, and some Gibbeted alive."[12] In the end, given what evidence we do have of the white South's violent, vigilante response to rumors and reports of slave rebelliousness, we have to believe that Cash's estimates are grossly unrepresentative of the numbers of slaves who were lynch victims.

Another observation drawn from anecdotal and not numerical evidence is that slaves seemed to suffer more grotesque lynchings than white victims, and often suffered immolation in a way that white victims simply did not. As one example, consider that when an interracial gang of rapist-murderers was captured by a posse in Chicot County, Arkansas, in 1857, all the black members of the gang were burned alive, while the white ringleader was shot to death.[13] Like the lynching of slaves generally, the act of burning slaves occurred early and persistently in American history. Both the slaves lynched in 1707 in New York and in 1797 in Scriven County were burned to death. Two Alabama slaves were burned to death by a mob in 1835, as was a free black man by a Saint Louis mob in early 1836. Five of the seven slaves killed in that three-month stretch in Georgia in 1862 were hanged and then burned. In April 1860 a Mississippi slave was burned by a mob, in May a Georgian slave, in August another Georgian "negro boy," and in February of the next year another in Harris County.[14]

Apologists for slavery sometimes denied that slaves were burned to death, but at other times they advocated the practice. When two slaves were burned alive after a spree of murder, rape, and kidnapping in Louisiana, the slaveholding diarist Bennet Barrow believed that "burning was even too good for them."[15] The Southern press shared Barrow's private beliefs and made such sentiments public fodder. After a slave killed a master, one Missouri newspaper urged its readers to "try the murderer with *fire!*"[16] An inflammatory editorial from a Tennessee newspaper in 1856 responded to an attempted slave revolt as follows:

> The crimes contemplated should be atoned for precisely as though those crimes had been attempted and consummated. Fearful and

terrible examples should be made, and if need be, the fag[g]ot and flame should be brought into requisition to show these deluded maniacs the fierceness and the vigor, the swiftness and completeness of the white man's vengeance. Let a terrible example be made in every neighborhood where the crime can be established, and if necessary, let every tree in the country bend with negro meat.[17]

This is precisely the kind of exaggerated panic that was symptomatic of what Armstead Robinson called the slave South's "epidemic of insurrection anxiety."[18]

What, then, can we conclude from these expressions and acts of violence; the punishment of those particular crimes of murder, rape, and insurrection; society's recourse to barbaric practices of immolation for black offenders; and, in the end, the anxiety of a slave society itself? We can begin by looking at the crime for which so many slaves paid with their lives at the hands of rabid mobs: the murder of their masters. According to Eugene Genovese, the "significance of slaves' murdering their master or overseers cannot be reduced simply to 'resistance to slavery.'" Even while granting that such action was significant because it defined the limits within which slaves were willing to acquiesce, Genovese concludes that such explosive action as murdering the master ultimately acted to reinforce the lesson of "acquiescence in the status quo." Since it was "an individual reaction to individual abuses," murdering the master was a form of protest that "set a model that reinforced the regime."[19]

The legal statutes of slave states seem to belie this reading, though. Although Brazil's Imperial Constitution of 1824 created more-liberal slave codes, banning whipping and other brutal physical punishments, its 1829 Criminal Code nonetheless made the punishment for a slave's murdering a master beyond appeal, even appeal for Imperial Clemency. In 1835 the Regency of Dom Pedro Segundo reinforced this law by passing an "exceptional law" stating: "The punishment of death will be suffered by all slaves, male or female, who kill by any means whatsoever, give poison, gravely wound, or commit any serious physical offense against their master, his wife, his descendents or forebears who may be living in his company."[20]

Even in the antebellum and colonial United States, where conditions did not permit the kind of perpetual slave unrest found in Brazil, there was an accentuated attention to slaves who murdered. In the South Carolina Act of 1712, for example, all cases of slave crime called for the court—made up of magistrates and freeholders—to "diligently weigh . . . and examine . . . all evidences, proofs and testimonies" before passing judgment on the accused slave. In "cases of murder," however, the court was permitted to make its judgment on the basis of "violent presumption and circumstances."[21] These stringent legal codes against slaves murdering masters, of property doing damage to property owners, betrayed the underlying fear that the regime was combustible, that a sufficient number of "individual reactions to individual abuses" could overthrow the slave system. A slave who rose to murder a master was a slave who had clearly exceeded the definition of slave. Moreover, the murder of the master, unlike the murder of an overseer, was a direct challenge to the system of property transfer. The 1835 law of Brazil clearly defines the most heinous acts as those perpetrated against the possible heirs.[22]

Lynch mobs were acting on the same perception that these slaves' acts undermined the very basis of a slave society. Mastery, like slavery, had to be an inheritable state for the society to make sense, but it was shown to be an apparently fragile status if the bondsman could wrest it from an individual master and his family. The "corner-stone" of the Confederacy, according to its vice president, Alexander H. Stephens, "rests upon the great truth that the negro is not equal to the white man, that slavery—subordination to the superior race—is his natural or normal condition."[23] A slave who killed his master or raped his master's wife had made himself equal to those he violated. Lynch mobs, then, acted with the kind of barbarity they did in lynching slaves because they, like the legal codes of the states they lived in, were intent on ensuring the hegemony and transmission of slavery and the white supremacy on which it depended. They killed those slaves who challenged the basis of the system through murder or rape of the master and his family—those slaves who, in other words, endangered the transmission of property from one generation to the next and the sanctity of white women and the legitimacy of the inheriting offspring they produced. Moreover, these lynch mobs resorted to burning because it took a particular kind of ritualized violence—"with deadly as well as shaming intent," as Bertram Wyatt-Brown notes—to render the slaves' presumptuous act negligible.[24] And burning literally did render the slave negligible, creating the conditions by which his very body would disappear in the act of its punishment.

It is worth teasing out the deeper meanings of that pervasive and fecund social anxiety that manifested itself in such profound violence. Herbert Aptheker's *American Negro Slave Revolts* offers example after example of white slaveholders who feel and express their fear of their slaves' rising up against them.[25] Moreover, as Winthrop Jordan notes, whites' fear of insurrection was not the fear of the loss of their servile labor, but rather the fear of being themselves subject to servility if not extinction. A successful insurrection, they felt, "loomed as total destruction, as the irretrievable loss of all that white men had won in America." As one colonial writer put it, what they feared from slaves was the "utter Extirpation" of whites.[26] The fear colonial Americans expressed was the same fear expressed by the press in the Old South. The *Clinton Gazette* did not feel it was protesting too much when it stated in 1835 that a handful of slaves was capable of bringing about "the total destruction of the white population of all the slave states, and the absolute conquest and dominion of the country."

It is, of course, the fear expressed by colonizers in other places, the fear that their work of cultivating the land and of civilizing the labor force will go for naught, that their great enterprise, which they represent to themselves as noble, will fail. To return us to the point I raised in the introduction of the previous chapter, what was at stake for them ultimately was their national identity; a people extirpated or subject to "absolute conquest" would not be Americans. It is worth remembering that, as Edmund Morgan has brilliantly elaborated, the very concept of "American freedom" was directly derived from the debased example of "American slavery." Virginians, Morgan writes, had a "special appreciation of the freedom dear to republicans" because in their slaves they "saw every day what life without it could be like." The presence of slaves continued to exert that same appreciation (and its concomitant fear) on Americans beyond Virginia.[27]

"OUTRAGES OF A POLITICAL CHARACTER": RECONSTRUCTION, 1865–1877[28]

If popular belief about the infrequency of slave lynchings is a result of historians' gross undercounting, the popular belief about the absence of lynching during Reconstruction is a result of historians' restrictive definitions of lynching, as we saw in the Introduction. Indeed, in the historical writing on lynching, Reconstruction is largely an absence or a counterpoint. But for a history of lynching, Reconstruction is much more than just the era preceding the age of lynching (1880–1930). The kind of collective violence performed against African Americans during Reconstruction was evidence of both the continuity and discontinuity in American life before and after the Civil War. The bodies of African Americans—previously owned, now free—became the battleground for crucial issues that arose during the Revolution and were left unresolved by the Civil War: issues about race and citizenship, about popular sovereignty and the state, about forms of social control. Lynching emerged as one of a series of forms of violence meant to resolve these issues.

At the core of the putative logic that was meant to protect slaves from lynching—a logic that failed in notable ways, as we have seen—was the belief that slavery itself was a system of social control, that the plantation was a site for regulating the labor of and exercising control over an enslaved populace. The plantation regime was buttressed by community mechanisms in the form of slave patrols, and state systems in the form of laws that disallowed slaves the possession of literacy, property, arms, and the claim of freedom. When the primary institution of social control was threatened, slaveholding states developed other mechanisms that would supplement plantation discipline during the Civil War, and replace it afterward. As soon as the Civil War began, Confederate states organized "home guards" or "committees of safety" or other forms of vigilante bands. In Georgia, for instance, vigilante groups often supplemented whatever laws were on the books, resolving "to ignore the existing legal structure and conduct their own patrols, believing the 'ordinary process of law . . . too slow to insure safety.'"[29] Both the patrol laws and the home guards would be replaced immediately after the war, the former with "Black Codes" and the latter with new vigilante groups created to terrorize African Americans. There was continuity, then, from slavery to Reconstruction in both the existence of state legal apparatus that essentially controlled the life options of black people, and extralegal vigilantes who controlled their very lives.

Without slavery as an institution to control the mobility and labor of African Americans, former Confederate state governments quickly evolved a set of "Black Codes," laws restricting the capacity of freed people to own or control their own property, including their labor power. In some states, these Black Codes forbad freed people the ownership of property and the rental of land; in others they imposed exceptional taxes on former slaves pursuing any occupation other than farmer or servant. In almost all states, these Black Codes required freed people to have labor contracts and severely punished vagrancy (which amounted, in many cases, to the mere absence of a labor contract). They forced black women and children to work outside of the home through harsh apprenticeship laws, and they prohibited collective bargaining. In effect, as Union general Alfred H. Terry noted, these Black Codes were attempts to resurrect "slavery in all but its name."[30]

It was precisely the goal of these Black Codes to do that, for the purposes of social control—in this case, the specific desires of the slave-holding elites to have unimpeded access to freed people's labor and to reinforce the mythology of white supremacy at the moment when it was most imperiled. A Georgian journalist writing in April 1865 prophetically represents the widespread belief that the *existence* of this social control (of labor and white supremacy) was more important than the *form* it took: "Keep the negroes in their proper places. Change, if you will, . . . the relations at present existing between master and slave, but beware how you attempt to change the relations existing between the two races. . . . Destroy, if you will, . . . the right of property in slaves, but keep the negro . . . subordinate and inferior . . . to the white man."[31]

The Black Codes did not last long, as it became clear that presidential Reconstruction under Andrew Johnson was a grotesque failure. Soon revoked by military officers during congressional Reconstruction, the Black Codes on the books were quickly replaced by vigilante groups in the field. The most significant of these during the first half of Reconstruction (the period from 1865 to 1873) was the Ku Klux Klan, formed in Pulaski, Tennessee, in May or June 1866 as a "social club," transformed some six weeks after its formation into a band of regulators, and then reorganized into a Conservative political terrorist weapon in the spring of 1867.[32] Until it putatively disbanded in 1869, and then was forcibly made subject to federal law by the Ku Klux Klan Act of 1871, the Klan committed innumerable acts of political violence against Republicans, scalawags, carpetbaggers, and African Americans.

Buttressed by imitators like the Knights of the White Camelia, the "Pale Faces," the Constitutional and Union Guards, the White Brotherhood, and the White League, the Klan and other paramilitary white supremacist organizations pursued a strategy of mob violence and terrorism meant to control elections and simultaneously to render the federal military presence and black freedom meaningless.

The Klan pursued a strategy of creating cascading violence, especially around black electoral activity and elections. During the elections of 1868, for instance, a Klan mob in Camilla, Georgia, killed approximately a score of participants in an unarmed black election parade. The majority of the two hundred murders committed in Arkansas during the three months leading up to the 1868 elections were committed by Klan mobs. Given these representative examples of Klan rampages and massacres, and given that they are only samples of the sort of regular activity in which the Klan participated, the number of victims of Klan violence almost certainly exceed the estimate by a leading historian of American violence of "over 400 Klan lynchings" between 1868 and 1871. We also need to remember that the Klan was only one of a number of like-minded white supremacist terrorist groups operating during Reconstruction. The Knights of the White Camelia, for instance, was equally committed to these sorts of massacres. In September 1868 a group of Knights in St. Landry Parish, Louisiana, horsewhipped an editor who criticized their interference in black political affairs, then shot four blacks who attempted to help the editor and had a dozen others arrested. That night, they took the dozen prisoners from the jail and shot them. The next day, the Knights roamed the parish and killed two hundred freed people.[33] To take one last example of organized mass violence against black Americans, residents of Vicksburg, Mississippi, created what they called the People's, or White Man's, Party, which won the municipal elections in the summer of 1874 by having roving armed gangs intimidate Republican voters. Later that year, armed bands of whites roamed the streets of Vicksburg and the surrounding countryside, murdering as many as three hundred blacks and threatening to lynch the black sheriff.[34]

In addition to these relatively organized massacres, Reconstruction also saw the introduction in the South of the urban race riot, although these "riots," as a congressional inquiry put it, tended to become "massacres."[35]

Usually inspired by a single incident, but reflecting the pent-up and seething state of race relations in circumscribed public spaces, urban riots erupted in several cities during Reconstruction. Some were minor, but others were deadly, as the precipitating confrontation led to rampaging mobs of whites entering black communities and killing the inhabitants indiscriminately. Forty-six were killed in the Memphis riot, and forty-eight in the New Orleans riot, both in 1866.[36] Riots in Charleston and Norfolk in 1865, and in Charleston, Richmond, and Atlanta by 1867, were less costly in terms of human lives but altogether made it clear that the work of spontaneous mobs was as lethal and as committed to the goal of social control as that of organized vigilante and terrorist groups.

The work of tabulating the number of victims is daunting. Despite congressional hearings into the "affairs of the late insurrectionary states," resulting in a thirteen-volume report, estimates of Reconstruction violence are impossible to ascertain. Consider the state of Louisiana, for example. In a riot in New Orleans in July 1866 thirty-four black and three white Unionists were slaughtered by a mob. The Freedman's Bureau official who counted seventy murders by February 1867 claimed that the number would increase exponentially if all the acts of violence could have been known and recorded. Between April and November, the months leading up to the elections of 1868, 1,081 recorded murders came to the attention of the congressional committee. Two parishes were particularly violent: 223 murders were committed in St. Landry and 167 in Bossier. Of those killed during that period in the two parishes, 200 and 162, respectively, were African Americans.[37] Of course, not all these fall under the category of "lynchings," but most are acts of mob violence and do qualify. In Louisiana in the decade following the Civil War, 70 percent of white homicides against blacks were committed by more than one person.[38] Taking into account the Freedman's Bureau reports of violence against former slaves, the congressional committee's tabulation of acts of political outrages, and the statistics from the numerous race riots in the era, historians might well decide that John Edward Bruce's estimate of "about 50,000 Negroes . . . slaughtered by the thugs, bullies and midnight assassins" of Reconstruction is not excessive.[39]

Whatever the number, it is enough to recognize the extent of collective violence against freed people and to discern the motives behind that violence. Some of these acts and motives constitute the continuity from slavery—to control the labor, the social options, and the bodies of black Americans.[40] In this way, we can see how the Klan and other vigilante organizations were committed to performing the work previously done by patrollers, home guards, and committees of safety.

But Reconstruction also gave birth to novel forms of and motives for mob violence. Both the occasions for violence—elections, black financial success, and political influence—and the forms the violence took—urban riots and massacres—were evidence of a changed terrain, where labor was "free" (and therefore required violent coercion), black men were enfranchised, and black people had the mobility to go to cities (and therefore had to be destroyed for the presumption of voting and moving).

Another way we can appreciate the continuity and discontinuity, from slavery to Reconstruction, in the practices of lynching black Americans is to see the relationship of extralegal violence to the state apparatus. The slave state explicitly sanctioned random violence against slaves in legal codes that permitted torture and murder, thereby implicitly creating a culture where violence against black Americans was acceptable and seen as unexceptional. Reconstruction was an attempt to provide a legislative response to that situation. The three key amendments gave the formerly enslaved their freedom, their citizenship, and their franchise. In the contestation over those rights putatively available to them, we see the battle over one of the key issues involved in lynching as an American practice—the issue of popular sovereignty. Would the state or the "people" determine the terms of social life? The body and the ballot of African Americans became in effect the last theater of the Civil War. The difference, then, is that whereas the slave state sanctioned those acts of violence against slaves and made those acts therefore part of the panoply of the state's punitive and disciplinary processes, the state during Reconstruction explicitly prohibited those acts and thereby made them one of the means for the "unreconstructed Southerners" to contest the state itself.

What such a suggestion means, let me affirm, is not simply that the state became effectively the guardian of black Americans' rights, and lynchers the only danger to them during and after Reconstruction. The Reconstruction state was a much more complicated, and conflicted, set of agencies that continued to rely on previous legislation and practices in circumscribing what constituted freedom for those who were formerly enslaved. The federal state, especially but not only during presidential Reconstruction, was considerably more concerned with reaffirming the unity of the nation, and ensuring the protection of other kinds of property (especially land), than it was in creating the conditions in which the rights granted by the amendments could be fully protected. The state, in other words, was not a unified or consistent agent in its enforcement of the laws that Congress passed.

What it does mean, however, is that those previous laws that permitted and promoted a particular kind of collective violence against enslaved people—laws we will more fully discuss in the Conclusion—were legally rendered null and void. Because those laws had been created to address particular kinds of imperatives and reflect certain kinds of white social power—imperatives that were *not* rendered null and void by the end of slavery—the terms of the battle now shifted. Those who believed in their continued right to form mobs and kill black Americans did so now with an added intent of explicitly contesting the state's right to proscribe that very activity.

Consider, for instance, the case of a mob in Knoxville, Tennessee, that hanged a black Union army private. First, they hanged him in front of the Freedman's Bureau, and then rehanged him in front of the local army commander's office. The mob then placed a sign on his corpse: "Hung to show the niggers and Freedmen's Bureau Nigger Officers what it takes to make a true Tennessean and whether they'd be run over or not."[41] The mob violence is directed against a person representative of the government (a private in the army) and performed as a taunt to the agencies representing the government (the Freedmen's Bureau, the army offices). The explicit terms of the action and the words the mob used to defend it were directed to and against the federal state. Here, they claim, is an action—the killing of black Americans—that used to represent the support, and now represents the contestation, of the state.

This development in the history of lynching is important because it set the terms for what lynching would mean in a state where it was difficult for people to use the frontier justice claim of an absent or immature legal enforcement and judiciary. Thereafter, those who rationalized lynching as a necessary form of justice would do so by claiming that the courts were flawed, full of technical loopholes, or simply inappropriate sites that further victimized the victims of the alleged crime. Lynchings in that kind of atmosphere became, sometimes explicitly, always implicitly, strategic contestations against the state, against its capacity for police enforcement, against its juridical power, against its ability to protect the rights of those it claimed as its citizens. It was truly in its post–Civil War manifestation that lynching became, in the words of Albert Bushnell Hart, "not simply extra-legal but anti-legal."[42]

The efforts African Americans made to protect themselves should also be seen as acts that challenged the state, in this case to perform its duties and uphold blacks' freedom, citizenship, and franchise. These efforts took several forms, ranging from organizing and agitating to armed self-defense. Shortly after emancipation, African Americans organized conventions that allowed for deliberation about social goals and the creation of community leaders. This organizing represented the preparation of black communities to enter into democratic citizenship, producing channels for communicating with the state and federal government, and ensuring that these communities had a voice in the systems promoting justice and rights. In the face of the extraordinary violence during Reconstruction, African American groups and communities produced petitions to make renewed claims to the justice they were denied. For instance, the petition presented to Congress and the Senate in 1871 from the "Committee of Grievances appointed at a meeting of all the Colored Citizens of Frankfort," Kentucky, lists 116 acts of terrorism and mob violence and challenges the Congress to uphold the laws they pass and protect the lives of those they represent.[43] Finally, in the absence of appropriate protection, black communities formed armed militias to protect themselves. Although there were armed black militias before emancipation, Reconstruction witnessed the emergence of militias designed to be a part of the public spectacle of black freedom, often at political events. What precipitated the massacre in Hamburg, South Carolina, in 1876, for instance, was the response of white mobs to a parade of Hamburg's black militia during a Fourth of July celebration.[44] In this final case, we see the dynamic between a novel form of black resistance and a novel form of white oppression in Reconstruction, between formerly enslaved people who arm themselves for protection and who celebrate the day commemorating American freedom, and the white mobs and complicit military forces that attack them because they had the effrontery to arm themselves and think themselves truly free.

The final point I wish to make here is that Reconstruction plays an important role as a trope in the discourse of lynching. We will see in Chapter Four the full role that the idea of Reconstruction played in the imagination of lynching apologists and critics at the end of the nineteenth century. For now, though, we can note that those apologists who claimed that lynchings were performed solely as a punishment for the crime of rape—a crime uniquely practiced by black men upon white women—regarded Reconstruction as the moment of birth for that crime. Two examples will suffice. During the "whole period of slavery," and throughout the Civil War, Thomas Nelson Page claimed, "the crime of assault was unknown throughout the South." "Then, came the period and process of Reconstruction, with its teachings . . . that the negro was the equal of the white," a teaching that flourished in the ravishing of white women, first by armed black militias and then by black civilians.[45] Myra Lockett Avary likewise states that the "rapist is a product of the reconstruction period. . . . He came into life in the abnormal atmosphere of a time rife with discussions of social equality theories, contentions for coeducation and intermarriage."[46] For these representative lynching apologists, Reconstruction stands as the moment when a prostrate South was raped in both metaphorical and literal ways, the moment when fears of black "servile insurrection" became fears of "Negro domination," with all that "domination" connoted sexually as well as politically.

Again, we will see the ways this particular discourse was formed and mobilized during the 1880s and 1890s, but it is important to recognize its rudimentary origins in the 1860s. We saw above what happened in St. Landry's Parish when the white supremacist Knights of the White Camelia lynched over two hundred African Americans in September 1868. The New Orleans *Daily Picayune*'s headline for that story—"Negro Rising in St. Landry/Program of Spoilation, Rapine, Conflagration, and Murder. . . . Conciliatory Policy of the Whites"—reveals how the trope of "rape" was invoked for virtually any form of black self-assertion, how the thought of black sexual violence consistently lurked in the recesses of what Wilbur Cash called "the mind of the South."[47]

I will end this section with a case that is representative of Reconstruction mob violence, and different primarily in that the victim was not killed and therefore able to testify about his trauma. Henry Lowther, a black man in Wilkinson County, Georgia, was jailed on trumped-up charges of gathering a black mob in order to murder another black man. He was joined in jail by twenty-four others who were arrested because they had gathered a group to protect Lowther. Members of the Klan interviewed him in jail to offer him the option of castration ("are you willing to give up your stones to save your life?"). Later, when he was interviewed by the subcommittee compiling the Senate report on Klan activity in the South, he noted that another man had been castrated in the same county ("whipped one of his seed entirely out and the other very nearly out"), and yet another in the adjoining county. In response to a question by a member of the subcommittee whether he had been charged with "any violence, any insult to any white woman," Lowther responded in the negative and noted that the Klan did say that he "was getting to have too much influence in the republican party there." The interview ended with the chair of the subcommittee again asking about the charges of Lowther's seeing a white woman, which Lowther again denied.[48]

This interesting case is both representative of Reconstruction-era violence (Lowther was punished, as others were killed, because of his affiliation with and role within the Republican Party) and a harbinger of the rituals that would become fully manifest in Progressive-era lynchings (the mob's allegations of interracial rape or sexual alliances and the focus on the emasculation of black men so charged). In both eras, victims of lynchings would be taken from jails, often, as in this case, with the complicity of the sheriffs, and in both eras these lynchings were intended as a challenge to the state. In addition, it is significant that Lowther was imprisoned for his work at arming black men and that the other black men were imprisoned with him for attempting to protect him with an armed guard.

Finally, we should note the interplay among the variety of motives addressed in this interview. The Klan charged Lowther with creating a black militia, the Senate subcommittee was struck by the rumors of Lowther's sexual alliance with a white woman, and Lowther knew that he was castrated because he was involved in Republican politics. Revealed in this tableau are two notable points: first, that the discourse of lynching depends on a form of ideological indirection (motives rumored are as important as the motives stated), and second, as I suggested above, we can see the budding discourse of lynching that would effloresce in the 1890s. The anxieties about black men's sexual alliances with white women were as manifest in the recesses of Congress as they were in the "mind of the South."

It is unlikely that we will ever have the kind of compilation of statistics of lynchings before the 1880s that we have of them after, and it is likely that the number of those killed by mobs during slavery and Reconstruction will never be known, but our knowledge of the existence of racial lynching before the 1880s is growing exponentially. It would be hard to find a historian claiming now, as Winthrop Jordan did in 1968, that the 1741 lynching of a black man in Roxbury, Massachusetts, was "perhaps the only such instance before the nineteenth century."[49] Yet and still, there is resistance to accepting that these acts of mob violence we have been discussing above are the "same" as lynchings during the Progressive era. Historians continue either to see distinctions that are defied by the evidence—"In Reconstruction, mob violence most often stopped short of murder, and when killing was involved, it happened without ceremony"—or to attempt to claim distinctions that seem tenuous or give undue credit to the claims of lynch mobs: "By contrast, lynching was 'ritualized murder' conducted under the claim that the mob was dispensing justice."[50] As we have seen, the claims of mobs are less significant than their actions; and their actions, during slavery, during Reconstruction, during the Progressive era, bespeak their desire to contain, terrorize, and control those whose lives they take with impunity. What happened to James Costello, for instance, during the 1863 New York City draft riots—when a mob of two to three hundred beat him to death with stones and fists, hanged him from a tree, and sliced off his fingers and toes—looks very much like the kind of "ritualized murder" that thousands would fall victim to during the fifty years after Reconstruction.[51]

That fifty-year period was an era in which mass transportation systems, mass media networks, and mass citizen participation colluded to produce an illusion of community, a delusion of white supremacy, and a confusion between state and civil society—all premised on a ritual sacrifice of someone whose ancestors were once enslaved by a mob of those whose progeny remained unreconstructed.

3

The Age of Lynching

In the spring of 1899, just outside Newnan, Georgia, Sam Hose was tortured, mutilated, castrated, and then burned alive in front of a crowd of about two thousand. The mob did its work methodically, different people cutting off each ear, different men removing each joint of his fingers. Only when they reached the work of emasculation did the mob of white men become boisterously chaotic, accidently cutting each others' hands in what one newspaper called "the delirious frenzy of the men to perform the bloody task." Following the torture and mutilation, the lynchers poured kerosene over Hose and the surrounding pine kindling and logs, and then lit a match that set ablaze the writhing man, who had been chained to a tree. An eyewitness noted that the flames immediately "darted up the man's clothing and ran up his back, burning away every rag, burning his hair away, singeing off his eyebrows." After feeding off and exhausting the kerosene on his body, the flame fell back to the ground and began its slow upward climb on Hose's body. As he struggled against the flames, Hose began to strike his hands against the chain binding him to the tree. The eyewitness describes the scene: "Piece by piece he beat the flesh off his hand, the fingers were stripped of flesh and sinews until the bones, protruding, were snapped by the blows." After twenty minutes of struggle, having broken the chain once and having been reattached to the tree, Hose lost consciousness and then life.[1]

What happened to Sam Hose had become a common occurrence by the turn of the century. In the previous two decades, hundreds of

African Americans had been hanged, burned, and tortured with exquisite design. What followed the lynching of Hose had also become routine, almost scripted. There was a public debate over just what happened to cause this lynching. White newspapers claimed that the crime he committed was rape and wanton murder; the local black community and black antilynching activists claimed that he had killed his boss in self-defense in a fight over unpaid wages. The Southern press defended the lynching as an act of chivalry in defense of the honor of the victims; the Northern and international press condemned the town and the region for its barbarity. For both the apologists and the critics of the lynching, the event was not an isolated incident, but a representative one. It was a story about not one man but a race, about not one town but a region, about not one country but an empire.

Indeed, the Hose lynching became an item of debate about the Spanish-American war. On one side, a pro-imperialist Georgia congressman spoke in the House of Representatives and used the Hose lynching to defend America's war of empire. He claimed that both the lynching of Hose and "the shooting of brown men in the Philippines" were done to "maintain the supremacy of the Anglo-Saxon race" and "in the name of civilization." On the other side, an anti-imperialist Massachusetts newspaper editor felt that the lynching exposed what was truly behind America's "world crusade," and that it mocked the "white civilization we would carry to the Orient and shoot into the hearts of the Malays if we cannot get it there otherwise."[2]

It was not just the name Sam Hose (not his real one, it turns out) that served to represent an abstract idea in political debates, in the midst of larger struggles about the meaning of chivalry and race and repression. His image also circulated in the course of these debates. The *Atlanta Journal* printed on its front page what a headline called "The First Picture of the Negro Yet Printed—Made from a Photograph Taken Yesterday for The Journal." A local Newnan newspaper later advertised a photograph of Hose "burning at the stake" for fifteen cents. In fact, not only pictures of his body, but his very body circulated in this society. A piece of his flesh, about the "size of a hen's egg," laid out on a bed of lettuce with onion garnish, was mailed to an outspoken critic of the lynching, and some of Hose's body parts were placed in pickling jars on public display.[3]

One of those body parts played an important role in the intellectual life of W.E.B. DuBois, who was on his way to the offices of the *Atlanta Constitution* with a "careful and reasoned statement concerning the evident facts" of the charges against Hose in order to prevent the lynching when he heard that Hose had already been lynched and that "his knuckles were on exhibition at a grocery store on Mitchell Street." DuBois returned to his offices at Atlanta University, letter undelivered, because, as he put it, he "suddenly saw that complete scientific detachment in the midst of such a South was impossible." Unlike DuBois, who succumbed to momentary despair in the beliefs that had hitherto guided his social activism, Ida B. Wells saw in the lynching of Hose yet another opportunity for her to address what she saw as the fundamental social function of lynchings—"to teach the Negro in the South he has no rights that the law will enforce." She continued her quest to make public the knowledge of what lynchings were, and the ways that lynchers constructed a deceitful cover story to hide what they were. Her expression of hope contrasts nicely with DuBois's expression of despair. She noted that she was publishing the pamphlet so that she could "give the public the facts, in the belief that there is still a sense of justice in the American people, and that it will yet assert itself in condemnation of outlawry and in defense of oppressed and persecuted humanity."[4]

What Sam Hose allegedly did and what happened to him would also define and reinforce the values of those who advocated lynching as much as of those who fought to end it. Tom Dixon based his representation of the black rapist in his 1902 novel, *The Leopard's Spots,* on a combination of Henry Smith, who was lynched in 1893, and Sam Hose. In a later novel, *The Flaming Sword,* an even more ambitiously racist novel—and that is saying something—Dixon portrayed the world of a decent white family utterly destroyed by a rapist and murderer who turns out to be Sam Hose's brother. It would be a crime that was punished by a fraternally similar lynching and would inspire the heroine who survives her ordeal to begin a campaign for a grander solution to the race problem. *The Flaming Sword* is a novel that mercilessly caricatures DuBois, alleges that Hose was inspired to rape after reading a poem by James Weldon Johnson, and ends its bitter description of what it calls "the Conflict of Color in America from 1900 to 1938" by advocating the repatriation of black Americans to Africa.[5]

What circulated in American society in 1899—contradictory information about the crime Hose allegedly committed, lurid accounts of the lynching itself, debates about the meaning of the lynching for the town, county, state, and nation where it occurred, and photographs, postcards, and physical pieces of Hose himself—is what circulated to varying degrees just before and just after numerous lynchings between 1880 and the 1930s. These were the years of the "age of lynching."

There are several reasons the period from the end of Reconstruction until the end of the Depression can rightly be called the "age of lynching." Emphatically, though, it is *not* because those six decades saw more lynchings than any earlier period of American history, for they did not. Although it is impossible to prove with extant data, it is highly likely that mobs and vigilante groups murdered more people during the dozen years of Reconstruction than in the half-century after. This time span likewise is not the epoch when lynching first established its conventional rituals, for those were evident in more than rudimentary form during the eighteenth and nineteenth centuries, although lynchings during the post-Reconstruction era did assume their most mature and brutal forms, and assumed them more regularly.

What makes this era rightly the age of lynching is that lynching assumed a new prominence and importance in American culture and became in effect a gauge of that culture. As the case of Sam Hose demonstrates, a lynching provided an opportunity for the entire society to situate the whole event in a variety of contexts—as a feature of race relations, a concern in domestic politics, or a consideration in international affairs. Lynching, in the age of lynching, became not just a practice but also a topic of legal and intellectual debate, and a symptom and metaphor for what America was and was becoming as a nation.

DEFINING THE AGE OF LYNCHING

It is not too much to say that Americans "discovered" lynching as a practice after 1880 in much the same way they discovered it as a term after 1835. Every sector of a rapidly expanding information society contributed to this growth in knowledge. Most responsible for this dissemination of information were the newspapers that made stories of lynchings a daily staple for their mass readership.[6] In addition to representing lynching in sensational ways, a point we will discuss more fully below, newspapers also helped to make lynchings calculable, which made the topic part of a public discourse of larger national questions. The newspaper most responsible for establishing the statistical coverage of lynchings was the *Chicago Tribune*. Exhibiting its new editor's faith in social science and the truth value of statistics, the *Chicago Tribune* in 1882 began producing an annual tabulation of lynchings.[7]

In 1900, Monroe Work, a Tuskegee social scientist inspired by the *Chicago Tribune*'s example, began to compile data for and produce semiannual reports. By 1915, these reports were being sent to the Associated Press and three hundred daily newspapers, and they were also annually published in *World Almanac*. By 1922, the reports were being sent to two thousand newspapers.[8] Both Work and Joseph Medill, the editor and owner of the *Chicago Tribune*, believed that this information, whose accuracy was unassailable since it was numerical, could help produce progressive social change—in the case of lynching, to help end it. The work this widespread information performed in changing public opinion—along with the work of civil rights activists and other anti-lynching advocates—attest to at least one source of increasing public opinion against lynching and in favor of federal legislation. What these statistical reports also produced was a set of data that revealed the extent and regularity of lynching in America, made it possible for people to see regional, seasonal, and demographic patterns, and enabled Americans to discern what mob violence bespoke about national character beneath the surface story of an individual lynching. By being published in newspapers, this information was not limited to social scientists but was available to a reading public who could use it to gauge the social climate, to determine, in the same way they used literacy rates or poverty indices, the degree of progress or civilization evident in the nation.

This era also marked the rise of antilynching advocacy and scholarship. Social activists—both individual intellectuals and civil society groups—began to publish editorials, articles, pamphlets, tracts, and books about lynching. In the last decade of the nineteenth and the first decade of the twentieth century, African American intellectuals, including such notables as Frederick Douglass, Ida B. Wells, and Mary Church Terrell, spoke out against lynching in nationally circulated periodicals and published tracts. The quarter century following the founding of the NAACP (1909) saw the rise of civil society groups' concerted antilynching agencies and campaigns. The NAACP committed itself to a legal struggle, as well as a moral one in the creation of the African American women's "Anti-Lynching Crusaders."[9] The Commission on Interracial Cooperation, formed in 1919, created the Southern Commission on the Study of Lynching and the Association of Southern Women for the Prevention of Lynching, the former an agency for the generation of knowledge about lynching, the latter an agency for moral persuasion and active agitation. The academic study of lynching was also inaugurated during these years, with the first book-length social science monograph published in 1905, and a clutch of books published later in the early 1930s under the auspices of the Southern Commission on the Study of Lynching. As the newspaper coverage revealed the extent and sensationalism of lynching to the masses, the essays in esteemed periodicals and books from university presses made lynching a pressing issue for intellectuals and activists.

These were also the years when state legislatures began to pass anti-lynching bills. In 1896, Ohio passed an antilynching law, while in 1897 Kentucky passed its own "act to prevent lynching and injury and destruction of real and personal property in this Commonwealth." By the beginning of the Depression, at least six states, including the Southern states of Alabama, Kentucky, Virginia, and North Carolina, made lynching a statutory crime, while four more states criminalized mob violence. In addition, Congress attempted to pass a federal anti-lynching bill. Including the most famous of those efforts—the 1922 Dyer bill, the 1934 Costigan-Wagner bill, and the 1937 Gavagan bill—there were sixty-one antilynching bills introduced between 1882 and 1933, and another one hundred and thirty between 1934 and 1940.[10]

We can call these decades the "era of lynching," then, not because of the spectacular rise of the practice, but primarily because of the remarkable circulation of information about the practice and, consequently, the way lynching became imbricated over so many other features of American life. Lynching became the subject of careful tabulation for social scientists and newspapers, the subject of study by scholars and intellectuals, the subject of activism for intelligentsia and civil society groups, the subject of legislation by state and national politicians, and, notably, the subject of debate about the prospects for postbellum African American life.

In addition, lynching in America during this era was as much an issue in debates about foreign policy as it was in those about domestic politics. In each American war, lynching became a symbol—in the case of wars of empire, a symbol of how America would treat conquered nations like the Philippines; in the case of wars against Germany, a symbol of the hypocrisy of a country claiming a moral defense of democracy as its motive—as in the *New Republic* article in 1918 asking whether lynching had become a part of "American Kultur."[11]

Lynching, then, was as public a fact as the large banner the NAACP flew outside its New York office on Fifth Avenue after each act of mob violence, a banner stating factually, "A Man Was Lynched Yesterday." And that banner, had the NAACP existed as early as 1882, would have flown on average at least once a week, every week, for five decades.[12] The information circulating during the era of lynching was based, in the end, on the substantial, enduring, and pervasive mob violence that marked these years.

We can note three distinctive developments in the form and dynamic of mob violence during the age of lynching. First, this is the period that witnessed the rise of what we can call the "total drama" of lynching. The total drama was largely a result of the media's framing of lynching stories. Newspapers gave a form and structure to these stories, starting with the rumors of the alleged instigating crime (usually rape, almost always presented in a sensational fashion), coverage of the manhunt, editorial predictions of the future lynching, accounts of the brutal lynching itself, and then editorial commentary lamenting or justifying the lynching. In fashioning this total drama—setting the scene, assigning motivations to actors, predicting action, and explaining or justifying it—newspapers provided both a titillating story—what Jacquelyn Dowd Hall called "an acceptable folk pornography" for a reading public—while also controlling the action of that story. They acted, then, as agents as much as recorders of the age of lynching, a point memorably made by one of Charles Chesnutt's characters, who calls them, in an apt pun, "noospapers."[13]

Second, this is the era that saw the substantial and regular rise of ritual lynchings of African Americans. While, as we saw in the previous chapter, we can find numerous lynchings of black people during slavery and a virtual orgy of collective violence during Reconstruction, it was largely during the age of lynching that we regularly find the practices and features we think of as part of the ritual lynching—torture, castration, immolation, mass spectatorship. This is also the era when it was widely acknowledged and documented—in the *Tribune* and Tuskegee statistics—that many more black people than whites were being lynched. It was the era, in other words, that recognized lynching as a racial practice.

Finally, this is the era that witnessed the rise and the assumption of hegemonic status of what can be called the "discourse of lynching," that is, the explanatory rationale for lynching provided by the practice's apologists. We will more fully discuss the discourse of lynching in Chapter Four, where we will see how the debate between lynching apologists and antilynching activists became a debate about the meaning of the practice (was it chivalry or genocidal racism, a gallant form of popular justice or the ruling elite's social control of a labor pool?), as well as a debate about the South and postemancipation African American life and character. It is worth noting, though, that for most African American intellectuals and antilynching advocates of all cultural backgrounds, lynching was, in the words of James Weldon Johnson, an "instrument for terrorizing Negroes, keeping them from voting, and in the position of 'inferior,' as well as an instrument of economic exploitation re-inforcing peonage in the cotton-raising sections of the country." Walter White, more succinctly, noted that lynching "has always been the means for protection, not of white women, but of profits."[14] The most honest lynchers, such as the Whitecaps of Lawrence County, Mississippi, agreed, noting in an 1893 "Declaration of Purpose" that their "first object is to control negro laborers by mild means, if possible, by coercion if necessary."[15]

These three major developments marked the age of lynching, but that should not lead us to believe that there was only one form or mode of lynching during this era. Historians have noted that the lynchings in these years differed in their motivation, in their procedures, in their structure. In addition, lynch mobs changed in size and strategies over the course of the age of lynching. We can begin by identifying the major types of mobs.

One of the first scholars to offer a classificatory scheme was historian John Ross, who divided lynch mobs into seven classes. Ross, who is to be praised for being one of the few students of lynching to stress the need for a capacious definition of the practice, discerned three primary "genera" of lynch mobs, based on level of organization: 1) those deriving from permanent organizations (which include the vigilante mob and the terrorist mob); 2) those that have elements of planning and collusion among the mob leaders (which include the organized mob, the private mob, and the secret mob); and 3) the "wholly spontaneous, unplanned outgrowth of crowd excitement" (which includes the hue-and-cry mob and the mass mob). Fitzhugh Brundage, in a foundational study of lynching in Georgia and Virginia, has identified four types of mobs operating during the age of lynching: terrorist mobs, private mobs, posses, and mass mobs.[16]

Terrorist mobs, often small but representative factions of larger organizations, like the Klan, performed lynchings in order to intimidate particular populations, sometimes on the pretext of what they claimed to be outright crimes, sometimes because of perceived violations of community mores, but most often simply to terrorize those groups. Private mobs (and secret mobs) were less-organized groups of between five and fifty individuals who pursued their victims with an aim of punishing alleged criminal offenses, acting with little media coverage, and indeed often cloaking their lynching with secrecy and themselves with masks. Posses, sometimes legally and sometimes spontaneously deputized, acted beyond whatever legal sanction they had when they murdered unarmed victims. These types of mobs infrequently performed the gruesome work usually associated with lynchings during this era—immolation, mutilation, and other symbolic gestures—but were more often content with the simple act of killing their victim. It was the last type of mob—the mass mob—that rigorously followed the pattern of ritual lynchings. Composed of large groups often numbering in the thousands, these mobs were not content with simply murdering the victim, which would not suffice to meet the symbolic and quasi-religious requirements of the rite. Instead the mob participated as a collective in selecting the symbolically appropriate site for the lynching, soliciting the participation of the family of the alleged victim of the originating crime, aggressively brutalizing the body of the lynch victim, and then memorializing the lynched corpse and lynching site.[17]

These mass mobs are the mobs most commonly represented in fiction, film, and historical studies. There is good reason why this is so. Although they do not predominate, they do represent a not uncommon occurrence. They were responsible for 39 percent of Georgia's lynchings and 43 percent of Virginia's. These were the mobs that performed the era's most notoriously infamous lynchings, which were motivated by a burst of xenophobia or anti-Semitism, such as the 1891 lynchings of eleven Italian immigrants in New Orleans and the 1915 lynching of Leo Frank in Georgia. These were the mobs that, motivated by a deep stain of racism, performed the innumerable lynchings of African Americans who were mutilated, hanged, shot, immolated, and killed by means and methods that were remarkable for their sadism. Most revealingly, 98 percent of the victims of mass mob lynchings in Georgia, and 94 percent in Virginia, were African American.[18] These are the mobs, then, whose racial lynchings were indeed *performances,* whose work was to produce a "grand spectacular show" to rival ancient Roman gladiators, as the editor of the *Vicksburg Evening Post* put it.[19]

THE ERA OF SPECTACLE LYNCHING

One of the first such "spectacular shows" took place in Paris, Texas, on February 1, 1893. Accused of raping and murdering a four-year-old child, Henry Smith was hunted down and finally found in Hempstead County, Arkansas. He was transported on a train to Texarkana, where a crowd of five thousand people were waiting. Prominent citizens of Paris addressed the crowd and asked that they not molest Smith so that he could be delivered directly to their town. A mob of 10,000 people were awaiting him at the Paris train station. They transported him on a carnival float through the town and then to an open field, where he was placed on a scaffold. After the crowd tore off pieces of his clothes, the father of the murdered child, the child's brother, and two uncles applied hot irons to Smith's flesh, burning first his feet and legs, and then rolled the freshly heated irons along Smith's stomach, back, and arms, before finally burning out Smith's eyes and thrusting the hot irons down his throat. After fifty minutes of such torture, those nearest the scaffold helped pour kerosene on cottonseed hulls they had placed under Smith and set them and him ablaze.[20]

Another such lynching occurred on October 27, 1934, in Jackson County, Florida, near the towns of Marianna and Greenwood. Accused of raping and murdering Lola Cannidy, a white woman who had been his childhood friend, Claude Neal was taken into custody by the sheriff, who transported him to an out-of-state prison in Brewton, Alabama, to protect him from the gathering lynch mob in Marianna. After the news of Neal's location was leaked, a group of local residents went to the Brewton jail and brought Neal back to Jackson County. In a wooded area about four miles from Greenwood, the group subjected Neal to two hours of torture. After castrating him and making him eat his penis and testicles, they slowly and methodically used a sharp knife to slice his sides and his stomach; they cut off many of his fingers and some of his toes, while also applying hot irons to his body. After murdering him, they dragged his body behind an automobile to the Cannidy house at 1 a.m., where the remnants of a crowd that had numbered from three to five thousand had been gathered for hours. There Neal's corpse was subject to further indignities, as Lola Cannidy's father shot three bullets into the forehead and the crowd plunged knives into the body. At about 3 o'clock in the morning, the mob took the corpse to the Jackson County courthouse and hanged it from a tree.[21]

Ida B. Wells wrote about the Paris, Texas, lynching in her 1895 publication, *A Red Record,* while the NAACP commissioned a white investigator to produce a record of the Marianna lynching, which the group published in 1934 as *The Lynching of Claude Neal.* Wells, who had already published an earlier pamphlet on lynching, intimated that there was something insidiously novel about the lynching of Henry Smith. The "white Christian people of Paris, Texas and the communities thereabout," Wells wrote, "had deliberately determined to set aside all forms of law and inaugurate an entirely new form of punishment for the murder."[22]

That "entirely new form" was the spectacle lynching, the public, communal ritual of torture, dismemberment, and hanging or burning. These are the lynchings, as I noted above, done by mobs of thousands, for which newspapers and radios announced the event, where photographs were taken of the body, and after which parts of the body became souvenirs. According to historian Grace Elizabeth Hale, the lynching of Henry Smith in 1893, which she describes as the "first blatantly public, actively promoted lynching of a southern black by a crowd of southern whites," was indeed the "founding event in the history of spectacle lynchings." For the next forty years, until the lynching of Claude Neal in 1934 "signaled the end of the gruesome southern practice," spectacle lynchings became the most resonant of the rituals of violence against African Americans. Lynchings, it is important to note, actually decreased in frequency after 1892, and spectacle lynchings, as we saw above, were not as common as the more private lynchings with smaller mobs. Yet these spectacle lynchings assume greater cultural power even as the actual numbers of lynchings decrease, because not only do they become spectacles for the participants in the significantly larger lynch mobs but they also become mediated spectacles for the consumers of the newspaper reports and photographs that circulated after the lynchings.[23]

It is these lynchings that most scholars implicitly discuss when they offer interpretations of the meaning of lynchings. Those who try to explain the causes of lynchings during the age of lynching generally align the ritual to changing material conditions of labor (economic fluctuations and depression, the uncertainty of a new market economy), to political developments (the structure and autonomy of Southern county governments, reactionary populism), and to new demographic conditions (a frontier ethos with rapid in-migration, the proportion of blacks in the population). Social psychologists have traced lynching to revivalist religious sensibilities, displaced aggression, and the emergence of an "authoritarian personality" in the mob leaders. In recent studies, historians and sociologists have argued that lynchings are to be understood as religious rituals of human sacrifice, as helping to ease class tensions within white supremacy in a consumer culture of segregation, and as part of a strategy for social domination—a "ritualistic affirmation of white unity," a mode for repressing black communities, and a means of controlling white women's behavior.[24] We will discuss these interpretations in the Conclusion.

Here we will address a somewhat different but I believe related question, which concerns not the causes of lynchings but how we may understand the lynch mob as an agent. I would like to suggest that in the first third of the twentieth century in the United States the lynch mob in spectacle lynchings constitutes an institution of American civil society.

I should clarify that I am making this argument about the kind of ad hoc lynch mob that was the most frequent agent of lynchings after Reconstruction. Organizations like the San Francisco Vigilance Committee in the 1850s, and imitators like the Montana Vigilantes in the 1860s and the Ku Klux Klan and other white supremacist groups in the 1860s and 1870s, have more recognizable features of civil society institutions. Here my focus is on those mobs that are not readily recognized as such. My claim is not that the ad hoc lynch mob is uniquely an institution of civil society during the age of lynching. Rather, I wish to show how, even in its more "disorganized" forms, the lynch mob of the age of lynching continued to exercise the same power as earlier vigilante and regulator groups, a power we can identify as constituting in some ways a "public."

In order to pursue this idea, let me turn briefly to some recent definitions of civil society. Whereas from the late-sixteenth to the late-eighteenth centuries the term "civil society" was synonymous with "the state," and in Hegel, Marx, Gramsci, and to some degree Habermas "civil society" still designates some of the features of the state proper, the term is now primarily used to describe those voluntary associations that are independent of and separate from the apparatus of the state and usually meant to provide a critical and discursive counterweight to the state. In this contemporary sense, civil society includes what Nancy Fraser calls that "nexus of nongovernmental or 'secondary' associations that are neither economic nor administrative." The members of these associations are not state officials, and even when state officials participate in particular institutions their participation is divorced from their official roles. In a recent revision of his original theory of the public sphere, Habermas notes that the "institutional core of 'civil society' is constituted by voluntary unions outside the realm of the state and the economy," and he lists such organizations as "churches, cultural associations, and academies," "independent media, sport and leisure clubs, debating societies, groups of concerned citizens, and grass-roots petitioning drives," as well as occupational associations and labor unions.[25] Contemporary voluntary unions in either formal institutions or more ad hoc organizations (groups of concerned citizens and grassroots petitioning drives) are "opinion-forming associations."[26] Their political influence is not as direct as it would be if they had the power of legislation, but it is considerable insofar as public opinion constitutes a genuine political force.

In that sense of civil society, then, we would certainly include those exemplary voluntary associations that arose during the first third of the twentieth century to combat, prevent, expose, and end lynching in America. Organizations like the Commission on Interracial Cooperation (CIC), the Association of Southern Women for the Prevention of Lynching (ASWPL), and the NAACP were at the forefront of the fight to reform public opinion and to mobilize political action against lynching. The CIC employed activist-scholars to undertake and publish reports and studies of the causes and meanings of lynching. The ASWPL dramatically undermined the major rationales of patriarchal chivalry offered as a defense for lynching. One of the first pamphlets the group published was titled *A New Public Opinion on Lynching.*[27] The NAACP, meanwhile, undermined the rationale of lynchers from the other side by demonstrating, as Ida B. Wells had done at the turn of the century, the rarity of rape as the alleged crime for the lynching. Against the widespread popular belief that, in the words of Rebecca Lattimer Felton, "it takes lynching to protect women's dearest possession from drunken, ravening human beasts," the NAACP reminded the American public that in only one-sixth of the lynchings in America was there even an accusation of rape. In addition, the NAACP conducted a publicity campaign and bravely lobbied for federal antilynching legislation.[28]

Is it possible to think of a lynch mob as an institution of civil society equal to the CIC, ASWPL, and NAACP? I can imagine several objections to this suggestion. First, it will be argued that the institutions of civil society are not destructive in the way that a lynch mob is; they produce rational discourse, whereas a lynch mob is organized only to inflict violence. Second, the lynch mob is not strictly an "opinion-forming association" in the way that a labor union or debating society might be said to be. Unlike the institutions that attempt to promote publicly acceptable opinions in a particular discursive form, lynch mobs torture and murder. Third, lynch mobs do not possess the apparatus or the enduring existence of the typical institution of civil society; indeed, they are marked by the spontaneity of their assembly. The objections, then, are that a lynch mob is spontaneously violent, irrational, disorganized, and ephemeral. Institutions, on the other hand, are constructive, rational, and organized to produce and retain legitimation. Institutions are marked by regular and expected patterns of behavior—that is, predictable agency—that govern and structure the lives of social actors within them.

I would like to suggest that these are implicitly the same kinds of objections that antilynching advocates were also struggling to answer. Apologists for lynching claimed that a clamor for swift and immediate justice in the face of an unacceptable crime drove the mob to its frantic action. The antilynching advocates, on the other hand, did not characterize the lynch mob *as a mob,* as a frenzied and inarticulate entity driven to spontaneous acts of unthinking violence. Jessie Daniel Ames of the ASWPL, for instance, claimed that one way to understand lynchers was to see them as "criminal devils, inherently wicked, and depraved," but another and more useful way, she intimated, was to believe that "lynchers are born into a social and economic system which turns them to acts of brutal violence." It was the social system that was in need of fundamental reform, not a few sociopaths in need of punishment. This was a point antilynching advocates stressed. In a study published under the auspices of the CIC, Arthur Raper noted that mobs "do not come out of nowhere; they are the logical outgrowths of dominant assumptions and prevalent thinking." There were seventy-five thousand Americans who joined a lynch mob in 1930 alone, Raper noted, and while they were members of a mob only one day in the year they "were most probably mob-minded every day in the year." And by "mob-minded" Raper does not mean that they were capable of becoming unthinking agents of violence but rather that they were in daily practice socialized to act out the white supremacy that is the reason for lynching.[29]

Antilynching advocates were intent on noting quite specifically how the lynch mob was a symptom of a social disorder by pointing out that lynch mobs were made up of business and civic leaders. They noted that the rituals of torture and dismemberment and display were established and regular; as one historian put it, the mobs performed "much as if their members had attended formal schools on procedures." They noted that lynchings tended to occur in counties where there was feared or perceived African American insurgency and they tended to be followed by a determined intimidation of the whole African American community. After Claude Neal was lynched, the lynchers, described by the local newspaper as "a well organized orderly mob," burned every shack owned by black people in the neighborhood before marching into town and starting a race riot. The leader of the race riot, according to the NAACP report, was a "young man from Calhoun County who has money and comes from a good family."[30]

To appreciate better the rhetorical force of the antilynching advocates, consider the difference in the reporting of the first spectacle lynching. Shortly after the lynching of Henry Smith, a member of the lynch mob published a pamphlet titled *The Facts in the Case of the Horrible Murder of Little Myrtle Vance, and Its Fearful Expiation, at Paris, Texas, February 1, 1893*. In that pamphlet, in his own words, and using the words of other apologists for the lynchings, the lyncher-turned-reporter writes that the rape and murder of Myrtle Vance "served thoroughly to madden the people." He described a people who were usually "peaceable, orderly, [and] quiet," but were by this crime "driven to madness, made wild to the point of savagery." The community was "goaded to madness by a deed demoniac." It is primarily the inflammatory nature of the crime, he suggests, that led to this collective temporary insanity.[31]

Ida B. Wells, on the other hand, noted that the "fury" of the mob that lynched Smith did not prevent its members from being fully "conscious that [each of them] will never be called to an account." And while she insists on noting the "shocking brutality and indescribable barbarism" of the mob's actions, she also insists on pointing out that the actions of the mob had the full "moral support" of the community. She exposed the role played by the corporations that publicized the event and facilitated the formation of the mob. The newspapers had announced that there would be a lynching three days before it occurred, and the railroads ran special excursions for those who traveled from distant towns and neighboring states. What particularly attracted Wells's attention was the coordination between those who lynched Smith and the civic officials who made it possible. The district attorney went to

Arkansas to retrieve Smith, and he himself turned Smith over to the mob, while the mayor of the town, she wrote, "gave the children a holiday so that they might see the sight." The mob, in other words, was characterized by a grim determination and had the approbation and active support of the officials of the state.[32]

The sociologist Oliver Cromwell Cox also noted that the typical lynching is "not primarily a spontaneous act of mob violence against a criminal." It is a more deliberate and more composed practice that assumes and reinforces the particular form of racial repression that characterizes the American South. Lynchings, he wrote, "serve the indispensable social function of providing the ruling class with the means of periodically reaffirming its collective sentiment of white dominance." And the lynch mob, he continued, is "composed of people who have been carefully indoctrinated in the primary social institutions of the region to conceive of Negroes as extralegal, extrademocratic objects." Not only are the individuals who make up lynch mobs so acculturated, however; the mob is in fact one of the primary means of perpetuating the mores and structures of feeling that necessarily debase black American life and lives. Lynching, Cox asserts, is a "special form of mobbing—mobbing directed against a whole people or political class." Lynching in these terms is not a spontaneous event, but a strategic ritual publicly affirming white supremacy and enforcing black terror, performed frequently (once a week for fifty years), involving masses of people (seventy-five thousand in 1930 alone), and effectively publicizing its primary political and cultural objectives. Lynching, as Cox forcefully puts it, is a "*social institution.*"[33] And it is a social institution, I would suggest, that is akin to other institutions that make up what we think of as civil society.

It was by redefining the lynch mob dynamic as *not* spontaneous and ephemeral that antilynching activists were able to suggest in what ways spectacle lynchings were calculated to produce a particular kind of publicity (of white supremacy in practice) and to generate a special kind of public opinion (in favor of white supremacy). Without pushing the analogy too far, we can see in what ways lynch mobs constituted something akin to voluntary associations, often supported by other institutions of civil society like the press and corporations like the railroad, and having a relationship with the state in the form of government officials who either abetted in or were apologists for the actions of the mob.

Let us now return to the discussions of civil society and see in what ways this understanding of the lynch mob as a voluntary association changes the dynamic of civil society as its most recent theorists have configured it. Fraser ends her critique of Habermas by distinguishing between "weak publics" and "strong publics," that is, between those civil societies whose "deliberative practice consists exclusively in opinion formation" and those "publics whose discourse encompasses both opinion formation and decision making." She concludes that "any conception of the public sphere that requires a sharp separation between (associational) civil society and the state will be unable to imagine the forms of self-management, interpublic coordination, and political accountability that are essential to a democratic and egalitarian society."[34] It is certainly not my intention to disagree with Fraser or to question her conclusion. In moving an "actually existing democracy" toward the egalitarian ideals of a participatory democracy, her call for multiple publics with greater strength in decision making is crucial.

I would only like to suggest that there has historically been another kind of public that has also thwarted efforts toward a more progressive democracy, what we might call a *coercive public*. This is the kind of public where opinions are indeed created and dispersed, where social identities are indeed formed and enacted, and where the public holds the power not so much to make decisions (which yet remains the office of the state) but to coerce the apparatus of the state in support of its agenda. The exemplary model of such a coercive public is the lynch mob.[35]

It has long been recognized that those who made up the apparatus of the state—the police, the judiciary, and the political representatives who were apologists for lynching—were also agents in spectacle lynchings. In a study of one hundred lynchings, Arthur Raper found that police officers directly participated in over fifty and actively condoned over ninety. In the lynching of Claude Neal, one of the speakers to address the lynch mob at the Cassidy home was a self-identified member of the Florida legislature. Not only were these individuals spectators, but they also acted in their official capacity to facilitate lynchings.

As Wells noted, the mayor cancelled school and the district attorney handed Smith over to the mob.

In addition, lynch mobs both directly and indirectly negotiated with state officials in order to create particular political conditions. For example, the same year Neal was lynched, a mob of several thousand in DeSoto County, Mississippi, refused to disperse until the commanding officer protecting the target of the mob's ire promised to use his influence to allow the father of the victim to act as the hangman at the execution. A trial was held, the jury pronounced the man guilty after deliberating for seven minutes, and the judge in the case sentenced the man, along with two alleged accomplices, to death. However, according to existing law the father could not be deputized as the executioner because he was not a resident of DeSoto County, so a state senator proposed a "hanging bill" that would permit a county sheriff to appoint any Mississippi resident as an executioner. (The bill passed by a vote of 18–15 and was then tabled in the face of public criticism.)[36]

This is only one of the numerous instances whereby mob activity created a hostile environment in which legislatures decided on measures to appease mobs, or, even more commonly, in which juries deliberated on the cases and decided the fates of alleged criminals. These jury decisions, frequently reached in minutes and under duress from a mob presence, are rightly called "legal lynchings," because of the force exerted by the mob, a force we have been describing as coercive and enduring.[37]

It was just this coercive role assumed by the lynch mob that antilynching advocates exposed in their publications. The issue of the *Crisis* that lamented the lynching of Claude Neal contained two cartoons that made clear the relationship between the lynch mob and the state apparatus. In one, a bloody arm representing the lynch mob extends an invitation to the lynching to the police chief, a Florida law enforcement official, and the sheriff. In the other, a public official and a rope-holding sheriff named "Givvum Upp" stand in front of a poster announcing the lynching and note that they do not need the help of the militia to perform this lynching. It was just this coercive role of lynch mobs that antilynching advocates and the politicians who supported them attempted to address by proposing federal antilynching legislation that would make local or state officers guilty of a felony if they did not protect an individual in police custody or if they conspired with a member of a mob to injure someone in custody. Antilynching advocates—no matter if they were exposing lynching activities or legislating, or if they themselves were members of voluntary organizations like the NAACP or members of Congress—saw that lynch mobs exercised an undue coercive, *political* influence, whether conscripting public officials or exercising control over police and judicial and legislative apparatus.

We can conclude by returning to that 1893 lynching of Henry Smith with which we began this section. Following the lynching, at least two extended accounts of the action were published by people who had been there. One pamphlet, *The Facts of the Case of the Horrible Murder of Little Myrtle Vance, and Its Fearful Expiation, at Paris, Texas, February 1, 1893,* "initiated a new genre of lynching narrative," according to Hale, in which the author was eyewitness and participant.[38]

The second pamphlet, *"An Eye for an Eye"; or The Fiend and the Fagot. An Unvarnished Account of the Burning of Henry Smith at Paris, Texas, February 1, 1893, and the Reason he was Tortured,* was also an eyewitness account, but was even more remarkable for the ways it used the lynching as part of a strategy of municipal recruitment. The booklet begins with an advertisement for a hotel in Paris, Texas, and ends with an advertisement for timbered land available for sale. The book concludes with a call, addressed "To All the Earth," in which the author invites anyone who shares the values of the townspeople, anyone who would "lose a week in hunting down and bringing back and burning alive any wretch of any color or clime, who is base enough to steal and outrage and murder any man's child, [to] come or write to us: for we have thousands of acres of land at $2 per acre." The book is selling a lifestyle and land, values and venues, based exclusively on the lynching. Lynching, in this case, is not only very much part of a consumer culture, as Hale indicates, but it also serves to advertise to Americans that it can be the very premise of community. Here is a book, then, that quotes the governor's indictment of the mob lynching only to impugn it, and then invites Americans to populate this town.[39] If your town does not lynch, move to one that will.

What the author does in this pamphlet, I am suggesting, is what lynch mobs implicitly do in all mass mob lynchings—advertise, create political opinions, and extend an invitation to believe in the values of popular sovereignty and white supremacy. It is rare to find published evidence such as that following the lynching in Paris, Texas, but such evidence does exist. Comanche County, Texas, for instance, published a newspaper-size brochure, recruiting residents from other parts of the nation. Comanche County had had a brutal lynching in 1886, which was followed by an expulsion of the entire black population, a case of what Elliot Jaspin calls "racial cleansing" in his study of this phenomenon throughout America. What the advertising brochure did in 1907, in inviting residents to move to a place that was "entirely and absolutely ALL WHITE"—"there is not a negro in the county, and the chances are there will not be any for many years to come," it continued—is precisely what the mob had done twenty years earlier. The mob acted on its belief that black people were the problem they needed to expel in order to create cohesion and community. The brochure reached the same conclusion as it described what it deemed the only way to deal with a "depraved and brutal race"—"the gallows" or "maceration and laceration and torture."[40] The mob and the county boosters did the same ideological work, and used or threatened the same sort of collective violence to do it.

The mass mob lynching that Wells saw as inaugurating "an entirely new form" in the early 1890s was coming to an end by the mid-1930s. Mobs were no longer able to act with the same kind of impunity as they had earlier. Indeed, the mob that wanted to lynch Claude Neal in 1934 was denied the opportunity to perform the actual torture and murder, which were done by a small group, and had to settle instead for the desecration of the corpse. As I noted earlier, lynchings had begun to decline much earlier, after reaching their highest levels in 1892 and 1893. There were a few notable moments when domestic and international events—World War I and the returning black soldiers from Europe, for instance—caused renewed spikes in the otherwise annual decline of American lynchings. By the second half of the 1930s, as the country recovered from the Depression, it also seemed to recover from the five-decade orgy of violence that had marked the age of lynching. The American media and antilynching activists gleefully recorded each moment as they approached what they hoped would be the epochal end of lynching in America.

By the early 1930s, they noted, there had occurred a "gradual decline in the number of states involved," as lynching became more and more a deep Southern phenomenon. At the same time, mobs changed in size and "in their methods," as they became smaller, more private, and more secretive. By the mid-to-late 1930s, these changes became even more pronounced. By 1936, mobs began to be less frenetic and "more orderly." As Congress debated a series of bills that would hold sheriffs and police forces liable for people detained in their jails and prisons, fewer and fewer lynch victims were abducted from police custody, or handed over by the police. Moreover, the discourse of lynching, and other justifications of it as a form of frontier justice, began to play a lesser role, as few victims of lynching were now being accused of any criminal offenses at all.

In the last years of the 1930s, the full drama of lynching, including the accusation, manhunt, and rationalization, began a serious decline. The ASWPL said the last manhunt took place in 1938. The organization also claimed that 1938 witnessed what it described as the "last lynchings in which mobs resorted to torture and the burning of the bodies of their victims." In sum, then, the lynchings that had defined the age of lynching—with large mobs justifying their activity through the lynching-for-rape discourse—had effectively ended. Mobs that did lynch were smaller and more private, more hidden, and more fearful of repercussions. They no longer announced their purpose and justification in newspapers or on radios. Indeed, they no longer even claimed that they lynched in order to protect white women's chastity or punish its violation. Given these changes, then, and given the changed economic and political conditions of the late 1930s, and given its own need to justify its antilynching activism, the ASWPL announced in 1939 that lynchings had "gone underground." Anticipating the debate the organization would have with the NAACP and Tuskegee in 1940, the ASWPL insisted that these changes—in mob size and strategy—raised some serious "doubts of the validity of designating as lynchings certain types of murder."[41] For the ASWPL, what had once been lynchings now were no longer lynchings because of the significant changes in the formal properties of those acts.

The ASWPL, of course, was also intent on recording what it called a "lynch-free year." Indeed, the group's motivation for changing the definition of what constituted a lynching might be directly tied to that desire, which, in turn, was connected to a desire to identify a society that was no longer mired in barbaric acts of ritual dismemberment and immolation. That desire, however, was to be thwarted. The 1930s, while witnessing these signs of decline in lynchings, and a declining overall frequency in the practice, also witnessed some of the most gruesome lynchings on record. In 1933, George Armwood was dragged, hanged, and then burned in Somerset County, Maryland, while David Gregory was dragged, dismembered, and burned in Hardin County, Texas. In 1937 and 1938, the same years that the ASWPL claimed that mobs had stopped resorting to "torture and the burning of the bodies of their victims," a mob in Crisp County, Georgia, dragged and burned to death John Dukes; another in Sharkey County, Mississippi, dragged behind a vehicle the burning corpse of Tom McGehee, and yet another mob used blowtorches to burn three African Americans to death in Montgomery County, Mississippi.[42]

Despite this spate of grotesque lynchings, it was nonetheless clear that the era of spectacle lynching was coming to an end.[43] The mobs were indeed smaller, the press coverage considerably more condemnatory. The public opinion that Ida B. Wells, the NAACP, Tuskegee, the Anti-Lynching Crusaders, the ASWPL, and other organizations had made it their mission to transform was slowly but surely changing. Lynchings, in a word, were no longer the effective kind of spectacle of terrorism they had been for the past forty or fifty years, although there continued to be scattered lynchings throughout the 1940s.

In 1952, the ASWPL, which had disbanded a decade earlier, finally got its "lynch-free year." Tuskegee, which had helped define the age of lynching through its tabulations and publication of statistics, marked the first year in the twentieth century with no recorded lynching. In 1953, after a second year without a recorded lynching, the Tuskegee Institute announced that it was discontinuing its annual tabulation of lynchings in America. The final report announced that lynching "as traditionally defined" had ceased to be a "valid index" or "barometer for measuring the status of race relations in the United States."

The report released by the Tuskegee Institute was not quite as hopeful as most media coverage of it would suggest. What Tuskegee said in the report is that lynchings were not the prime barometer of race relations because other economic and social criteria were better suited for the assessment of racial inequities in America, like employment numbers and the level of political participation, education, and health. Another point that Tuskegee insisted on making was that lynchings had come to an end for reasons that were positive (there had been "significant changes in the status of the Negro"), as well as for reasons that were wholly negative (that racial terrorism had now assumed new forms). Indeed, what large mobs had done before was now done through "other extra-legal means of control, such as bombings, incendiarism, threats and intimidations."[44] The violence meant to act as a form of social control and terrorism, in other words, had evolved so that it required less collective ritual and fewer people. Individuals, paired assassins, and small groups could now do with bombs and drive-by shootings what mobs had done with ropes and kindling.

Lynchings after the 1930s never returned to the levels of frequency or barbarity they had reached during the nineteenth and first half of the twentieth centuries. There continued to be isolated cases that came to national attention in the 1950s, with the lynching of Emmett Till in 1955 and John Mack Parker in 1959, and then with a spate of them in the mid-1960s in a rearguard struggle against the civil rights movement. But the age of lynching was clearly over.

Lynchings neither began nor ended with the age of lynching, of course. Let me again clarify that I am not arguing for a clean break between earlier periods in the history of lynching and the "age of lynching." There was an undeniable and important continuity from the end of the Civil War to the end of the 1930s and after. What was exceptional about the age of lynching, as I have suggested, is not that it was the historical moment that witnessed the greatest number of lynchings, nor was it particularly exceptional in the brutality of the lynchings that defined it. There were, of course, new technologies of communication that lynchers employed to publicize their actions even more widely, and new kinds of machinery (automobiles, blowtorches, and electric drills) that they used to perform their savage work. But those were incidental changes that simply enhanced earlier technologies and strategies.

Rather, what made the age of lynching distinctive is that a particular type of society was born then—a society in which two regions of the country achieved postbellum reconciliation through a tacit agreement about the fate of African Americans, a society in which mass media, mass transportation systems, government officials, and business elites cooperated with and abetted mobs that were too frequent in appearance, too regular in strategy, and too pervasive to be thought of as spontaneous or ephemeral. It is worth noting that the age of lynching is flanked by a major set of federal legislation at its origin (the end of Reconstruction) and another at its decline (the end of the Depression). The extralegal action of mobs organized in communities was a small-scale war against new legal codes and newly extended federal power. The Fourteenth Amendment could define who was a national citizen, and the Fifteenth who could vote as one, but a lynch mob resisted both by insisting on its power to define who could and could not belong in a town, in a community, in this world.

The earliest slave codes, as we saw in Chapter Two and will discuss more fully in the Conclusion, created a culture that permitted and encouraged violence against people of African descent, and the work of antebellum mobs participated in that culture. The work of mobs during the age of lynching, on the other hand, following on the example of Reconstruction-era mobs and white supremacist organizations, became the work of resistance to the change wrought by the end of slavery and the beginning of federal citizenship. It was the work of those who hanged and burned their victims on courthouse lawns in order to show the powerlessness of the state that attempted to upset a culture of collective racial violence that had been encoded in laws and hearts for too long merely to be legislated away with a few amendments.

What the spectacle lynchings of the age of lynching produced, then, in addition to spectacles of humans being tortured and mob-murdered, is an agency deeply representative of much unspoken public sentiment (that sometimes was spoken and even written, as we saw). The agency took a form—the mob as a civil society organization—and participated actively in the major debates in the age of lynching: debates over the role of legal apparatus in crimes against community, debates over what constituted community itself, debates over federal legislation to curtail lynching, and debates over the very meaning of lynching. Those debates are the subject of the next chapters, where we will see how mobs and their apologists created a particular cultural discourse of what lynching meant to that society and that age.

4

The Discourse of Lynching

In June 1998 three young white supremacists in Jasper, Texas, committed an almost unimaginably cruel murder by dragging an African American man behind their truck until his body almost disintegrated; they then left what remained of his torso in front of a black church. It was later discovered that they had written up a plan to initiate a white supremacist cult with a ritual murder of a black man. As they chained their victim to the truck, the three young men stripped off his pants and underwear. Gazing at the work they were about to commence, one of them declared: "That's what they used to do when a black man got caught messing around with a white women, in the old days."[1] The victim of their horrific crime, James Byrd, Jr., had not been "messing around" with a white woman, nor had they suspected that of him. They had in fact chosen him at random, having picked him up hitchhiking while they drove home from a night of drinking.

What is remarkable about this episode in the history of American lynching is that it reveals the depth of what I am calling the discourse of lynching—that is, the mythology or foundational narrative that has given structure and meaning to lynching in America for the past century. The three white supremacists were motivated to act by a mythology of black men's insatiable sexual desire for white women, and a mythology of white men's sacred duty to protect white women through violent actions against black men. Like other lynchers of a century earlier, these three young men in the 1990s were roused by a discourse that made them view black male sexuality as an omnipresent danger, and inspired them, also like their ideological ancestors, to stand in awe and fear and in an attitude of violent vengeance at the sight of a black man's genitalia. In the act of stripping their victim and alleging things they well knew to be false, these three lynchers demonstrate precisely how the discourse of lynching operates, how it masks real motives (to establish white supremacy) through a mythic evocation of what lynchers of an earlier era called "the usual crime."

Lynching, then, has a discourse, a changing set of myths, narratives, and imagery that allows lynchers and their advocates to claim the high ground of justice, chivalry, and morality. A *discourse,* as I am using the term here, structures the ways a group of people imagines an event. A discourse defines the parameters of, and assigns the meaning to, that event; a discourse likewise defines the group of people who use it to justify their participation in that event.[2] The ascendant discourse of lynching, the one with which I began this chapter and which hereafter I will call the "lynching for rape" discourse, defined all the participants in the scenario through the act of rape: white women as vulnerable victims, white men as righteous avengers, and black men as ravenous animals. Whoever wished to challenge the lynching for rape discourse was liable to the charge of being against chivalry, against family, against the rights of self-defense, against morality, against virtually everything decent. The discourse of lynching, then, determined not just the meaning of the event but also the terms of debate over the event. Moreover, it has always been the lynching advocates who have mobilized the discourse of lynching that delimited the possible responses of antilynching activists.

It is to that history that we now turn in this chapter, to see how the discourse of lynching evolved. We will examine the factors that went into the formation of a series of discourses of lynching; how these were developed to suit different conditions; how select elements of discourses survived the demise of the rest of the discourse and how these elements assumed a place in newly emergent discourses; and, finally, how these discourses were so purposefully mobilized to motivate lynchers and embolden their defenders. Two points are worth noting at the outset. First, the lynching for rape discourse is only one of the evolving discourses of lynching. Because, however, it is also the ascendant one, the one with the most historical resonance, sufficiently evocative in our own day to inspire the hateful work of three white supremacists and the gratuitous rhetoric of one would-be Supreme Court Justice, the history I offer is largely a history of how other discourses evolved into the lynching for rape discourse. Second, the history of the discourse of lynching is the intellectual history of the terms of debate created by lynching advocates and contested by antilynching activists; it is also a history of the work of ideological myth-making, an exposé of the ways particular conflicts are hidden, certain social fissures papered over, and other, apparently more salient differences configured as meaningful.

THE FORMATION OF THE DISCOURSE

In 1880, three years after the withdrawal of federal forces from the South, a Charleston newspaper noted that it had long expressed its positive opinion on the "subject of lynching negroes who commit outrages on women." These sentiments, the editor concluded, "are not new and they have been often times expressed." It is true that neither the practice nor the defense of lynching black men alleged to have committed rape was particularly new, and rudimentary versions of the defense of lynching may have been expressed even earlier than the editor supposed. Enslaved African Americans were lynched throughout the eighteenth and nine-teenth centuries, often for an alleged rape of a white woman, and some-times these lynchings were defended on the grounds of the alleged crime. In a notable case in Mississippi in 1841, for example, two runaway slaves from Louisiana were burned to death for allegedly committing a series of murders and rapes as they made their way along the Red River. A Mississippi newspaper editor writing belatedly in 1854 retold the story with vigor and claimed that the case demanded no less brutal or exem-plary a punishment since the crime of rape appealed "to every noble feeling, to every generous sympathy, to man's high sense of inexorable justice."[3] Nonetheless, while there are scattered examples of people justi-fying lynching for rape in the mid-nineteenth century, and earlier, it would not be until the end of Reconstruction that there emerged a discourse that would exert an enormously influential role in motivating lynchers, inspiring their apologists, and fashioning a coherent worldview with its own history and morality. That discourse borrowed from and augmented the earlier discourses.

We saw in Chapter One that there emerged during the Revolutionary War two major claims made by lynching apologists—the frontier justice claim with its assertion that justice can be delivered by self-proclaimed groups in the absence of the conventional judicial apparatus of civilized societies, and the popular sovereignty claim that the people can execute acts of justice because they never fully surrender their will to their elected or appointed representatives. Both vigilante groups and vigilance committees drew on these claims and used them to defend the work they did, sometimes in genuine frontier conditions where there were no courts, and sometimes in urban conditions where they claimed the courts to be lax or corrupt.

In addition, we have seen that these two claims were sometimes buttressed by claims of military necessity. The case of the Bedford militia was an early example during the Revolutionary War, as was then General Andrew Jackson's summary executions of two Indian chiefs and two British agents accused of fomenting Indian rebellion during the Seminole War in 1818. An even more egregious but ambiguous case is the Civil War massacre at Fort Pillow on April 12, 1864, when General Nathan Bedford Forrest led his Confederate forces against the Union-held outpost on the Mississippi River, capturing the fort and then murdering in cold blood up to three hundred Union soldiers after they surrendered, many of them black.[4] Cases of wartime summary executions are complicated and might at times be better described as military massacres in violation of the laws of war rather than as lynchings. The important point for us to note, though, is that the claim of military necessity, and concomitantly the language of war, had an undeniable appeal that could be evoked in situations that were less clearly moments of war. In recent times, we have seen the government suspend the civil liberties of those deemed enemies or "enemy combatants" in the cases of the "War on Drugs" and "War on Terror" (although, notably, not the "War on Poverty"). Prolynching advocates did not always draw on the language of war, but some did and others often implied it to indicate the sort of crisis that permitted extralegal action. Rebecca Lattimer Felton serves as an example of someone who evoked war imagery in her advocacy of lynching when she urges white men to protect "poor maidens [who] are destroyed in a land that their fathers died to save from the invader's foot." The enemies before were the invaders, the enemy now what she calls "the heathen at home." In either case, she casts the South and her maidens as besieged, embattled, and in battle.

Another factor that contributed to the lynching discourse, one that was largely the contribution of the regulators, which antedated the term "lynching" if not the actual practice, is the idea of a community's right or obligation to control those who violate its understood values and mores. What popular sovereignty was to democratic theory, communal values were to statutes—the informal but higher authority that governed a people. Advocates of lynching frequently note that lynchers uphold mores that are inscribed more deeply than any other laws, and that these values—values like chivalry and the sanctity of home and hearth—are to be protected whether or not the government or courts have in place means or laws to protect them. Following the example of different kinds of regulators throughout American history, including the Klan in some aspects, lynch mobs often asserted as their prerogative the correction of misbehavior by deviant or defiant members of the community. By the end of the nineteenth century, the means of correction used by lynch mobs were much more severe than those used by earlier regulators, and the kinds of misbehaviors that lynch mobs "corrected" were either allegations of spectacular crimes or unspecified breaches of racial mores.

The allegation most popular in the post-Reconstruction lynching discourse, of course, was rape. Although there is no one historical episode or intellectual forebear to which we can trace the origin of justifying lynching by reference to rape, the case that did the most to make "lynching" a nationally recognized term also introduced the embryonic form of that lynching for rape discourse. The 1835 Vicksburg, Mississippi, lynching and purging of the city's gamblers was cast into dynamic gendered terms. In explaining the "dire necessity" of the Vicksburg citizenry, the local newspaper wrote: "We had borne with their enormities, until to have suffered them any longer would not only have proved us destitute of every manly sentiment, but would also have implicated us in the guilt of accessories to their crime." It was "manly sentiment" that drove them to lynch the gamblers, and not to have done so would not only have made the citizens destitute of manhood, but would have them "accessories," in a word, pimps to this crime. And this crime, whatever its actual nature, was sexual. The *Vicksburg Register's* language—"in the name of our insulted laws—of offended virtue, and of slaughtered innocence"—is language written in the register of rape even though the actual crime was gambling.[5]

Here we see what would become the stark gendered dynamics of the lynching discourse, which represented lynching as a patently patriarchal practice, a defense by men of women, through violence. In later forms, primarily during and after the 1870s, the discourse of lynching will straightforwardly state that those who lynch are protectors of women and those who are lynched debauchers of them (and, of course, "women" in that discourse always could mean only "white"). It is notable that one of the earliest defenses of lynching also used the language of rape, and even more notable that the crime the lynchers punished was so obviously not rape. This apparent anomaly demonstrates the ways that the rhetoric of rape was used to register the most offensive type of crime, one for which there was no defense. Someone could murder in self-defense, could perhaps be driven to theft by hunger, but nothing could justify rape. Moreover, rape was seen to be worse than either murder or theft. While theft could be seen as an abstraction, to an extent, and not irreversible (property can be returned), rape was neither; in the terms of the debate over it, rape rendered the raped woman irredeemable and stole from her (and, in patriarchal values, her father or husband) something that was lost forever. It was common for lynching advocates to claim that rape was worse than murder because it assaulted the soul as well as the body of the victim, not a surprising rhetorical strategy in a patriarchal culture where a woman was valued for her capacity to deliver an honest heir, where centuries of religious scripture and secular writers celebrated chastity as a greater possession than life, for a woman. Finally, rape, according to the patriarchal dictates that governed the understanding of the crime, was perceived to be a crime against family, that haven in a heartless world, and one to which any man with a family was therefore susceptible. It was a crime without any means of defense, a crime that left the victim worse than dead, and one that struck close to the heart of any man with a mother or wife or daughter. In the midst of a culture holding such values, it was obvious how effective the rhetoric of rape could be, no matter what the crime. It was a metaphor for the nadir of human debasement. It was also a charge that was, in the words of

British Lord Chief Justice Matthew Hale, "easily to be made and hard to be proved, and harder to be defended."[6]

While it was rape that lynch mobs claimed to punish, it was the specific form of rape that violated racial mores that was indeed punished. This fact is almost too obvious to mention in a country where consensual interracial sexual relations, even within the sanctity of marriage, remained illegal in more than a dozen states until 1967, in a land where almost the only men who suffered capital punishment for interracial rapes were black men. If the law and the courts supported these racial mores, what could we expect of the extralegal mobs who felt the law and the courts to be too lenient? As further evidence of how obvious it was that lynchings were to punish black rapists of white women, consider those prolynching advocates who espoused the justice of their cause by claiming that it was the nature of the crime and not the race of the alleged perpetrator that drove them to lynch. In the Mississippi lynching of 1841, the apologist claims: "Had the perpetrators of these awful crimes, for which they terribly atoned, been white men instead of negroes, they would have met the same fate."[7] That white men would be lynched for this crime is the hyperbole to support the necessity of what actually happened and to whom it actually happened. This rhetorical device of insisting that race is incidental and not causal in lynchings for rape would also reappear in the post-Reconstruction discourse, and reappear in a way that actually insisted that race was in fact a central determinant.

In summary, then, the rudimentary rhetorical elements that would coalesce into the lynching for rape discourse were largely in place by the eve of the Civil War. The major claims of frontier justice, popular sovereignty, and the regulators' rhetoric of communal values had been clarified and given sanction by repeated usage. The charge of rape, the rhetoric of rape, and the language of imperative necessity (usually in the form of the rhetoric of war) were available no matter what the actual or alleged crime or social state might be. We can conclude our discussion by looking briefly at one antebellum example of the not quite complete but nonetheless mature deployment of the discourse of lynching in order to see it at an earlier stage, twenty years before it came to fruition.

In 1859, a lynching apologist in Missouri defended the lynching of four slaves in the course of three days in Saline County. A farmer and justice of the peace, James M. Shackleford wrote several letters in the local newspaper making the claims that lynching was necessary because the legal "penalty for rape" was "inadequate to the crime"; and that it was an expression of the people's sensibilities about proper justice. "An enlightened public opinion," Shackleford wrote in a proverbial phrase Tom Watson would echo a half-century later, "is the voice of God." Having deployed the two major claims justifying lynching (frontier justice, popular sovereignty), Shackleford then lists a series of revolutionary and military events that he describes as equivalent moments of "mob law." It was "mob law," he wrote, when Jackson hanged the two British agents, "mob law when the men of Boston disguised themselves as Indians and threw the tea overboard," "mob law when the people of France hurled the Bourbons from the throne, and crushed out the dominion of the priests and established a new order of things." With these noble precedents, he concludes, "I know no reason why we should not have a little mob law in the State of Missouri, and County of Saline, when the *occasion imperiously and of necessity* demands it." The immediate occasion was the slave's alleged raping of a white woman, but the imperious necessity likely was to be traced to the larger social crisis in the county and the state—the alarming number of slaves who had escaped from Saline County (at least a dozen in the year and a half prior to the lynchings) and the memory of John Brown's raid into Vernon County to abet the escape of eleven slaves. For Shackleford, the lynching was also a way to quell what he called a "spirit of insubordination" evident in the "negro population that required a terrible example to be set them."[8]

In response to a social crisis precipitated by the fear of slave insurrection, and a raid by John Brown, Shackleford invokes military precedents that suggest that Saline County is in the equivalent of a state of war, that the justice system is inadequate, and that the lynching is finally an expression of communal values that are not just revolutionary but divine. When another newspaper, the *Lexington Express,* questioned this logic, it was called a "negro-outrage-loving," "antisouthern," and "contemptible" newspaper hopelessly filled with transparent "negroism."[9] These were precisely the terms of debate that would follow Reconstruction after the Civil War—between those who aligned themselves with the South and those who were disowned by it, between those who saw rape as a metaphor for their political and social crisis and those who were vilified as pimps to black rapists ("negro-outrage-loving") because they did not understand this reasoning, between those who were apologists for and those who were critics of lynching.

THE DISCOURSE ASCENDANT: THE REBIRTH OF A NATION

Ida B. Wells, the greatest of all antilynching activists, pointed out that "the greatest of all Negroes, Frederick Douglass" was the first to trace the emergence of the intellectual justification of lynching.[10] In a pamphlet published in 1894, Douglass noted that there were "three distinct periods of persecutions" of African Americans and three distinct "sets of excuses for their persecution." The first excuse was what Douglass called the fear of "insurrection" when African Americans, as Wells noted, were slaughtered indiscriminately at the perceived threat of urban disorder. Eventually, the "story" of insurrection "at last wore itself out" when it became obvious that there were no insurrections, that whatever violence occurred left only black victims, no black rioter was ever apprehended, and no dynamite ever exploded. "It was too much to ask thoughtful people to believe this transparent story," noted Wells, "and southern white people at last made up their minds that some other excuse must be had."[11]

The second "excuse," born of and during Reconstruction, was the fear of what Wells termed "Negro Domination," and Douglass "Negro supremacy," by which both meant the fear that African Americans armed with the franchise would destroy white American government and civilization. To prevent that supremacy or domination, white terrorist groups—"the Ku Klux Klan, the Regulators, and the lawless mobs"—maimed, mauled, and murdered black would-be voters. Having rendered the franchise meaningless by dint of "fraud, violence, intimidation and murder," the white South finally achieved a more stable form of disenfranchisement through state constitutions and more covert forms of intimidation. With that accomplishment, as Wells put it, the "white man's second excuse became valueless."[12]

The third and final rationale offered for the continued assault on African American lives was the charge that "Negroes had to be killed to avenge their assaults upon women." Both Wells and Douglass expose what they hold to be the malice involved in the fabrication of that charge. All these "excuses" reveal what Douglass calls "design, plan, purpose and invention" called "into being by a well-defined motive." Wells notes that all the institutions and powers of the society— "legislators, preachers, governors, and bishops"—cooperate in "intently, maliciously, and constantly" propagating these "falsehoods." Given its constant reiteration, and given the "unanimity, earnestness and apparent candor" of those who made the accusation again and again, it was not long before the account became widely accepted—not long, as Wells put it, for the world to accept "the story that the Negro is a monster which the Southern white man has painted him" to be.[13]

What Douglass calls "excuses" are not simple rationales or justifications, declarations of why something was done, but rather a set of ideas that both justify and motivate the deed while implicitly delineating a social world in which that deed makes sense. These "excuses" are operative in the sense that they are apparently neutral statements that promote particular courses of action; and they are ideological in that the work they do is primarily to screen the real motives for that action. Douglass notes that these fabrications are precisely intended to preoccupy "the public mind with an issue entirely different from the real one in question." And, he concludes, these "excuses" reveal what he calls the "American method of reasoning in all matters concerning the Negro"— that is, the account "inverts everything; turns truth upside down, and puts the case of the unfortunate Negro inside out and wrong end foremost."[14] What Douglass and Wells call "excuses"—these apparently simple statements that contain within them a constellation of associations, some hidden and some obvious, and doing the work of masking the real motivations and political aims behind the purported ones—are what I am calling discourses; and the third and final excuse is precisely the lynching for rape discourse. This lynching for rape discourse was widely accepted, by those who lynched, by those who defended the lynchers, and, most tellingly, by many who criticized lynching and its advocates.

What, then, is this lynching for rape discourse, what are its terms, its logic, its source of appeal? As with any myth, the discourse is largely a product of popular imagination rather than intellectual labor, a form of knowledge more the result of the accumulation of informal stories than any formal course of study. It also operates in the same way as popularly generated knowledge, by evocation, by connotation, more than by systematic or direct means. There were some intellectuals, however, who did make a concerted effort to mount a comprehensive case for the discourse and they prove invaluable in revealing the connections and associations explicitly in their writing that the majority implicitly make in their minds.

Thomas Nelson Page provides a paradigmatic case of an intellectual who synthesized and put into a complete and contextual framework the lynching for rape discourse. In a book published in 1904, Page, the best-selling and most successful Southern novelist in the last quarter of the nineteenth century, renounced his earlier novelistic representations of African Americans as simple and devoted retainers and fully committed himself to the black rapist myth.[15] The argument he makes depends a great deal on certain rhetorical maneuvers, a strategy of implication, a back-handed way of making insidious associations, and some unsubtle innuendo. It is, in other words, a mendacious effort to give coherence to what, at certain revealing moments, even Page himself seems not to believe.[16]

The major rhetorical structure of the argument is fairly straightforward. Page begins by constructing a syllogism: white Southerners lynch rapists, black men commit rape, and therefore white Southerners lynch black men. Thereafter, Page offers two historical accounts (one of the rise and evolution of rape, the other of the rise and evolution of lynching), and then he provides two sociological interpretations (explaining the social conditions that make black men rape and white men lynch). The structural logic of Page's text serves a greater purpose since part of his whole enterprise is to create the illusion of parallel activities (rape/lynching), parallel sympathies (blacks' for rapists, whites' for lynchers), and ultimately parallel responsibilities (blacks' for ending rape, whites' for ending lynching). This parallelism gives the appearance of being evenhanded and fair while not so subtly creating a nefarious set of associations that place the full blame for black rapists on all black people and, in the end, indicting the religious, intellectual, and cultural values of African American life as essentially fostering and cultivating rapists.

From the outset, Page is aware of the flaws in his syllogism since lynching was not confined to those who would avenge acts of rape. By

1904 it had been made eminently clear that lynching was a response to a variety of alleged crimes and perceived violations of racist mores (of which less than one-quarter were allegations of rape). Nonetheless, Page circumvents these facts by consistently presenting rape and lynching in a cause and effect relationship. He talks about rape as "the brutal crime which has largely brought about the frightful crime of lynching"; he produces an image of "ravishing and lynching spreading like a pestilence over the country." And he makes perfectly clear the relationship between the one and the other: "The crime of lynching is not likely to cease until the crime of ravishing and murdering women and children is less frequent than it has been of late." In the end, rape certainly becomes what he calls "the causing crime." Lynching is reduced to merely an "effect." Page feels compelled to make that association in order to undo the other link so obvious to Americans, the link between race and lynching. Many of his readers, he claims, might have a "feeling" of the mischief of lynching, which "has undoubtedly been due mainly to the belief, that the lynching has been directed almost exclusively against the negroes," which in turn produces a "latent idea" that lynching has a "political complexion."[17] Having disposed of this argument by acknowledging this misguided "feeling," wrongheaded "belief," and inaccurate "latent idea" that suggests the apparent connection between race and lynching, Page then hastily and thereafter declares the real connection between crime and lynching.

With his syllogism now in place, Page then produces a historical account of the evolution of black rape. Like others, both antilynching and prolynching advocates, Page begins his historical account by noting that black Americans did not commit rape prior to the Civil War—"the crime of rape was substantially unknown during the period of slavery"—or during the Civil War when, as Frederick Douglass noted, African Americans "had every opportunity to commit the abominable crime now alleged against" them. Indeed, writes Page, no "race ever behaved better than the Negroes behaved during the war." Rape, then, was "the fatal product of new conditions" brought about during "the period and process of Reconstruction," with what Page calls "its teachings": the main three being the "teaching that the Negro was the equal of the white, that the white man was his enemy, and that he must assert his equality." These teachings took effect and manifested themselves first in the crime of rape when presumably Northern "members of the Negro militia ravished white women; in some instances in the presence of their families." As a result of these "teachings" and this example from the conquering North, previously docile former slaves began to commit the hitherto unknown crime against white women. "The first instance of rape, outside of these attacks by armed Negroes, and of consequent lynching," notes Page, "occurred in Mississippi, where the teaching of equality and of violence found one of its most fruitful fields." The crime of rape, then, concludes Page, can be traced directly to "the teaching of equality and the placing of power in the ignorant Negroes' hands."[18]

As the author of several books in which black retainers were faithful and wholly committed to their white masters, Page was somewhat loath to condemn the entire generation of African Americans who lived through Reconstruction's teachings. He was, after all, someone who fully endorsed and had profited from the plantation romance and the stock characters who populated it. Later in the book, he would spend several pages fondly reminiscing about "Uncle Balla," the black carriage driver on the Page plantation, who was "the guide, philosopher, and friend of [his] boyhood," and "recall with mingled affection and awe [his] mammy's dignity, force, and kindness." To circumvent this problem, Page posited that rape arose again once that favored generation was superseded by a new one that was sadly not the beneficiary of the school of slavery. "As the old relation, which had survived even the strain of Reconstruction, dwindled with the passing of the old generation from the stage, and the 'New Issue' with the new teaching took its place, the crime broke out again with renewed violence."[19]

What was not in doubt, though, was that rape was the crime that begat lynching. With the rise of rape during Reconstruction, by black militia and civilians alike, "lynching, in its post-bellum stage, had its evil origin." Page's parallel history of the evolution of lynching required him to make that crucial connection to what he called "the causing crime" and then to explain how it came to be that so many lynchings were performed for other reasons. As he himself acknowledges, "though after the war lynching in the South may have begun as a punishment for assault on white women, it has extended until of late less than one-fourth of the instances are for this crime." The story he tells to explain this anomaly is that lynching became unmoored from its justifiable roots and was therefore corrupted. "Even though lynching is not now confined to the punishment of this crime, this crime is the one that gives the only excuse for lynching." Implicitly, Page then defends lynching for rape instead of considering the possibility that there were always other motivating factors.

The second problem Page confronted was the sheer brutality of fin-de-siècle lynchings, where mobs tortured and mutilated and immolated their victims. Such excessive violence seemed grossly inappropriate for a form of what he is essentially calling chivalry. His answer is both to downplay the violence—he refers to the Henry Smith immolation in Paris, Texas, in 1893 as "perhaps, the second or third instance of burning in the country after the war"—and to place responsibility for the increased mob violence on the black rapists. "For a time, a speedy execution by hanging was the only mode of retribution resorted to by the lynchers; then, when this failed of its purpose, a more savage method was essayed, born of a savage fury at the failure of the first, and a stern resolve to strike a deeper terror into those whom the other method had failed to awe."[20] The mob, in other words, acted rationally in choosing to castrate, torture, dismember, and burn African Americans in order to produce a greater deterrent effect on that "causing crime."

Having completed parallel histories of the rise and evolution of rape and lynching, Page turns to the social context that makes lynching justifiable. He rehearses three justifications that had become commonplace by 1904: 1) the "ordinary course of the law" had proved no deterrent to the crime in question; 2) citizens were rightly dismayed by "the constant delay in the execution of the law"; and 3) the court system was ungallant if not vicious in requiring "the innocent victim, who, if she survived, as she rarely did, was already bowed to the earth by shame, to relate in public the story of the assault—an ordeal which was worse than death." But the final and most compelling reason that white Southerners were driven to lynching was, as we might expect in Page's logical morass, the fault of black people whose crimes and "the unnamable brutality" attending those crimes rendered white people literally insane. These "unnamable horrors . . . have outraged the minds of those who live in regions where they have occurred, . . . upsetting reason, [and] swept from their bearings cool men and changed them into madmen, drunk with fury and the lust of revenge."[21] Lynching happens, then, because white people are driven to it by the failures of the legal system and the actions of black people.

When Page finally turns his attention to the social conditions that produce black rapists he deploys his most insidious rhetorical devices. First, he makes insinuating suggestions about all black people, much as he had used innuendo to inflame the passions of his readers by noting that the "unnamable horrors" and "unnamable brutality" are not just unnamable but unprintable. With comments like the following—"the facts in the case were so unspeakable that they have never been put in print. They simply could not be put in print"—Page manages to make these facts inflammatory by making them titillating. This is a wonderful demonstration that the stories of rape and rumors of rape were what Jacquelyn Dowd Hall memorably and brilliantly called the "folk pornography of the Bible Belt." Page uses a similar strategy to malign black people when he opens his book and his chapter on lynching with exactly the same sentence, which certainly insinuates just what it appears to be denying: "To say that Negroes furnish the great body of rapists, is not to charge that all Negroes are ravishers." In the end, he manages to suggest that "all Negroes" are certainly responsible for rapists by noting "the absence of a strong restraining public opinion among the Negroes of any class," and the complicity of the black intelligentsia. Not only have intellectual "leaders of the Negro race . . . rarely, by act or word, shown a true appreciation of the enormity of the crime of ravishing and murdering women," but the spiritual leaders in black churches condone and give sanction to rapists, both by failing to provide for them a practical moral code and by harboring and refusing to surrender black criminals to white police. Indeed, concludes Page, "the real sympathy of the race" resides "mainly with the criminal rather than his victim," and the crime of rape will simply not be "done away with while the sympathy of the Negroes is with the ravisher." While not all black people were ravishers in Page's portrait, all were sympathetic to ravishers—no different than those in more rabidly racist depictions, like R. W. Shufeldt's. This writer fantasizes that the last living black man in America, tied to a stake and feeling the heat of flames licking at his flesh, with the "surgeon's knife actually pressing upon his scrotum," would nonetheless "seize his victim and outrage her if it lay within his power to do so."[22] Black men, in this discourse, are congenitally rapists, by instinct, by genetic predisposition, and by the voting power and beliefs in equality that Reconstruction gave them.

This image of the black rapist, on which the lynching for rape discourse so obviously depends, arose during the late nineteenth century. One notable historian of the South, Joel Williamson, dates the rise of the black rapist motif to 1889, when both the charge of black rape and the act of lynching for it "commanded a new and tremendously magnified attention," and dates "the death of the image of Negro as beast" to 1915.[23] Without necessarily requiring that kind of precision, we can note that the rise of the black rapist motif coincided with the creation of the myth of the Lost Cause, that intellectual movement that attempted to defend and apotheosize the Confederacy, a product also of the 1880s and 1890s. A major tenet of that Lost Cause mythology—what David Blight describes as its most important "article of faith"—is "the disclaimer against slavery as the cause of the war." Page too belatedly joins his voice to those Southerners who vociferously argued this point. What is most revealing, though, is that Page is more forthright in stating just what was at stake in this argument. It is "important to make it clear that the right [of secession] did exist, because on this depends largely the South's place in history," he writes. "Without this we were mere insurgents and rebels; with it, we were a great people in revolution for our rights." Page foresees a historical trend that will stamp the South as a backward civilization if it is believed that the Civil War was about slavery.

> It is not unlikely that in fifty years the defence of slavery will be deemed the world over to have been as barbarous as we now deem the slave-trade to have been. There is but one way to prevent the impending disaster: by establishing the real fact, that, whatever may have been the immediate and apparent occasion, the true and ulti-mate cause of the action of the South was her firm and unwavering adherence to the principle of self-government and her jealous devotion to her inalienable rights.[24]

The issue, for Page and for the other creators and defenders of the Lost Cause myth, is whether the South fought for timeless political ideals about liberty or for the mere protection of an exploitative economic system—for precious principles or precious property.

There are additional issues in Page's apologia, though, and they are integrally related to the discourse of lynching. For one thing, the political issue of "inalienable rights" is part and parcel of the issue of the popular sovereignty claims on which lynching apologists rested their arguments. Even more important is that this final commentary in Page's book again reveals his primary strategy of divorcing political actions (Civil War, lynching) from what seem to be their "immediate and apparent occasion" (the desire to own and kill black people) in order to offer a more exalted and chivalrous "true and ultimate cause"—in the case of the Civil War, the protection of sacred rights; in the case of lynching, the protection of womanhood. And for Page, and other Lost Cause prolynching proponents, there is an intimate connection in the chivalry exhibited in both causes.

The reason the contributors to the lynching for rape discourse repudiate the idea that the South fought the Civil War to defend slavery, then, is precisely that they wanted to elevate the justifications for both causes to unassailable (and common) grounds. Another writer of the same epoch reveals this connection more strikingly. In her 1906 paean to the Lost Cause, *Dixie After the War*, Myra Lockett Avary approvingly quotes Confederate Vice-President Alexander Stephens's sixteen-year-old nephew, who declared that he was off to the Civil War to "fight for the fair sex," and then offers her rejoinder to disbelievers: "And to this day some people think we fought to keep negroes in slavery!" In her discussion of lynching, Avary likewise notes that the "rapist is a product of the reconstruction period," and that mob murder is a response only to the crime of rape, and, as such, "lynching seems to eradicate the evil for which administered." The chapter on lynching is entitled "Crime Against Womanhood."[25] Not so subtly, then, Avary makes defense of womanhood the cause of the Civil War as much as it is the cause of lynching. The Lost Cause is supplemented by the still not yet lost cause of lynching; both are emblems of Southern chivalry.

To get an idea of how crucial this point was to the lynching for rape discourse, we can turn to the antilynching activists who challenged this representation. For Frederick Douglass, for instance, it was imperative to demonstrate the continuity from slavery to lynching, first by noting the moral legacy of slavery. The "sentiment left by slavery is still with us," he writes, "and the moral vision of the American people is still darkened by its presence." Lynchers are, in the end, he writes, the products of that culture: "They have had among them for centuries a peculiar institution, and that peculiar institution has stamped them as a peculiar people." Moreover, the evocation of slavery in the antilynching critique of the lynching for rape discourse is an outright exposé of the claims of chivalry. Slavery, Douglass concludes, "was a system of unmitigated, legalized outrage upon black women of the South." His immediate point is that no white man was ever lynched for raping a black woman—and thus demonstrating that lynching is not performed to avenge rape and defend womanhood—but his larger point is that those who held slaves and fought a war to protect that right are no more chivalrous than are those lynchers whose complete absence of "respect for human life" is the result of their living in a slave culture. Pauline Hopkins likewise demonstrates the continuity from the era of slavery to the era of lynching. She compares "these days of mob violence, when lynching is raising its head like a venomous monster" to antebellum slavery and notes that the "atrocity of the acts committed one hundred years ago are duplicated today, when slavery is supposed no longer to exist." Lynching and concubinage—the attacks on black men and the rape of black women—are both "nothing new. Southern sentiment has not been changed."[26]

This challenge to the representation of slavery as it is found in the lynching for rape discourse reveals just what is at stake for the advocates of either side. The image of slavery in the lynching for rape discourse is of a period when black men did not rape (that came during Reconstruction), a period when black people were faithful retainers (Avary notes that "my affection is for the negro of the old order"), a period when white people were in control.[27] The most effective metaphor for the loss of that control was the loss of the ability to protect their women, an ability the South fought a war to protect, according to Avary, and an ability recovered now only in occasions of mob violence, according to Page and Avary. In contrast, the image of slavery in the critique of that discourse is of an epoch when white men did rape black women (as they continued to do), an epoch that created an American culture of racial violence, and an epoch to which can be traced the motives and methods of postbellum lynchers: the desire for social control.

Let me end this section by briefly discussing the primary work that the lynching for rape discourse performed, the work, that is, that was both an expression and an example of the social control lynching sought to maintain. I noted in the introduction to this chapter that a discourse defines discernible roles to social actors. In the case of the lynching for rape discourse, rape is what black men are predisposed to committing, what white women are thereby vulnerable to having committed on their bodies, and what white men chivalrously avenge in lynching. This renders white women beholden to white men and fearful of black men; it renders the violence done to black men as justifiable; and it retains for white men the power of controlling their women (through fear and chivalry) and their former slaves (through fear and violence).[28] What this discourse seems utterly to ignore is the role of black women. Rape and lynching appear to be a triangular affair, with everyone but black women assigned a place. That, however, is deceptive, for in covert ways the discourse of lynching for rape contains at its heart a vicious representation of black women that holds them ultimately responsible for the whole cycle of rape and lynching.

To see the subtle work of the discourse in assigning black women ultimate responsibility, we can return to a point made by Thomas Nelson Page, who declared that "the Negro does not generally believe in the virtue of women. It is beyond his experience." Again, with the insinuating innuendo that is his trademark, Page is saying that women's virtue is beyond black men's "experience" because they never find it in black women. Philip A. Bruce is much more thorough in spelling out the full logic, at which Page only hints. Black women, according to Bruce, "are less modest as a class at the present day than they were before the abolition of slavery, since they are now under no restriction at all." Without the beneficial social control of white planters, black women, Bruce concludes, have become wanton and are therefore fundamentally responsible for the rapes black men commit, in at least three ways.

First, they not only fail to provide a suitable domestic morality for their men but indeed spur their men to a life of crime. "Their moral influence over their husbands is often pernicious," writes Bruce, and "much of the crime which the latter commit is secretly or openly instigated by the wives, who frequently go so far as to be active accomplices themselves." Second, and this is the point Page was emphasizing, the failure of black women to be chaste gives their husbands no examples of womanly virtue. Having no "perception of personal dignity or the pangs of outraged feeling," the black man simply cannot "gauge the terrible character of this offense against the integrity of virtuous womanhood." Therefore, the "average plantation negro does not consider rape to be a very heinous crime," Bruce concludes, because he is "so accustomed to the wantonness of the women of his own race." Finally, black women are responsible for black men's raping white women (and therefore of black men's being lynched) because of what Bruce calls their "corrupting sexual influences." Black men are made insatiable because black women are insatiable. It is an infection that earlier writers had used to defend white slaveholders who found themselves seduced by the slave women they owned. The "heaviest part of the white racial burden," notes Avary in an almost paradigmatic case, "was the African woman, of strong sexual instincts and devoid of a sexual conscience, at the white man's door, in the white man's dwelling."[29] Black women were doing to black men after slavery what they had done to white men during slavery.

We can see, then, the logic and work of the lynching for rape discourse. White men lynch because black men rape, and black men rape because black women incite them to it. The ultimate responsibility for lynching rests at the feet of black women. Using elements borrowed from the discourse of the Lost Cause, employing rhetoric inherited from earlier discourses justifying lynching as an act of popular sovereignty and an expression of communal support against violators of communal mores, the lynching for rape discourse became an almost unassailable constellation of ideas that worked to motivate lynchers, derail their critics, and assign particular roles to every segment of the society. Those forces that arraigned themselves against lynching attempted to undo this discourse, to reveal its false logic, and to challenge the particular roles that defined those critics. It is worth noting that black women's antilynching groups had to be committed to defending black women's sexual reputation as well as criticizing lynching; and white women's groups, like the Association of White

Women to Prevent Lynching, made part of its mission the critique of the logic of chivalry and denounced "the mob as a false protector of Southern womanhood."[30] It was the peculiar power of the lynching for rape discourse—because it did create roles for all social actors—to demand of its critics that they first challenge their imputed role before they could challenge lynching as a practice. Having seen the terms and logic and operative force of the discourse, we can now turn to the ways this discourse was mobilized and how it served to direct the terms of debate over lynching for the rest of the century.

THE DISCOURSE MOBILIZED: AN AMERICAN CULTURAL NARRATIVE

It would be difficult to overstate the enormous power of the lynching for rape discourse. Although critics of that discourse demonstrated through the use of statistics and facts that the discourse was simply wrong in its major presuppositions, its unperturbed defenders continued to ignore that criticism and repeat with renewed energy the main tenets of that discourse. What had been cast as "unnamable" because it would offend the virtue of the reader now became unnamed because it was widely enough known not to require naming; it simply became "the usual outrageous crime."[31] We can perhaps best appreciate both the widespread power of that discourse, and therefore the challenges faced by its critics, by discerning the range of different arenas where that discourse assumed a prominent, almost hegemonic place. For the sake of brevity, we can focus on three arenas of intellectual debate—medicine, politics, and the academy—to discern how each social arena accepted and contributed to the discourse.

The medical profession weighed in on the public debate about rape and lynching in the May 1893 issue of the *Virginia Medical Monthly*. In a representative exchange, important because it was between the president of the American Medical Association and a professor of surgery in Chicago, the president asks the professor to provide supplementary medical proof of what both agree to be undisputable facts—that black Americans are "deteriorating morally and physically," and that the primary sign of that regression is black men's predatory raping of "innocent, mutilated, and ruined female victims." Both correspondents are, in the end, mildly critical of lynching, although sympathetic to lynchers—the president feels that newspapers too glibly report the lynching and ignore the crime that led to it, the professor feels that burning black men is barbarous but that he would also do it "under like circumstances."

What is most telling, though, is how thoroughly both accept the premise that lynching is performed for rape and that black men are habitually (indeed physiologically) prone to raping white women. The professor ends his disquisition by advocating an apparently less barbarous punishment than lynching that he believes would help curb this peculiarly racial crime: medical castration "supplemented by penile mutilation." But the more significant contribution to the debate for our purposes is the medical diagnosis offered by the doctors. The reason black men are prone to rape, the doctor concludes, is that they have a "distinct tendency to reversion to type, which reversion is especially manifest in the direction of sexual proclivities." Held in check before by the "inhibiting influences of slavery," the black man's reversion is now unhindered by any social agency and driven primarily by biological imperatives, by "hereditary influences," and by "animal propensities" that even the usually ameliorating act of "cross-breeding" fails to reduce.[32] In addition to its being a failing of morals and civilization, black men's raping attests to the failings of genetic inheritance. So weighs in the medical profession to make its unique and authoritative contribution to the lynching for rape discourse.

If the contribution of the medical profession to the lynching for rape discourse was to make the problem of rape pathological and physiological (and to some extent thereby suitable only for medical professionals), the contribution of politicians was to make the discourse a representative form of political demagoguery. Two South Carolinian gubernatorial candidates exemplify the way this discourse was mobilized for political purposes. In the gubernatorial campaign of 1892, Ben Tillman proclaimed: "There is only one crime that warrants lynching, and Governor as I am, I would lead a mob to lynch the negro who ravishes a white woman." Twenty years later, Cole Blease employed the same discourse, making even more explicit what Tillman had unsubtly implied: "Whenever the constitution of my state steps between me and the defense of the virtue of white womanhood, then I say to hell with the Constitution!" So certain was he that this sentiment would impress his constituency that one of his campaign posters contained the slogan "A Governor Who Lauds Lynching."[33] Both candidates won their elections. So, too, did Jeff Davis (not the former Confederate president, who died in 1889), the gubernatorial candidate in Arkansas in 1903, who explained away his having pardoned a black man by noting that in Arkansas "when we have no doubt about a negro's guilt we do not give him a trial; we mob him. . . . The mere fact that this negro got a trial is evidence that there was some degree of doubt of his guilt." Davis was elected to an unprecedented third term in 1904, and the next year he took the occasion of President Theodore Roosevelt's visit to state publicly that lynchings would happen wherever "true manhood has a representative or virtue a worshipper."[34]

The lynching for rape discourse provided a fine campaign strategy because it allowed the candidates to align themselves with a principle more important than the constitution they eventually have to swear to uphold. Instead, they claim connection to a greater cause—chivalry, and, by implication, white supremacy—which is more directly meaningful to the voters. A Southern newspaper editor, commenting on a lynching in a different state, echoed this sensibility when he argued that lynchers claimed an allegiance to "a law more potent, more majestic, more unchangeable than any in the statute books . . . the common law . . . written not on tablets of stone, nor in the sections of her Code . . . but graven on the hearts of her men who have any manhood in them."[35] The discourse appealed to and implied a certain kind of populism, a rhetoric stating that the actions of the masses are more effective and manly than the institutions of the society, which by implication are more effete and less virile.

But it was not just on the way to or on the steps of the governor's mansion that Southern politicians could trumpet these sentiments. On the floor of the Senate in 1907, then Senator Ben Tillman offered a more graphic and personal version of this discourse. He first offered the traditional images of the stock characters in the lynching for rape discourse—black men whose "breasts [were] pulsating with the desire to sate their passions upon white maidens and wives," and a white woman victim, "her body prostituted, her purity destroyed, her chastity taken from her, and a memory branded on her brain as with a red-hot

iron"—and then concluded with a stirring narrative of familial dysfunc-
tion: "I have three daughters, but so help me God, I had rather find
either one of them killed by a tiger or bear and gather up her bones and
bury them, conscious that she had died in the purity of her maiden-
hood, than to have her crawl to me and tell me the horrid story that she
had been robbed of the jewel of her womanhood by a black fiend."[36]

Another senator, the first woman to become one, Rebecca Latimer
Felton, spoke with even more venomous power in her most famous
speech at the annual meeting of the State Agricultural Society of
Georgia in the summer of 1897. Felton's peroration is the most memo-
rable and oft-quoted part of her speech—"If it takes lynching to protect
woman's dearest possession from drunken, ravening human beasts, then
I say lynch a thousand a week if it becomes necessary"—but the intent
behind it was what gave substance to that bloodthirsty cry. And the
intent was to disenfranchise black men, whose raping of white woman
was in her mind symbolic of the raping of the body politic. Felton
claimed that the crime of rape among black men "had grown and
increased by reason of the corruption and debasement of the right of
suffrage, [and] that it would grow and increase with every election
where white men equalized themselves at the polls with an inferior
race." The logic, then, was that rape would decrease with black
disenfranchisement, which was being accomplished in virtually
every Southern state by constitutional means in the 1890s and would be
effectively achieved in Georgia within a decade of Felton's speech.[37]

The contribution of politicians to the discourse of lynching, then, is
threefold. First, as apologists for lynching they put the discourse into a
public forum—state and federal congresses—whose primary function is
to create the laws that lynchers violate. This situation exemplifies how
greater law matters to these politicians and their constituents to such a
degree that the advocates of lawlessness become the chief executives of
law in their states. Second, they use the discourse to appeal to voters
who are swayed by what sounds like a reform and populist rhetoric but
is in reality a white supremacist agenda. We know that a promising bira-
cial populism crashed on the shoals of racism; we see how conservative
politicians employ a discourse that borrows elements of populist
rhetoric to help in that wreck. Third, politicians use that discourse to
create an association between the crime of rape and the one meaningful

activity in the political arena, the act of voting. When blacks vote, they become rapists. When whites vote, they elect representatives who are apologists for extralegal violence against black rapists. The lynching for rape discourse mobilized a political sentiment that ultimately helped disenfranchise black people.

The third arena of social activity, the academy, is the one where we might expect to find some dissent to the discourse. A place of putatively more liberal leanings, with a stated commitment to freedom of thought and expression, the university in the South should have been the source of the kind of criticism that was absent or anemic in the media, the pulpit, and most of civil society. Two famous cases—one at Emory in Atlanta and the other at Trinity College in Durham—thoroughly demonstrate just how much free debate was stifled in the academy precisely when it came to discussing the logic of the discourse of lynching.

In 1902, Andrew H. Sledd, a professor of Latin and Greek at Emory College, published an article in the *Atlantic Monthly* in which he excoriated politicians and editors who were apologists for lynching, calling them "blatant demagogues, political shysters, courting favor with the mob; news sheets, flattering the prejudices and pandering to the passions of their constituency." He directly challenged the lynching for rape discourse by declaring that rape was not alleged in the vast majority of lynching cases, and that lynchers, rather than being chivalrous Southern gentlemen, were rather members of "our lower and lowest classes." Those politicians and newspaper editors he criticized (including Rebecca Felton) wrote with such force in denouncing him that Sledd finally resigned and left for further study at Yale with a financial "settlement" to assuage the guilt of the Board of Trustees of the college.[38]

A year later, John Spencer Bassett, a faculty member at his undergraduate alma mater, Trinity College, raised a similar furor when he published an article in *South Atlantic Quarterly* in which he asserted the rights of African Americans, prophesied their eventual social equality with whites, and condemned those white politicians and newspaper editors who employed the discourse of lynching as a strategy to foment what he called "race antipathy." Josephus Daniels, owner and editor of the *Raleigh News and Observer*, who had in fact defended Sledd's right to freedom of thought and expression a year earlier, attacked Bassett and defended the discourse of lynching as the "glory of Southern manhood and Southern chivalry." He pointedly excluded Bassett from that fraternity, claiming that he was unfit to write "from the standpoint of a Southern man." Bassett's brethren at the Smithfield Methodist Church likewise felt that he was unfit to worship with them, as they resolved to dismiss him for what they called statements "unjust to our southern institutions, and southern sentiments, and . . . compromising and humiliating to southern Anglo-Saxon manhood and womanhood." A trustee of Trinity College, John F. Bruton, concurred and averred that Bassett's article would incite black rapists to act: "Every published declaration like those of Dr. Bassett quickens the pulse of the black man."[39] In the end, Bassett was not fired from Trinity, largely because the president of the college interviewed Bassett and permitted him an occasion to rephrase and downplay every statement that had proved antipathetic to his critics. Three years later, Bassett resigned from Trinity and left the South to teach at Smith College in Northampton, Massachusetts.

The academy, then, proved to be subject to rather than critical of the influences of political and media demagogues, and thus a site committed to repeating rather than investigating the claims of the discourse. The academy was also the bulwark of apologists for the discourse of lynching: some were zealots who wished to purge wayward faculty who had the temerity to doubt the truth of the discourse, and some were moderates whose graceful writing and authoritative status made the discourse more respectable. John Carlisle Kilgo, for example, the president of Trinity College, who spoke eloquently for freedom of speech during the Bassett hearings in front of the Board of Trustees, nonetheless managed to rein in the opinions of at least one faculty member in his somewhat coercive interview with Bassett. But Kilgo was no less an apologist for lynching. He had in fact published an article a year before the Bassett case in the very journal Bassett founded, *South Atlantic Quarterly*, in which he defended lynching, exalted Southern women, and proclaimed that the repeated lynching of black men "cannot be charged to racial prejudices."[40]

While white academics might lose tenure or church membership for criticizing the discourse, black intellectuals faced the threat of losing their lives to the mob activity they denounced. In 1887 the black weekly *Montgomery Herald* published an editorial that mocked the lynching for rape discourse, claiming that mobs would soon "lynch every colored man that looks at a white woman with a twinkle in his eye," and implying that interracial sexual relations were consensual and a result of the "growing appreciation of the white Juliet for the colored Romeo, as he becomes more and more intelligent and refined." The editorial provoked the town leaders of Montgomery to call a public meeting and form a committee of ten prominent citizens who would visit the editor, Jessie C. Duke, and give him eight hours to leave town (which he had already done before the committee's visit). In 1892, Ida B. Wells published an account that likewise challenged the lynching discourse on its most basic grounds—"Nobody in this section of the country believes the old thread bare lie that Negro men rape white women"—and instead claimed that many "poor blind Afro-American Sampsons [*sic*]" are lynched because they are "betrayed by white Delilahs." In response to Wells's editorial, a mob destroyed her Memphis newspaper office, and two white-owned Memphis newspapers advocated lynching and castrating the offending writer (they did not know that Wells was a woman). Six years later, another black editor, Alexander Manly, would be threatened with lynching and run out of Wilmington, North Carolina, for criticizing Rebecca Felton and noting the hypocrisy of white men's lamenting "the virtue of your women, when you seek to destroy the morality of ours." In 1927 E. Franklin Frazier likewise touched a raw nerve when he claimed that the lynching discourse was delusional and that white women suffered hallucinations of being attacked by black men—hallucinations, he concluded, that were "projected wishes." Local Atlanta newspaper editorials attacked these ideas with vigor, and Frazier received death threats. Frazier had to leave the South hastily to avoid a threatened lynching.[41]

Here, then, we see the effect of the lynching discourse on several sectors of society. The ruling elites in the medical profession, the government, and the academy all contributed to the discourse and ensured that any criticism from within those institutions was regulated, and any from without threatened with extinction. The success of that discourse is measured ultimately in the ways Americans practiced lynching and interpreted the meaning of the practice. The most tragic measure, of course, is the amount of blood spilled of those whom the discourse maligned and cast beyond human sympathy, the direct victims of lynch mobs, and the potentially threatened victims of those who shared their race. A second tragic measure of the discourse's success is the ways it foreclosed debate about African American life and the ways, in the words of Ida B. Wells, it "closed the heart, stifled the conscience, warped the judgment, and hushed the voice of press and pulpit on the subject of lynch law."[42]

Faced with this hegemonic discourse, critics of lynching had to resort to strategies that were largely determined by the discourse. One can hear in their repetition, decade after decade, the disheartening effect of their having to state, over and over again, the raw statistics that proved that the allegation of rape was infrequent, having to defend the race against charges that stained with their very mention. Those who knew better nonetheless felt compelled to repeat the rostrums of the apologists in order to gain a hearing and avoid the fate of those critics who dared speak the truth. When Booker T. Washington, for instance, wrote in criticism of lynching, he began by accepting that lynching had been "instituted some years ago with the idea of punishing and checking outrages upon women," before going on to show that current lynchings in 1899 were motivated by less noble principles.[43] When Congressman Thomas E. Miller, a black political leader in South Carolina, wished to speak against the what he called the "slanderous, and most damnably false" charges against African Americans, he had nonetheless to tame his rage by referring to white women as those "walking emblems of American purity."[44] Presumably, because he continued to live and to live in South Carolina, no one heard the sarcasm in his voice.

This, then, is the discourse that circulated and helped form the society of the age of lynching, but, unlike the age of lynching, this discourse did not end. It continued to exercise the minds and motivate the acts of those who continued to believe the variety of myths on which it was based—the myth of the Lost Cause, the myth of black sexuality, the myth of chivalry, the myth of white supremacy. It inspired mob leaders who used what Lillian Smith denounced as its "obscene, perverse imagery" to whip up the fury of those murderous mobs who did the work of lynching.[45] And it continued to do so—masking raw racial domination under the rhetoric of gallant chivalry—and continues to do so for a significant minority of Americans for whom those Jasper, Texas, lynchers of 1998 presumed to speak and inspire to form another white supremacist community.

Conclusion

The Meanings of Lynching

One of the first representations of a lynching in American film appears in D. W. Griffith's *Birth of a Nation* in 1915. The lynching is performed off-screen, but the body of the lynched man is brought on-screen by the triumphant Klan and left on the steps of the lieutenant governor's house as a statement for "blacks and carpetbaggers." The black victim, Gus, is lynched for his desire, cast as an attempted rape, for a white woman named Flora, who leaps to her death rather than succumb to his advances. The lynchers identify Gus as the assailant when they see an imprinted image of his menacing face in the eyeball of the dead Flora. Even dead, Flora nonetheless is able to reveal the identity of the brute who would destroy the flower of white womanhood.

African American filmmaker Oscar Micheaux challenged this representation of lynching in Griffith's movie in his 1919 film *Within Our Gates* in several ways. First, Micheaux shows us the work of the mob as they lynch an African American bystander while waiting to catch the person they believe to be the actual criminal; during this first lynching, because we have a superimposed picture of the actual hanging while the victim is being beaten by the mob, the lynching is present, not off-screen. Second, he shows us the lynching of the entire falsely accused Landry family, revealing the ways that mobs are frenzied forces, quite unlike the calm, deliberative Klan in *Birth of a Nation*. Third, by showing us what happens to the Landry family's bodies ("incinerated in the bonfire"), he reveals the barbarity of the mob, whose cause is not so noble as Griffith wished to present it.

Fourth, Micheaux shows us the role newspapers play in enflaming mob activity by having the scene of the original crime replayed through the newspaper's falsifying narration. Finally, as Toni Cade Bambara notes, Micheaux echoes the rape scene in *Birth of a Nation* by having a white man attempt to rape a black woman, setting the record straight, Bambara concludes, "on who rapes who." The fact that the rape is prevented by the discovery that the rape victim is the daughter of the would-be rapist evokes both the long history of miscegenation and white-on-black rapes (as opposed to the short history of black-on-white rapes lynching apologists fabricated) and reveals the familial ties across race in the same way that Griffith's film revealed familial ties across regions in his Civil War battle scenes.[1]

This debate in film in the second decade of the twentieth century, like the political debates between prolynching apologists and anti-lynching advocates, is ultimately a debate about the meaning of lynching. Each proposed a story to account for the action. Griffith promoted the account of prolynching apologists that lynchings were acts of chivalry and honor, while Micheaux followed the example of antilynching advocates to reveal the deceitfulness of this "surface" account and to show that lynchings were acts of terrorism. Modern students of lynching approach the question of the meaning of the practice in much the same way as Micheaux and the antilynching advocates. They want to discern the deeper motivations behind the "surface" story, the unspoken, sometimes unspeakable, imperatives that drove people to perform the violent acts they did.

I will here survey three recent and exceptionally useful accounts that assess lynchers' hidden motivations. These accounts, as we will see, all draw on the form and model of lynching from what we have called the "age of lynching." After seeing what these interpretations teach us, we then approach the question of meaning through a different strategy that is less interested in the motives that drove the practice and more attuned to the historical origins of those motivations. When the primary concern of a study is the persistence of a practice, its evolution over a long period in a nation's history, as ours is here, the origins question is the one more likely to help us comprehend what that practice means to the nation in which it has evolved and endured.

THREE INTERPRETATIONS

At the outset, we should note that most general interpretations of what lynchings mean attempt to explain only those lynchings that occurred during the age of lynching, and frequently only spectacle lynchings. Those interpretations of lynching tend to try and discern the *purpose* of the lynching through an elaboration of either the *scene* or the *agents*.[2] Those who focus on the *scene* see the hidden meaning of lynching in the environmental circumstances (seasonal and crop fluctuations) and social conditions (economic, political). These are the interpretations that trace lynchings to concrete social practices around conditions of labor, politics, and demographics. Those who focus on the *agents* explain what lynchings mean by attending to the lynchers and discerning what motivated them, whether it was principles of Southern honor, psychosexual fixations, or mythic and religious beliefs.

I will focus here on three such interpretations, each of them in its own way quite compelling. The three interpretations account for lynching as a practice that reflects lynchers' attitudes based on one of three spheres of human thinking and action—identity, economics, and religion. The questions these scholars ask are: what motivated lynchers to do what they did, and what can we say lynchings mean, given those motivations? These interpretations cover a great deal of ground in terms of motive, whether it is solidifying particular types of social identities organized around race and gender, or reinforcing class and labor status, or ritually reenacting sacrificial practices at the heart of religious traditions. They also reveal different ways of comprehending what it is lynchers attempt to protect when they perform their lynchings— conservative, patriarchal models of domestic relations, or access to cheap labor, or a social order they believe reflects a divine categorical imperative to punish. Although the scholarly interpretations I am discussing here are relatively new, appearing in the last decade or two, antilynching activists for the past hundred and twenty years have been employing the categories identified here in similar ways. We can turn, then, to the first of these interpretations.

In the late 1970s, Jacquelyn Dowd Hall brought a remarkably important and illuminating feminist sensibility to the study of lynching in her biography of Jessie Daniel Ames, the founder of the Association of Southern Women for the Prevention of Lynching (ASWPL). Hall set out to write a "narrative of violence against black men in which neither black nor white women were displaced." Her argument in that groundbreaking book, *Revolt Against Chivalry,* is that the "racism that caused white men to lynch black men cannot be understood apart from the sexism that informed their policing of white women and their exploitation of black women."[3] If we were to identify precursors of Hall's, we would say that she followed in the footsteps of her biographical subject, Ames, who in turn drew on the inspiration provided by the Anti-Lynching Crusaders of the 1920s, a group of African American women who set out to agitate against lynching. But the pioneer who inaugurated the analysis of lynching by demonstrating the ways lynching was connected to racial and sexual terrorism is, of course, Ida B. Wells.

Like Wells, Hall is carefully attuned to the ways lynching apologists spoke a partial truth when they declared that black men accused of raping white women were lynched. Both Wells and Hall were alert to the deceptions both of fact (mobs lynched for a plethora of reasons, and rape was the allegation for lynching in only a minority of cases) and of ideology. Lynching, they both saw, was a form of controlling populations of women and men through strategies of spectacle, rumor, and the creation of a pervasive climate of fear. Hall's important insight, developing a point implicitly made by Wells, was that lynching and rape were employed together in an overarching strategy of terrorism. Racism that manifested itself in lynchings of black men operated to intensify what Hall calls the "sexual hierarchy" of Southern society, while at the same time the "rape scares" that helped mobilize mobs and popular opinion functioned "as a means of both sexual and racial control."[4]

Lynching, then, served to assert particular political goals for those who practiced it—terrorism during Reconstruction, white solidarity during the Populist era, and antimodernism in the midst of modernity.[5] In addition, lynching served during each of these periods as a way of controlling black mobility, black political organizing, and black independence. It also served, and this is Hall's significant contribution, to produce a "dramatization of cultural themes, a 'story' white southerners told themselves about the social arrangements and psychological strivings that lay beneath the surface of everyday life."[6] Explicating what we called the "discourse of lynching" in Chapter Four, Hall demonstrates in just what ways the story of lynching for rape operated in the everyday lives of white and black Southerners.

Obviously, the lynching itself effectively dramatized the dangers faced by black men who dared transgress the sanction against interracial sex. Less obviously, but as important, the threat of rape that these stories made their essential premise served to keep white women as "a subordinate group in a state of anxiety and fear." These stories were meant to intimidate and make beholden to their saviors white women as much as they were to make black communities fearful. And, as we saw in Chapter

Four, black women in the end bore the most brutal brunt of the effects of this discourse, as they were cast as the lascivious cause of white men's and black men's lust. Lynching and rape, then, were inexorably connected in every way. Black men were lynched for putatively raping white women; white women were cast as perpetually in fear of rape; white men were justified in raping black women; and black women were cast as the cause of the whole complex of rape and lynching. Exquisitely showing the connections that the discourse of lynching for rape attempted to submerge or hide, Hall concludes that the "ritual of lynching" did indeed serve as a "dramatization of hierarchical power relationships based both on gender and on race."[7]

Hall's contribution to our contemporary understanding of lynching, to our appreciation of the ways a particular social practice can produce and reinforce a set of social roles, was truly groundbreaking. All modern students of lynching remain indebted to her analysis. Hers was the first modern study to excavate the lynching discourse and demonstrate how that discourse, and the practice it defended, controlled a society through sheer violence and an accompanying pornographic mythology. She was the first to plumb the depths of that discourse and reveal the ways that every person of whatever race, class, and gender was implicated in that discourse and thereby controlled by its dictates. Hall's analysis was so fruitful and useful for later scholars primarily because of her emphasis on connections (how all are implicated by a single discourse), and her alertness to the ways that gender and class, lynching and rape, operated in a single system.[8]

The next interpretation was less concerned with how to decipher what lynchers said, because it believed that the discourse was entirely a ruse to mask and hide a particular kind of social relation. Walter White spoke for many of his antilynching predecessors and peers when he noted in 1929 that the lynching-for-rape discourse was a "red herring," a way of hiding the true cause of lynching, which he identified as the white South's desire for "economic ascendancy over Negro labour." Lynching, he mordantly concluded, "has always been the means for protection, not of white women, but of profits."[9] He was anticipated, joined, and echoed by other antilynching activists who emphasized that lynching was a strategy for controlling black labor and thereby ensuring the continuing exploitation of the surplus value of that labor. Modern scholars of lynching have continued to explore the background economic conditions of lynchings. Those scholars who have focused on what I called *scene* above, especially sociologists, have attended to how lynchings can be explained as a form of terrorism that is particularly meant to regulate and control a pool of labor and thereby stabilize the region's economic conditions.

In the most thorough analysis of lynchings using these terms, *Festival of Violence*, Stewart E. Tolnay and E. M. Beck identify three intertwined functions of lynching in the South: "first, to maintain social control over the black population through terrorism; second, to suppress or eliminate black competitors for economic, political, or social rewards; and third, to stabilize the white class structure and preserve the privileged status of the white aristocracy." Tolnay and Beck conclude that the most robust interpretation that the data support is the one connecting lynching to cotton culture, by which they mean a "constellation of factors including arrangements of land tenure, a strong dependency on cotton as the primary cash crop, and a reliance on black labor." They conclude that generally "economic factors were important in motivating lynchings," and that more specifically there was a strong correlation between the frequency of lynchings and the economic cycles of cotton—fewer lynchings when cotton prices were high, and more during economic downturns. They also conclude that there was a strong correlation between lynching and the seasonal cycle of cotton culture—with the most lynchings occurring when the "need for labor was greatest," and therefore the time when landlords most wanted to exercise and demonstrate their "increased control over labor."[10]

Historians and sociologists focusing in particular on the cycles of production continue to develop and refine these findings. In a stimulating and insightful book on "the culture of segregation," *Making Whiteness*, Grace Elizabeth Hale offered what is perhaps the most creative and innovative approach to understanding the relationship between lynching and the economics of the South by changing the focus from production (the control of labor) to circulation and consumption. Hale begins by noting the tensions, fissures, and contradictions in Southern society that arose and appeared in the period between the 1890s and 1940s as the South developed and expanded a modern "consumer culture" that challenged and required new defenses in its "culture of segregation." As the consumer culture expanded in the South, it produced what Hale describes as a "disjuncture" in the society that used stereotyped black imagery in advertising new goods (thereby implying a white consumer), while at the same time creating new spaces (railroads, gas stations, restaurants, movie theaters, and general stores) where this new "geography of shopping" also depended on black consumers. She then explores in what ways white and black Southerners struggled over this terrain, as blacks resisted and whites tried to assert a new strategy of "racial control over the new spaces of consumption."[11]

Having examined the ways that Southern whites attempted to control these spaces through several means (the placing of signs, the mounting of advertising campaigns, and the inculcation of a set of racial mores), Hale turns finally to lynching, which, she argues, "became increasingly bound up" between the 1890s and 1940 in the "very practices of a modern culture of consumption." Her argument is that these spectacle lynchings cannot be understood as regressive actions against modernity, a frontier strategy in an age that no longer had a frontier. Instead, they have to be understood as part of modernity itself and "intertwined with the practices of an emerging consumer culture," since they depended on "modern transportation and printing technologies" and became a key strategy for resolving "the contradictions within the culture of segregation." Spectacle lynchings became "a southern way of enabling the spread of consumption as a white privilege." Because of their dynamic, lynchings became sites of violence that helped "create a white consuming public" in the very act of defending and reinforcing "the structure of segregation where consumption could take place without threatening white supremacy."[12]

The irony at the heart of lynching in a culture of segregation is that lynching required a violation of the rules of that culture; in other words, lynching required the mingling, and most intimate mingling, of a black body among whites. The important thing about what Hale calls this "transgression of segregated spaces"—the introduction of a black body into an otherwise exclusively white society—was precisely that it was not random or chaotic, but rather a "controlled inversion of this practice of racial separation." It was done at the whim and will of the white mob, and it was precisely done to reinforce the values for which that mob stood. If one of the fears that a consumer culture created was that black people might create their own economic and social enclaves in the spaces they occupied, lynchings worked to deny "that any space was black space, [as] even the very bodies of African Americans were subject to invasion by whites."

More importantly, these spectacle lynchings also worked to make the modern consumer culture consistent with the earlier economic system of the South—slavery. Lynchings effectively reversed the "decommodification of black bodies begun with emancipation," because lynchings provided white Southerners an opportunity to purchase parts of black bodies, fingers, toes, and other mementos of the lynching. As Hale puts it, not only did "blacks themselves become consumer items," but the very "sites of their murders became new spaces of consumption." A lynching, then, operated to make the present expansion of consumer culture (where one could buy new things in new places) congruent with the system of consumption that made the South what it was (where one could buy black people because they were first and always property).[13]

Hale concludes her study by showing how spectacle lynchings helped resolve other tensions in Southern society, including gender and class tensions. Since a new consumer culture created new opportunities for women, lynching, with its standard story of chivalry in the service of a threatened white womanhood, served to reinforce old roles. Lynching, as Hale puts it, "helped reconcile the ambiguity of gender difference at the heart of a society in which the primary boundary was the color line." In addition, lynchings, as assertions of a unified white community, seamless in its solidarity in the presence of a menacing black body, "also helped ease the class tensions within white supremacy." In other words, the fact that a lower-class white person could not enter the consumer culture with the same vigor or aspirations as an affluent white person came to matter less given the importance of their shared identity—both could, in a word, consume black lives. Lynchings, then, "subverted segregation, separation as culture, in order to strengthen it," and to make those spaces of the expanding consumer culture that much less riven by class and gender divisions within white communities.[14]

Hale focuses on the tensions between consumer culture and the culture of segregation—understanding how a social order attempted to create a particular order where certain things belonged in one place, and others in another. The most recent new interpretation of lynching as a social practice has likewise drawn on the culture of segregation as the fundamental grounds on which lynching can be understood, but the focus in that interpretation has shifted from the economic, material conditions from which lynchings arose to the religious, otherworldly traditions that Southern segregationists believed required a particular kind of ritualized violence to maintain.

In 1929, at the same time he diagnosed the economic motive in lynching, Walter White had simultaneously discerned the religious imperative in the practice. He did not believe that "lynching could possibly exist under any other religion than Christianity" because only Christianity had so thoroughly drawn "the colour line and thus set up an elaborate array of invidious distinctions which assure the white Christian of his immense superiority." In addition, White continues, it is the specific form of evangelical Christianity in the Southern states that has provided the impetus for lynching. "No person who is familiar with the Bible-beating, acrobatic, fanatical preachers of hell-fire in the South, and who has seen the orgies of emotion created by them, can doubt for a moment that dangerous passions are released which contribute to emotional instability and play a part in lynching."[15]

Two scholars—the historical sociologist Orlando Patterson and the historian of religion Donald Matthews—have each recently offered a cogent interpretation of lynching as an avatar of Christian ritual sacrifice. The religious interpretation of lynching does not necessarily conflict with the earlier interpretations of lynching, but rather asserts that the source of consolation that comes to lynchers is effectively a dangerously misguided reading of the role of sacrifice in Christian salvation.[16]

Patterson asserts that lynching is effectively a "sacrificial ritual" that performed "vital social and cultural functions for Southern postbellum communities." The particular kinds of lynchings that qualify as sacrificial rituals had to include three factors: torture, mass attendance, and burning. And these kinds of lynchings he dates from the end of Reconstruction, when he notes an escalation of lynching of African

Americans, to as late as the 1930s.[17] Those spectacle lynchings, occurring during what we have been calling the "age of lynching," performed what Patterson describes as "powerful functions in the symbolic universe of postbellum Southern culture and religion."[18]

The first function required a sacrificial victim who represents sin. The ex-slave, as Patterson notes, became the "most exquisitely appropriate representational object" of sin because of the enduring Western beliefs about both blackness and enslavement. Blackness had become symbolic of evil and the devil in Christian iconology, and the purging of that evil, in the minds of lynchers and their theological apologists, could be effected by killing a black person. Moreover, Patterson reminds us that the Latin word *redemptio* means to "purchase a slave out of slavery into freedom." Lynchings, then, became acts of redemption in that they killed the icon of evil (the black person) at the same time that they liberated out of slavery those who were redeemed (by killing the emblem of slavery in America, the black person).[19]

If one function of lynching in this scenario was to relieve the existential sense of guilt in Southern religious communities, another was to address the historical moment that rendered that guilt unbearable—and that is the loss of the Civil War. Confronted with an inexplicable problem—how to explain the defeat of "a God-fearing, chosen people with a proud martial tradition"—the Lost Cause ideologues produced a robust account in which that defeat could be traced to Satan and could be offset only by the exorcism of that group of people whose blackness, again, associated them with evil. Free African Americans, Patterson mordantly notes, "became to the body politic what Satan was to the individual and collective soul of the South." Both had to be excised, and the new "civil religion" of violent racism answered that need. The lynching of black people in the years after the war became both "expiation and atonement" for the Southern mobs that obeyed the tenets of that religion.[20]

Patterson's argument, then, is that lynching was a demonstrably ritual act that reveals something about the "secular religion of racism" that supported it in the American South and the Christian religion from which he argued it emerged. Patterson demonstrates how lynchers actively performed what can only be seen as acts of consecration, especially to give sanction to places that were not consecrated in more orthodox ways, such as churches. Lynchers, he notes, often used the traditional means of making a site more appropriate for a ritual act by employing "fire as a consecrating agent." Fire is also essential for Patterson's argument about lynchers as cannibals. Drawing on the phys- iological connection between smell and taste—he cites a psychophysi- cist who comments that "there is no true sensory inhibition between olfaction and taste"—Patterson then concludes that the lynchers who were "suffused with the odor of the lynch victim's roasting body" were literally participating in a "cannibalistic devouring of his body."[21]

That act of ritual cannibalism, argues Patterson, is to be traced to the religion in whose name the lynchers performed their deeds. Christianity, he maintains, is not "simply a profoundly sacrificial reli- gion," but rather a religion founded on an act of human sacrifice. Fundamentalist sects emphasize the idea of Christ as a "suffering victim who sacrificed his life for the salvation of sinners," and Southern funda- mentalists drew on this imagery and conception of sacrificial violence in their lynching murders of African Americans. Patterson traces this emphasis on human sacrifice back to what he considers an unusual development in Christianity, which, unlike other religions, did not sepa- rate two distinct forms of atonement. In other religious and spiritual practices, the process of ridding a soul or communal body of an alien evil requires two separate acts: first, a sacrificial ritual of aversion, in which the alien evil is expelled or exorcised; and second, a sacred ritual of purification or propitiation, in which the soul or communal body is purified anew. Christianity, Patterson argues, incorporates both rituals into "the single sacrificial act of Christ's crucifixion and the surrogative rituals pertaining to it, most notably the Eucharist."[22]

Patterson, then, sees lynching as not an aberration but a fulfillment of Christian values as understood by fundamentalist sects and their doctrinal apologists. These sects and apologists created a social system (segregation) that they supported by regular ritual acts of violence against the segregated. "Jim Crow," concludes Patterson, "rose to power on, was suffused with, and had as the very center of its doctrine not just the permanent segregation and subjugation of Afro-Americans but their demonization, terrorization, and humiliation." The "central ritual of this version of the Southern civil religion" was "the human sacrifice of the lynch mob."[23]

For Patterson, then, lynching could be explained by specific historical markers (the defeat of the South in the Civil War), a psycho-religious means of coming to terms with that historical event (Lost Cause mythology)—which produced a social order (the civil religion of segregation) that required the violent ritual sacrifice of African Americans as symbolic of evil—enslavement, and the cause of that original historical humiliation that began this cycle of retribution. Lynching in this religious melodrama is what the fundamentalist Christian South used to answer for a specific loss in the hope of a particular racial atonement.

Where Patterson emphasizes the connections amid a series of historical events, their memorialization, and the religious attempt to provide answers for them, Matthews focuses more on just how much of what he calls the "Southern rite of human sacrifice" pervaded almost every aspect of Southern culture. Matthews attends in particular to the ways that Southern churches emphasized the idea that at the "heart of salvation were the metaphors of retributive justice," while at its center was a "symbol of torture and death"—but not, like Patterson, to indict a particular brand of Christian apologetics (although he does do that), but rather primarily to show how this subterranean stream of thought informed "the very logic of the predominant white Christian understanding of the Universe."[24]

Like Patterson, Matthews argues that Southerners thought of segregation as a "religious system"—what he calls "segregation *as* religion." Matthews notes that Southern evangelicalism, which was "ever alert to contamination," was inevitably drawn to "nurture segregation, because the holiness of one [evangelicalism] supported the holiness of the other" (segregation).[25] Matthews differs from Patterson in that he sees segregation as a strategy used by Southerners to "protect" white women by putting black people at the margins of society, although this expressed reason actually masked an entire complex of puritanical ideas. For Matthews, the "fusion of southern Protestantism with prohibition, repressed sexuality, and the canonization of white women all combined to blur distinctions between sacred and secular where race was concerned." Matthews does not see this as a conscious process whereby lynchers justified their acts in these terms. He argues that this was instead inscribed into their very ways of imagining their world. "They could not understand, although they could sense, that lynching resolved violence within the social system by attributing its source to African

Americans and then punishing a representative (a vicarious substitute) of that class in order to achieve 'peace.'"[26]

Matthews's analysis of the "connection between the South's most dramatic act of brutality and the pervasive drama of salvation preached from pulpits throughout the region" reveals the profound contradictions inherent in the "violent logic" that moved people to lynch for a religious imperative.[27] The first contradiction is, of course, that Christians are violating one of the most fundamental of laws and commandments—thou shalt not kill. Matthews, like others before him, explains this contradiction by noting the divine madness that seized lynchers. "Such moments," he writes, "suggest an ecstatic seizure that excites humans to violence, which in itself somehow *justifies* them in *transgressing* justice." Matthews differs from earlier commentators who had largely seen this "ecstatic seizure" as either a fraudulent pose or a temporary insanity. Matthews sees it instead as part of a religious strategy that lynchers sincerely believed. "The many crowds and vigilantes who punished the violation of taboo in blood somehow understood in their solemn silence, or grim satisfaction, or in the ecstasy that demanded the shout of 'glory,' that when enacting their own theater of the sacred transgressive, they were engaging the Transcendent and entering the realm of the *sacred* abyss."[28] Like Patterson, Matthews sees that lynching for evangelical Southerners was not an aberration of their beliefs, but, sadly, a confirmation of them.

A second contradiction is one that Matthews rightly notes would have confounded "white Christian understanding" had it ever made it to consciousness. In believing themselves to be repeating the ritual act of human sacrifice at the heart of Christianity, lynchers essentially made the lynch victim into a martyr, and in turn into someone whose sacrifice was essential to their salvation. Now, white lynchers might well have believed that the black lynch victim was essential to their salvation, but they repressed the connection between that victim and the one they worshiped on Sundays. In other words, white lynch mobs celebrating in such "dramatic and public fashion" this act of human sacrifice seemed unaware, and would have been horrified to discover, that in their act "the Christ had become black."[29]

For Matthews, the fundamental fault line that lies unexamined under the social order he describes is the very concept of punishment—

the righting of wrong through an act that is expressly meant to redress one action through an akin act that opposes it. Matthews follows Patterson's example and asserts that observers to lynchings became "participants through inhaling the stench of burning flesh," but what they participate in is not cannibalism, per se, but rather a social, religious act of punishment. And that concept of punishment, Matthews maintains, is the most vexing one for our ability to understand social relations and divine history. He concludes that "the full meaning of religion and lynching may not be understood until we seriously confront the meaning of punishment itself, the status of those punished, the complicity of the punishers in defining what is punishable, and the full ramifications of punitiveness."[30]

Both Patterson and Matthews are equally interested in seeing in what ways certain attitudes associated with religion—sacrifice, salvation, punishment, atonement—are brought to bear in American lynching. They are, in other words, as attuned to the ways we can think of "religion as lynching," to quote Matthews, as they are to the ways lynching serves as a religion for Southern fundamentalist evangelicals from the end of Reconstruction to the Great Depression.[31]

These three general interpretations, representing the most robust attempts to understand the *meaning* of lynching, are all compelling and all informative. They together reveal the ways that the spectacle lynchings from the 1890s to the 1930s served fundamental social roles in the region where they most often occurred. These lynchings operated to control the ways people thought and acted by controlling the stories they told themselves about their social identities (their gender, race, and class status). These lynchings worked to resolve the contradictions of a society whose expansion of its commercial base and its consumer culture put severe stress on the social order of segregation and white supremacy. These lynchings also worked to relieve the trauma and ennui of religious angst in the South in the wake of the rupture that came with the loss of the Civil War.

There are places where these interpretations do not entirely agree with each other—on the question of whether lynching was a resistance to or constitutive of modernity and the emergence of a newly empowered nation-state, for instance. There are also places where earlier commentators have made important points that might have helped modify some of these interpretations. We saw in Chapter Three, for instance, the ways that writers like Wells and Cox challenged the idea of mobs as driven by "fury" or "madness," emotions at least akin to the sort of religious "ecstasy" or spiritual "seizure" on which to some extent the religious interpretation relies. Nonetheless, each of these interpretations, and all of them together, work well to show us the possibilities for understanding what drives lynchers to do what they do, and what they believe or delude themselves into believing they are serving in those acts.

These three general interpretations inform us how lynching was a social practice that served a set of particular ends for a society whose resort to extralegal violence reveals both its fissures and its resources, both those fault lines that expose the society's fragility and the power lines that gave it considerable force to move people to what they believe is sanctioned violence. They show us what is at stake for lynchers and their apologists, and the general forces that moved them to action: the desire to maintain particular identity relations, labor conditions, or religious values. They have identified the specific values that did indeed mobilize masses of lynchers at a specific crucial moment in American history. The moment that concerns each of these interpretations, of course, is the age of lynching and the era of segregation.[32]

Because they do focus on the era of segregation, these interpretations are somewhat limited, if our wish is to apply them to lynchings in other eras in American history. Lynchers did indeed exhibit psychosexual fixations when they castrated and emasculated black men regularly during the age of lynching, but not so much when they hanged horse thieves on the frontier. They were clearly driven by religious beliefs when they immolated victims tied to a stake in acts of communal purification, or when they lynched Jewish and Irish-Catholic Americans, but not so much when they murdered Welsh miners, British agents, and Indian chiefs during presumed wartime conditions. Given our focus and strategy in this study—that is, primarily to trace the evolutions in the practice of lynching over time—what can we make of these general interpretations of a specific moment, albeit arguably the most significant specific moment in the history of American lynching?

I suggest that these general interpretations have identified and teased out the deeper meanings of three conceptual categories that can indeed help us find another way to see the meaning of lynchings in the *longue durée* of lynching from the Revolutionary War to the present. The three values, motives, forces that they focus on—the policing of social identities, the protecting of an economic system through the control of a labor pool, and the developing of a justificatory religious ideology—strike me as the most fruitful concepts to discern what lynchings are and mean. What I will do in the final section is turn to an earlier moment and a different institution than segregation that arguably first established violence in the service of policing identities, supporting economic systems, and drawing on religious sanction—the era and institution of American slavery. Here we can turn to the second question about meanings: the question of origins.

SLAVERY AS THE ORIGINS OF LYNCHING

Is a general interpretation that attempts to account for the causes or meaning of lynchings over the course of two and a half centuries even possible? It is clear that no single meaning will explain that long history of lynchings. Having conceded that, we can nonetheless attempt to affirm some unifying elements in different kinds of lynchings that help us comprehend just what forces might be at work in that history. We will proceed by first listing the types of lynchings we have surveyed in this book, and then teasing out the hidden meanings in the most popular justifications for those lynchings, before suggesting that a potent meaning of lynchings is to be found, ultimately, in a place where it is most frequently denied that lynchings occurred—American slavery.

We can begin, then, by looking at what lynchings are, and what they *are*, of course, is not one thing. In this brief survey of two centuries of extralegal collective violence, we can distinguish at least six different forms of lynching.

First, there have been lynchings associated with military conditions and performed by militia either during times of war or in imagined states of siege. The person after whom lynching is named falls into this category. These are lynchings that are sometimes better understood as crimes of war rather than as lynchings, but at other times they are clearly lynchings that draw on the conventional defenses of summary justice.

Second, there have been lynchings performed as acts of punishment on wayward members of frontier communities, although, as I suggested in Chapter One, those vigilante groups sometimes fell victim to their own rhetoric, punishing their critics and enemies and failing to recognize the establishment of a more mature legal apparatus in their midst.

Third, there have been lynchings performed in order to regulate the mores of deviant members of the community. This is assuredly the form of lynching most commonly practiced, and it had its existence in regulators of various stripes who antedated and then were called lynchers after the term associated with Colonel Lynch came to dominate. This was the type of lynching meant to control the activities of people deemed in defiance of widely held communal values—and those values came to include and then be subsumed in white supremacy.

Fourth, there have been lynchings that were more or less bald attempts at usurping power within certain locales, what Richard Maxwell Brown called "western wars of incorporation" where lynchers performed work necessary to ridding the frontier of those who opposed or stood in the way of capitalist centralization. This would include vigilante groups like the 1856 San Francisco Vigilance Committee.

Fifth, there have been lynchings that were concerted actions of a campaign to purge a locale—town, city, county—of a population deemed illegitimate in some way. This includes such efforts as the 1835 Vicksburg campaign to rid the city of gamblers, the various urban race riots of the late nineteenth and early twentieth centuries, and the startling number of counties recently unearthed by Elliot Jaspin in which communities intent on "racial cleansing" performed lynchings as part of the process of exiling African Americans beyond their boundaries.[33]

Finally, there have been lynchings in which white Americans controlled the political activism, social mobility, and physical lives of African Americans, from slavery through the age of lynching and beyond. Depending on how one looks at things, these lynchings can be understood as racial instances of other forms of lynching—lynchings for those who defy community values, or lynchings as part of exiling a population or even lynchings for economic incorporation. Another way to see them, though, is as lynchings performed primarily as a form of racial terrorism, intended as rites for demonstrating the subordinate status of people of African descent and reproducing white supremacy.

That is how the majority of African American intellectuals saw lynchings—from Ida B. Wells and Frederick Douglass at the end of the nineteenth century to the leaders of the NAACP and the authors of *We Charge Genocide* through the twentieth century. It was finally the way that lynchings came to be understood in the wider society. In the words of President Truman's Commission on Civil Rights in 1947, lynching was "the ultimate threat by which his inferior status is driven home to the Negro." It was, they concluded, a "terrorist device" that reinforced "all the other disabilities placed upon him."[34] At the end of the age of lynching, then, the executive branch of the federal government began to understand the role of lynching in the panoply of racial oppressions faced by black Americans.

These, then, are at least some of what lynchings *are*—extralegal, collective acts of violence done in the name of necessity, community, capital, and race. Within that framework, lynchings *mean* what they seem to mean. Sometimes, lynchers are patently clear about their motives, as they were in some cases of frontier justice and, less frequently, in cases of racial terrorism. Sometimes they hid their motives behind the exalted rhetoric of popular sovereignty or the more homely rhetoric criticizing the current state and apparatus of justice. In those cases, lynchings mean what their practitioners were wary of stating. Here, I think, is where we can follow the examples provided by Hall, Hale, Patterson, and Matthews, and find the deeper, unstated motives that lynchers and lynching apologists reveal in the defenses of their actions.

While lynchings mean what they seem to mean—as acts done in the name of necessity, community, capital, and race—they also mean more. And the "more" is what the rhetoric and the practice of lynchers reveal in the claims they proudly make (popular sovereignty) and the ones they frequently deny (racial terrorism). Here, I think, we can examine the two most resonant defenses of lynching in order to discover what specific terms they establish that help us better understand just what is inherently at stake for lynchers.

The claim of popular sovereignty has clearly earned a special place in the discourse of American lynchers. It was perhaps the earliest, and has remained the most common, claim for those who wish to take the law into their own hands. We saw in Chapter One the several problems with the claim, both in its logic and in its historical application. Here we can focus on what it provides for lynchers. Let us consider one representative statement of popular sovereignty, one popular enough to be published in the widely read *Lippincott's Monthly Magazine*. According to the author, Maurice Thompson, "Government has always jealously guarded its right of eminent domain, not only in the estate, but in the living body of its citizen. The mob assumes the same imperious radical sovereignty." The mob, in other words, is equal to the government, for the reasons we have heard before—that the people elect or are the power behind the government and can therefore elect or empower themselves to pursue alternative courses.

More importantly, though, the author makes this right equivalent to the right of self-defense. "If a man may take the law by force, and with impunity kill the seducer of his wife or daughter," Thompson asks, "why may not a community do a like thing to the negro who commits an infinitely greater outrage?" Thompson asserts that there is no difference between a lynch mob's activity and an individual act of passion when a criminal is caught in flagrante delicto—"he has, single-handed, lynched the wrecker," a murder that is "as surely [a] lynching as the hanging of a negro by a mob." Both, according to Thompson, derive their authority from the "human well of impulse, the ancient and ineradicable source of self-defence."[35] A Jacksonville newspaper editor pursues the same logic when he justifies vigilantes in Tampa by claiming that "the people have acted as the Anglo-Saxon has always claimed the right to do in self-protection." Or, as a New York newspaper put it in supporting the vigilance committee, the vigilante work was demanded by "self-preservation."[36]

As an aside, it ought to be noted that the right to self-defense is not eternal in American or "Anglo-Saxon" law. In a fascinating history, Richard Maxwell Brown has demonstrated the shift from the "duty to retreat" in English common law—where every individual was responsible for withdrawing from a confrontation or threatening situation—to the principle of "no duty to retreat" in American law. In the words of an Indiana judge who in 1877 rejected the English law, "The tendency of the American mind seems to be very strongly against the enforcement of any rule which requires a person to flee when assailed." Of course, those who claim the right to self-defense do not generally invoke the law but claim instead, as a Washington court did in 1917, that it is "human nature" or, in the words of a Wisconsin court in 1909, a "divine right."[37]

What is more important, and striking, is the logic that a "mob" either has a "self" or possesses the same rights as a "self." Here, I think, might be the first key term in understanding the dynamic of collective mob violence. The "self" that feels a right to murder the seducer of a wife or daughter in self-defense is augmented by feeling the right to kill the seducer of the wives and daughters of neighbors and fellow same-raced citizens. The "self" in this patriarchal sensibility is now the protector of all the race's women. We can, I think, invoke here the findings of anthropologists and feminists that women are thought of as property, a medium of exchange between men in patriarchal cultures. Lynchings for allegations of rape, then, are performed to protect a right in property, just as they more openly are for other alleged crimes that involve property of other sorts, including material ones like money and goods, and immaterial ones like honor. We see, then, how the "self" is now empowered to protect all those people and things thought to constitute an extension of selfhood.

Having now teased out the implications in the key terms used by the apologists who use the popular sovereignty argument, let us turn to the terms we can discern in the frequently denied defense of racial terrorism. The key term, not surprisingly, is race. Even when apologists attempt to evade the implication that lynching is performed against black people—frequently by saying that the lynching would have been done no matter the race of the alleged rapist—they almost always and incessantly place blackness as a central feature of their argument. We see above how Thompson evokes the concepts of "citizen," "community," and "mob"—each of which he ultimately asserts has a "self" that emerges when it is called on to defend its rights against the "negro," whose only agency for Thompson is criminal.

In other words, blackness in Thompson's defense is what gives rise to violence that in turn gives a sense of "selfhood" to the mob performing it. Scholars have long written about the ways that white racial identity is created through this dynamic of either exploitation or violence against black people. We can see then that what W. E. B. DuBois first called the "wages of whiteness," and what contemporary cultural critics have called the "property in whiteness," is also an extension of that selfhood that requires protection.

Summing up, then, we can see that lynching becomes an act of self-defense. The mob is an *augmented* self, a collective that acts as a single agent, and the mob's actions defend what is ultimately a *constituted* self—that is, a self defined by its property, including its women and racial identity. The claim of popular sovereignty has always depended on a particular rhetorical force to produce unanimity, create community, and quell internal dissent. Lynching too accomplished those ends, through an act of rhetorical and physical force that defined those who were or were not part of the community, or the nation, between those who were Self or Other.

We see, then, that these two rationales are not truly separate, but fundamentally connected. The claim of popular sovereignty—the right to exceed the laws on the books in order to defend the society that produced those laws—is part and parcel of a property in whiteness. If we accept that premise, then we can ask a different question about the *meaning* of lynching. Instead of asking what force guides and motivates lynchers (religion, race, or economics), we can ask what political conditions produced the ethos that fed the rationales for lynching. Where, in other words, did a property in whiteness and the idea of popular sovereignty find an opportunity to cohere and form a worldview? The answer to that question, in this nation, is American slavery. Slavery, I argue, can be seen as the root of lynching in two specific ways. First, slavery produced a world where the ideas of popular sovereignty and white supremacy could and did cohere and form an enduring worldview. Second, slavery also produced a society that formally created what we can call a culture of vigilantism.

Let's begin with a point that many lynching apologists emphasized, that lynching was neither prevalent nor a product of slavery. "We deny that lynching is a legacy of slavery," began one representative editorial in the *Wesleyan Christian Advocate*.[38] The reason for that denial was not hard to find. It is governed by the same logic that led lynching apologists to trace the practice to Reconstruction and no earlier. According to their account, as a postbellum practice, lynching constituted punishment for the actual crime of rape, which emerged after slavery ended, which had in turn been a salutary institution that prevented such outrages from happening while it existed. The point that slavery and lynching were equally forms of racial terrorism and social control was clearly unpalatable to those who romanticized their lost plantations and their previously indentured retainers. Because their narrative of lynching for rape was meant to defend slavery as much as it defended lynching, it relied on a clear break between black behavior before and after slavery.

African American intellectuals challenged that narrative on the most fundamental grounds. As Ida B. Wells put it in a representative statement, the practice of lynching "is like unto that which prevailed under slavery. *The very same forces are at work then as now.*" Or, in the words of Pauline Hopkins, the "difference between then and now," between the period of slavery and "these days of mob violence, when lynch-law is raising its head like a venomous monster," is "so slight as to be scarcely worth mentioning."[39] I believe that Wells and Hopkins and others who echoed them were doing more than insisting that racial lynchings were a form of terrorism meant as a social control over the labor and lives of black people, and, as such, part of the trajectory of racial oppression traceable to slavery. I believe they were making a larger point about slavery as the institution at the root of lynching. Phrasing it differently, we can say that they are hinting that the *meaning* of lynching is to be found in slavery.

I have suggested above that there are two ways that slavery can be seen to be the root of lynching. First, slavery produced the conditions in which the ideological and intellectual rationales for lynching were originally formed and began to cohere. Second, slavery created a culture in which extralegal mob activity received legal sanction. Slavery, then, gave the lynchers and their apologists their two most robust ideological defenses (property in whiteness and popular sovereignty), and gave the lynch mob its first relationship to the nation-state.

We saw already in Chapter Two how Edmund Morgan exposed the origins of American "freedom" in American "slavery," by showing how those who came to define republican liberty—and thereby produce the conditions for popular sovereignty—did so because they saw in the life of the slave what life without freedom could be like. Or, as Vincent Harding put it, the paradox of black slavery's being "introduced into the colony of Virginia at the same time that the House of Burgesses came into being" demonstrates that slavery and "representative government" were "planted together."[40] Freedom, then, was an idea that emerged out of slavery, as was, ultimately, whiteness ("white" was a term that came to be used only in the 1680s in legal statutes, replacing "English" and "Christian"). The institution of slavery, then, produced the property in whiteness, the supremacy of it, at the same time as it produced the sensibility of freedom, first for the colonial generations, and then for all white people in the generations after the Revolutionary War.

It is crucial to understand that this development was fundamentally a formal and legal one, not just the emergence of a vague sensibility among a people. Laws throughout the colonies spelled out what rights did not inhere in people who were first indentured, then enslaved, and then emphatically African. And, implicitly, those were the rights that did or came to inhere in people who were not. Consider, for example, a Virginia statute of 1639: "All persons except Negroes are to be provided with arms and ammunition or be fined at the pleasure of the governor and council."[41] Here was a representative case of the ways rights were apportioned by race, defining the freedoms of whites through the denial of them to "Negroes." Eventually, those laws, by about 1660, came to define freedom itself as inherently the property of whites, at the same time and inasmuch as it became the presumption that it was not the property of blacks.

We saw above the role that the concept of "self-defense" has played in American jurisprudence and the rhetoric of prolynching apologists. Again, consider another representative Virginia Act of 1680: "If any Negro lift up his hand against any Christian he shall receive thirty lashes." Here was the right of self-defense removed from a class of people against another class, which inherently then comes to possess that same right. We see, then, the ways that the law created not just a general sense of freedom, but a specific set of rights—especially involving the rights to a *self*, an armed self, a self free to defend itself— that defined what constituted freedom by identifying what bodies were denied it (and, in being denied it, were thereby not "selves"). What slavery and the laws creating it produced, in sum, was a suite of beliefs about selfhood, property, whiteness, and freedom that were the essential prerequisites for the emergence of lynching's most resonant defenses. Slavery produced the ideology of lynching.

But these defenses of lynching required, of course, a lynching to defend, and here, I believe, is where we can even more profitably see the ways slavery created the structural conditions for lynching to flourish.

As we have seen, lynching apologists often defended summary justice by claiming that the state failed to mete out appropriate and appropriately speedy justice, especially in the cases of what they claimed were heinous crimes. Post-Reconstruction lynchers often hanged their victims in front of courthouses, or sometimes on the very scaffolds built by the state, as a way of demonstrating their defiance. Lynchings were both a mimicry and a subversion of the state's monopoly on capital punishment. Critics of lynching made the case that lynching violated law and order and produced anarchy in its mocking of the state's solitary power. The relationship between the state and the lynch mob was largely antagonistic. Under slave law, however, that relationship was not.

To begin, it is important to see how the state apportioned the very rights at stake in lynching—the right to defend, to punish, and to murder. An Act of the Virginia legislature in 1669 aptly claims that masters have precisely those rights: the right to murder their slaves, by accident or while punishing them. According to that Act, "it cannot be presumed that propensed malice (which alone makes murther Felony) should induce any man to destroy his own estate."[42] Here the focus is on the rights of property, as the legislature worked on the assumption that what was property ("estate") was subject entirely to the unlimited will of those who owned it. Murder of a slave, then, was not murder because the person committing whatever act it was (essentially the prerogatives of ownership) occupied the social space that was allowed selfhood, self-defense, and the rights of agency against all things that constituted the extensions of self.

Virginia legislators, however, did not wish to limit that property in whiteness only to those who had property in slaves. By 1705, Virginia had refined the 1669 code beyond the provision that masters could kill their slaves with no fear of prosecution: refractory slaves were now subject to capital punishment by essentially any citizen of the state. Once a proclamation was made public that a runaway slave was in the area—this required two justices of the peace to authorize the sheriff to post a notice on church doors on the Sabbath—the law states that "it shall be lawful for any person or persons whatsoever, to kill and destroy such slaves by such ways and means as he, she, or they shall think fit, without accusation or impeachment of any crime for the same."[43] The apparatus of the state, then, operated essentially to empower the people to perform the work of capital punishment, at random, in mobs, and with complete license to inflict whatever suffering they saw fit in their actions.[44]

What is crucial to notice is the direction in which the law operated. It worked outward from the plantation, which had pretty well its own sovereignty and left slaves' lives subject to the whims of their masters, to the society at large, where slaves could be subject to the mastery of any white citizen of the state. It is that kind of monopoly—the reproduction of white supremacy from plantation to public, where planters' practices and mores became state law—that made any society into a *slave* society.

It is perhaps worthwhile to make the obvious point that slavery in the American historical experience is not static or uniform. It has clearly different features in different eras (colonial, Old South), different cultures (rice, tobacco, cotton), different geographies (urban, rural), and different regions of the country. There is no *one* slave society in America, nor would I wish to suggest that there is. What I am arguing, though, is that the slave laws, first created by the earliest colonies, especially in Virginia, and meant to regulate the racial economy of slavery, control the enslaved population, and determine just what range of activities were "legal" in regulating that population, produced a society that assumed certain prerogatives and rights about the place of collective, unrestrained violence in the service of upholding slavery. Those social norms, prerogatives, and rights became effectively a set of cultural imperatives that constituted both those societies where those laws were produced (colonial Virginia, for instance) and those societies where that culture was established and reestablished, in laws and practices.

It is that kind of slave law, I argue, that created lynch mobs, not as extralegal entities challenging the state's orderly dispensation of justice, but as licensed free-roaming bands of white citizens with no restraint on their capacity to maim and destroy, legally sanctioned by virtue of the status of their agents (white "persons") and the nonstatus of their victims ("slaves").

Let me clarify what I am arguing here, and what I am not, about the relationship of the state apparatus to lynching. I will begin by noting two pertinent points that historian Bertram Wyatt-Brown makes about how common law and lynch law "were ethically compatible." His first point is that there were no real differences between "legal public hanging and the communal rite of lynching" insofar as both practices "exercised the spectators." His second point is that common law "enabled the legal profession to represent traditional order," while lynching "conferred upon ordinary men the prerogative of ensuring that community values held ultimate sovereignty."[45]

About his first point, there can be little disagreement about how both public executions and public lynchings meant much the same to the spectators, who, even in the case of state-run executions, were sometimes participants. As early as 1763, the *Boston Gazette* reported that a mob was so incensed by a slave's alleged rape of a white child that they cut down the body of the executed man, after he had been hanged by the state, and dragged it through the streets.[46] In what Michel Foucault calls the "spectacle of the scaffold," there is little difference whether the state or a private party is performing the execution.[47] Wyatt-Brown's second point is about lynching as a statement of popular sovereignty that supplemented rather than subverted the power of the state. The state regulated one kind of social order, while lynch mobs regulated the communal values that were supremely the source of that order. Both these points are well worth making.

The point I am making, though, is that the state did not simply tolerate lynchings as a supplemental practice, nor allow spectators to participate in public executions in a way that would later be replicated in lynchings. The argument I am making is that these laws of the colonial states and of the early American republic created a *culture*—of white supremacy and of the legitimacy of popular violence against African Americans—that would endure and evolve into the postbellum culture that would produce the kinds of lynching practices with which we are more familiar.[48]

Slavery, then, produced an ideology of the popular sovereignty of white people and a culture of vigilantism that together inexorably gave rise to lynching and its defenses. Both were necessary features—the ideology and the culture—and both were produced and codified by laws that gave whiteness its property value in the same act as it gave directed collective violence its meaning. The laws of slave states produced a code of which denied rights constituted slavery, and therefore which assumed rights constituted freedom. That freedom, as we saw, began as a freedom over property, including and especially a property in whiteness, and became a freedom that rested on the rights to defend that property either individually or collectively ("person or persons," "he, she, or they") by performing acts of violence that were sanctioned exclusively on the basis of that property in whiteness.

Lynching, in other words, was not just a means of social control that replaced slavery. It was a product of slavery. Everything we have suggested that gave lynching its *meaning*—that it was collective and directed violence, that it possessed a particular ideology emphasizing property in whiteness and popular sovereignty—is to be traced to the slave state that produced it. It was during slavery that the lynch mob was given its primary ideology and form. It is important to note that the form of collective, directed violence we find in slave society is encoded in laws; it was not yet extralegal. The state later developed an antagonistic relationship with the lynch mobs that usurped its exclusive power, and rendered them illegal. Originally, though, the slave state produced and, through law, formally empowered that lynch mob. That same state, those same laws, also defined the almost limitless range of power that the mob could exercise against the member of an identified group ("to kill and destroy" by "such ways and means as he, she, or they shall think fit"). The slave state in its laws and the culture of vigilantism that was produced through those laws created what Daniel Jonah Goldberg, in another context, called a "world without restraint."[49]

The *meaning* of lynching, then, or at least a meaning of lynching when it is considered in the *longue durée* in American history, is not only that mobs were motivated by particular sets of concerns (conserving racial and gendered boundaries, economic prerogatives, and religious imperatives), which they certainly were in particular instances and epochs, but that lynchings are first and foremost and enduringly a product of slavery, of slave laws, and of an ideology and culture of vigilantism that emerged out of those laws. *Meaning* here does not focus so much on immediate motive, but rather on the sources and origins of the practice—origins and sources that gave the practice its first and most lasting expression of defining the agency of violence for a Self (who could kill and destroy) at the same time as it negated the rights and very existence of the Other.

I can imagine an immediate objection to this argument, and I can also imagine some fruitful implications in it. The objection is that the forces that drive people to lynch exist everywhere, not just in America, and that we find lynchings in cultures that have a history of slavery and in cultures that do not. Given the universal existence of vigilantism, why should we believe that the laws created in colonial slave society matter in creating the ways that lynchings are conceived and performed in America? Let me answer this objection by agreeing with its premise and contesting its conclusion. The premise is entirely right: the motives to lynch, and lynchings themselves, are indeed found in a range of societies; this argument does not constitute another attempt to assert American exceptionalism.

The conclusion, however, is wrong. Even in the case of a practice that has many forms in many different kinds of cultures and nations, we should strive to understand the particularities in each society that gave lynching its specific imperatives and helped define the forms it took. For us to understand what matters in a society, we need to attend not so much to the large principles that the society claims, such as freedom, as we do to see what forces and institutions specific to that society acted on those principles and gave shape to its practices. In America, slavery—as a practice, a legal code, a foundation for ideas about freedom, a model for apportioning rights and racial identities—was the particular institution that gave lynching its primary impetus, controlled its evolution, and provided lynchers their fundamental way of imagining their right to punish.

Before turning to the fruitful implications of this argument, let me add a cautionary note about deriving the meaning of a practice from tracing its origins. Quite simply, the fact that lynching had its origins in slavery does not *explain* the later manifestations of lynching. It has been the resolute argument of this book that lynchings evolve and change, that they are employed in quite different historical contexts, reflecting manifestly different dynamics, and done for different reasons. The meaning of each lynching is not that it reflects the imperatives of the slave society when the culture of vigilance coalesced, nor is its only significance that it continues to reinforce the values that the slave society gave it. We must not confuse the specific current utility of a practice with its historical origins.

What identifying the origins of a practice does is help us understand the primary structural and ideological forces that gave the practice its first impetus and formed it into a recognizable shape. By locating and surveying the grounds on which the practice originated on American soil, I believe, we can also appreciate to what extent that practice continued to occupy some of that same terrain in later manifestations. To put it another way, we can see to what extent the original impetus that gave rise to lynchings—a state-sanctioned mode of policing and punishing people who refused to accept their definition as slaves—might be residually present in later lynchings. In understanding the origins of lynching in slavery, we are better able to identify the vestiges of those origins in the lynchings that apparently had nothing to do with slavery.

Now, let me conclude by noting two major implications for our understanding of lynching that come when we shift from focusing on how lynching buttresses one particular American institution—segregation—on how it instead originates from another—slavery.

First, the trajectory of the history of lynching changes considerably. We would not view lynching as the product of frontier sensibilities that was adapted to racial repression at the end of the nineteenth century. Instead, we would see lynching as the grounds of struggle between a state that for two centuries created its foundations by sanctioning mob violence and a state that then revoked that sanction because it wished to control all forms of violence within its domain. Reconstruction, then, becomes a key moment in the history of lynching since it constitutes the moment when the culture of vigilantism created by a slave society confronted the modern nation that no longer needed to buttress its economic system through that particular kind of violence.

Likewise, we would not think of lynching as becoming "racial" when it began to be employed primarily against people of African descent in the 1880s. We have already seen that, empirically, this premise is false; African Americans were lynched during slavery and Reconstruction. More important, though, we would have to reassess in what ways lynching was "racial" in all manifestations insofar as it was the product of a culture of vigilantism that was fostered for the very reason of reinforcing racial identities. We have seen that lynchers sometimes resorted to calling their victims "white Indians" as a way of contesting their whiteness, and at other times lynched those whites they deemed too sympathetic to other racial groups, including people of

African descent. Given the efforts of lynchers to deny the property in whiteness to those who patently had it, might we not conceive of lynching as a strategy that was formed to permit white people to police black lives and that it retained that dynamic to some degree when applied to people who were not black?

Second, our understanding of the usual explanations for American lynching, its motives and background rationales, would likewise change. We have seen the development of the most common and deeply held rationales for lynching, the imperatives people claim for taking the law into their own hands: the frontier, where they held that they had no other options for dispensing justice, and popular sovereignty, because it was their birthright, their heritage, the final statement of their freedom. Our interpretation would allow us to trace the ways that those who conquered ever more distant frontiers did not go to those frontiers without the baggage of the society they left behind. The Americans who set out to conquer the series of frontiers that would constitute the making of America took with them models of governance and a culture of vigilantism that were created by the slave society on the first frontier on American soil.

Likewise, if we accept that the "freedom" they claim is largely a product of slavery, its terms and significance wrought out of the denial of specified rights to an enslaved populace, then we can examine more critically just what was "popular" about the sovereignty based on racial identity created through laws that protected a property in slaves and whiteness. The sense of freedom that defined popular sovereignty—a people free to elect and defy their representatives—was a product of slavery in form (freedom was the opposite of slavery) and in the suite of rights claimed by a free people (precisely the rights that slaves were denied). This fiery American anti-authoritarianism might not be so much a product of heritage, Anglo-Saxon or Scotch-Irish, as various prolynching apologists claim, as it is the product of a formal law that defined a particular kind of violence against a specific victim in order to hide the inequalities among those of the same racial heritage, a heritage of whiteness created at the same time, and in the same process, that created blackness and slavery.

By appreciating the ways that American lynching had its origins in American slavery, we tell a different story of what lynching represents in

American history. If lynching is indeed, as I have argued, largely shaped in its forms and ideologies by its origins in slave society and law, then we can understand lynching, lynchers, and lynch victims in new ways. Lynching as a practice has as its most significant moment of development that moment when lynch mobs were transformed from agents of the state to agents contesting the state's exclusive right to punish. Lynchers can be conceived not as agents who claim to represent community values and mores against formal technologies of justice, but rather as agents originally formed through laws that protected property, material and immaterial, before being transformed into agents of a coercive civil society contesting the state that gave it its original mandate. And lynch victims, finally, can be seen as the individuals whose bodies became the terrain on which the struggle between the state and the now-extralegal mobs waged a battle over the rights that defined citizenship—the rights to life, due process, self-defense, the rights (in a word) not to be a slave.

Let me end by returning to that 1705 Virginia statute that permitted slave owners to kill truculent slaves, and the general populace to destroy runaways. In that statute, the Virginia General Assembly ratified the racial basis of slavery in the colony by defining who could be "held as real estate." The next sentence in the statute rewrites the 1669 Act by declaring that any master who accidentally kills a slave in the course of correction "shall be free of all punishment . . . as if such accident never happened."[50] It is a curious law that can change something that happened (an event) into something that "never happened" (a nonevent). That law rendered the juridical status of the slave as negligible as the fires lit by the mobs rendered his body. That law defined who was a slave; it was someone to whom something did not happen.

The law that gave those who possessed a property in whiteness the right to maim, torture, and kill with impunity those who were deemed simply property—the law that created the culture of lynching—also created a way of thinking about violence and the very concept of action itself that deeply informed future lynchings. The innumerable lynchings in American history, enacted on people of different races, for different motives, using different techniques, and defended through different rationales, shared this in common: they had their origins in a society whose laws made murder not murder, and events not events.

Epilogue

American Lynching

We can end by returning to the question with which we began this book: How "American" is lynching? It is American insofar as it was a practice that defined "Americans" for those willing to use collective violence against those they would exclude from the terms of citizenship and community. It is American insofar as the most important divisions in American life, divisions over property, race, social class, labor, and gender, have been invoked at various times for various purposes to explain or justify lynching. In particular, it is American insofar as it became a peculiar practice of regulating and controlling one racial population in order to assert a particular kind of white supremacy. What is perhaps most distinctively "American" about lynching is that its apologists produced a discourse that explained different social roles and promoted both actual and discursive violence in order to exalt those who occupied some of those roles and control and debase others.

That discourse of lynching, created from a mélange of nineteenth-century scientific racism, white supremacist folkways, and Lost Cause romanticism in the 1880s, remains sufficiently compelling that some second-wave American feminists have evoked it in the altogether noble cause of challenging rape and other forms of violence against women. It remains sufficiently forceful that it can be revived in times of racial crisis, as happened in the mid-1970s, as a "resurgence of racism" was "accompanied by a resurrection of the myth of the Black rapist" in the backlash against the Black Power movement generally.[1] It remains sufficiently resonant for three barely literate white supremacists in Jasper, Texas, to know and cite and act on it more than a century later.

Finally, lynching is American insofar as we have an enduring history of the practice from the origins of the nation to the present. In this book I have promoted an argument that would help us see more clearly, I hope, just how continuous that history is, and just how much it has defined the nation. That argument goes against the grain of the most common representation of the history of lynching. That representation, explicit in some historians' works and implicit in most others, is that lynching is a practice marked by discontinuity. The most important tenet in that argument is that lynchings did not occur against people of African descent during slavery and Reconstruction, and that it ended as a practice in the 1940s, to be replaced by something new, like "hate crimes." This argument, I believe, leads to a historical vision of American lynching that is marked by disjuncture and discontinuity, and that in turn leads to the assumption that lynchings for racial terrorism are isolated because they occupy one specific historical moment (1880s– 1930s) and are therefore disconnected from the earlier history of the practice.

By affirming the lynchings that did occur, frequently and consistently, during slavery and Reconstruction, we are better able to see the connections between the age of lynching and the trajectory of lynching history that preceded it. And by returning to the origins of lynching created in the two earliest institutions of American life—the Virginia House of Burgesses and slavery—we can see better the longer continuities in the practice, and the true sources of its imperatives. We can then see that those lynchings that became a form of racial terrorism during the age of lynching were neither isolated from, a new development in, nor unrelated to, the forms of lynching earlier in American history. Appreciating the origins of lynching also lets us see in what way American slavery created yet one more underappreciated rift in American society. That rift, evident in the 1790s debates about the course of the new nation, virulent during the 1830s and full-blown in the Civil War, became a battle between a slave state that first legally sanctioned mobs to carry out unrestrained terrorism and a modern state that attempted to pass laws proscribing a sanction that by then had assumed the status of a right as fundamental and valuable for its practitioners as the properties they used it to protect.

PREFACE: AN AMERICAN ICON

1. Philip Dray, *At the Hands of Persons Unknown: The Lynching of Black America* (New York: Random House, 2002), p. 191. Mark Twain, "The United States of Lyncherdom," in *Mark Twain: Collected Tales, Sketches, Speeches, and Essays, 1901–1910* (New York: Library of America, 1992), pp. 479–86, esp. p. 486. Twain's essay was written in 1901, published posthumously in 1923; he sent it to an editor as a proposal for the multivolume work but changed his mind about the project. See L. Terry Oggel, "Speaking Out About Race: 'The United States of Lyncherdom' Clemens Really Wrote," *Prospects: An Annual of American Cultural Studies*, Volume 25 (New York: Cambridge University Press, 2000), p. 129.

2. Richard E. Rubenstein, *When Jesus Became God: The Struggle to Define Christianity During the Last Days of Rome* (Orlando, FL: Harcourt, 1999), pp. 3, 195, 212. Michael Ignatieff, *The Warrior's Honor: Ethnic Wars and the Modern Conscience* (New York: Henry Holt, 1997), p. 142. The Afghanistan case is complicated because the Taliban mob claimed they were performing an execution, and in a state where there is no recognized authority the lines between execution and lynching become blurred.

3. Lewis Blair, "Lynching as Fine Art," *Our Day* 13.76 (1894): 307–14, esp. pp. 307, 313. James Elbert Cutler, *Lynch-Law: An Investigation into the History of Lynching in the United States* (Longman, Green, 1905), p. 1. Ida B. Wells, *A Red Record* (Chicago: Donohue & Henneberry, 1895), p. 14.

4. B. O. Flowers, "The Rise of Anarchy in the United States," *The Arena* 30.3 (September, 1903): 305.

5. National Association For the Advancement of Colored People, *Thirty Years of Lynching in the United States, 1889–1918* (New York: NAACP, 1919), p. 5. "The Great American Specialty," *Crisis* 27.4 (February 1924): 168. "My Country, 'Tis of Thee," *Crisis* 41.11 (November 1934): 342.

6. I would like to thank Nathan Connolly for his helpful suggestions in thinking about the implications of these politicians' claims.

7. Steven Lee Myers, "Bush, at Commemoration, Says Nooses Are Symbol of 'Gross Injustice,'" *New York Times* (February 13, 2008).

INTRODUCTION: THE STUDY OF LYNCHING

1. Owen Wister, *The Virginian: A Horseman of the Plains* (1902; repr., New York: Oxford University Press, 1998), pp. 284, 283.

2. Hubert Howe Bancroft, *Popular Tribunals, Volume 2*, in *The Works of Hubert Howe Bancroft* (San Francisco: History Company, 1887), Volume XXXVII, p. 670.

3. W. Fitzhugh Brundage, *Lynching in the New South: Georgia and Virginia, 1880–1930* (Urbana: University of Illinois Press, 1993), p. 291.

4. Jacqueline Goldsby, *A Spectacular Secret: Lynching in American Life and Literature* (Chicago: University of Chicago Press, 2006), pp. 11, 282. Christopher Waldrep, ed., *Lynching in America: A History in Documents* (New York: New York University Press, 2006), p. xvii. Waldrep, in this anthology and, especially, in *The Many Faces of Judge Lynch: Extralegal Violence and Punishment in America* (New York: Macmillan, 2002), is rigorously attentive to the radical ambiguity in the term "lynching," and nobody has done a finer job of showing the varying ways it has evolved and been contested.

5. Gore Vidal, "Lincoln, Lincoln and the Priests of Academe," *United States: Essays, 1952–1992* (New York: Random House, 1993), pp. 669–700, esp. p. 691. The author does recognize that footnoting such a quotation fulfills its truth!

6. Of course, hanging is only one mode; the next verse in Holliday's song focuses on "the sudden smell of burning flesh." But the point I wish to make is not simply that there are different kinds of victims, and different ways they have been dispatched.

7. Brundage, *Lynching in the New South*, p. 1.

8. Ben Tillman, January 12, 1907, United States Senate, *Congressional Record*, 59th Cong., 2d sess., 1441; qtd. in Waldrep, *The Many Faces of Judge Lynch*, p. 120. Rebecca Lattimer Felton, *Atlanta Journal* (August 12, 1897); qtd. in Brundage, *Lynching in the New South*, 198. Coleman Blease, in Bryant Simon, *A Fabric of Defeat: The Politics of South Carolina Millhands, 1910–1948* (Chapel Hill: University of North Carolina Press, 1998), pp. 32–33.

9. Linda O. McMurry, *Recorder of the Black Experience: A Biography of Monroe Nathan Work* (Baton Rouge and London: Louisiana State University Press, 1985), pp. 124–25.

10. Stephen J. Whitfield, *A Death in the Delta: The Story of Emmett Till* (Baltimore: Johns Hopkins University Press, 1988), pp. 24–25.

11. Waldrep, *The Many Faces of Judge Lynch*, pp. 127–50.

12. James Elbert Cutler, *Lynch-Law: An Investigation into the History of Lynching in the United States* (Longman, Green, 1905), p. 276.

13. Waldrep, *The Many Faces of Judge Lynch*, pp. 183, 12. Waldrep's definition is more nuanced and useful than Cutler's.

14. Edmund S. Morgan, *Inventing the People: The Rise of Popular Sovereignty in England and America* (1988; repr., New York: W. W. Norton, 1989), p. 59.

15. It is worth noting that Cutler, whose restrictive definition contemporary historians use to discount Reconstruction-era violence as lynchings, did himself believe that lynch-law reigned during Reconstruction; his view, however, is deeply informed by a romantic rendering of the work of the Klan during Reconstruction. See Cutler, *Lynch-Law*, pp. 137–54, esp. pp. 152–53.

16. Waldrep, *The Many Faces of Judge Lynch*, pp. 67, 79–80. Richard Slotkin, *Regeneration Through Violence: The Mythology of the American Frontier, 1600–1860* (1973; repr., Norman: University of Oklahoma Press, 2000), p. 207, notes that some Puritan writers, like William Hubbard, who wrote about King Philip's War, used "outrage" instead of "war" because it was a term more "appropriate to the subhuman nature of the Indians." In addition, as I will show below, the terms "lynching" and "lynch-law" did appear frequently in newspapers accounts of anti-Black violence during Reconstruction.

17. Waldrep, *The Many Faces of Judge Lynch*, p. 78.

18. Albion W. Tourgée, *A Fool's Errand*, ed. John Hope Franklin (1879; repr., Cambridge, MA: Harvard University Press, 1961), pp. 246, 149, 99. And even more telling, Tourgée refers to "Judge Lynch" to define the threat of "rope and fag[g]ots" faced only by antebellum abolitionists.

19. "North Carolina. Great Excitement over the Recent Lynching-Kinston in a State of Siege-Outrage in Duplin County by Negroes," *New York Herald* (January 30, 1869). "Trouble in North Carolina. Lynching and Outrages," *Cleveland Plain-Dealer* (January 30, 1869). "North Carolina. The Recent Lynching Outrage," *Cincinnati Daily Enquirer* (January 31, 1869). "North Carolina. Discovery of the Secrets and Organization of the Ku Klux Klans" *New York Herald* (September 16, 1869).

20. "Lynch Law. An Outrage Upon a Lady Committed by Two Inhuman Fiends—They Are Captured," *Cleveland Plain-Dealer* (August 28, 1869). "A Black Fiend, an Atrocious Outrage near St. Louis, Threats of Lynching the Culprit," *Indianapolis Sentinel* (July 1, 1875). "The Lynch Law Case in Harford County," *Baltimore Sun* (July 24, 1868). "Lynch Law in Arkansas," *Baltimore Sun* (August 8, 1877).

21. Waldrep, *The Many Faces of Judge Lynch*, pp. 72, 73.

22. Ibid., p. 84.

23. "Ku-Klux Klan," *New-Hampshire Patriot and State Gazette* (April 8, 1868).

24. Brundage, *Lynching in the New South*, pp. 6–7. Cf. William Cohen, *At Freedom's Edge: Black Mobility and the Southern White Quest for Racial Control, 1861–1915* (Baton Rouge: Louisiana State University Press, 1991), pp. 211–12: "In Reconstruction, mob violence most often stopped short of

murder, and when killing was involved, it happened without ceremony. . . . By contrast, lynching was 'ritualized murder' conducted under the claim that the mob was dispensing justice."

25. Tourgée, *A Fool's Errand*, pp. 255, 193.

26. For other opinions on Reconstruction lynching by earlier historians and commentators, see Cutler, *Lynch-Law*, pp. 152–53; and James Weldon Johnson, "Lynching—America's National Disgrace," *Current History* 19.4 (January 1924): 597. Cutler argues that the "application of lynch-law under the anomalous conditions in the South . . . rendered the reconstruction period a distinctive period in the history of lynch-law." Johnson traces lynching back to slavery and finds in Reconstruction a "recrudescence of lynching."

27. The account of this incident in the Atlanta riot lynching is taken from Edward L. Ayers, *The Promise of the New South: Life After Reconstruction* (New York: Oxford University Press, 1992), p. 436. None of those murdered during the 1906 Atlanta riot are listed in the NAACP report. NAACP, *Thirty Years of Lynching in the United States* (New York: NAACP, 1919). Cf. Appendix A in Brundage, *Lynching in the New South*, pp. 270–80. For a fuller narrative of the Atlanta riot and the newspaper rumors of an epidemic of black rape, see David Fort Godshalk, *Veiled Visions: The 1906 Atlanta Riot and the Reshaping of American Race Relations* (Chapel Hill: University of North Carolina Press, 2005). Many "race riots" or political pogroms were spurred on by the same lynching discourse that mobilized mobs to kill individuals, including those in Atlanta (1906) and Wilmington (1898). See, for instance, an editor for a Birmingham, Alabama, newspaper who claims that "all these race riots have been caused by the attempts of negro men to override the race line and to make white women the victims of their lustful passions." Qtd. in Philip Resnikoff, "A Psychoanalytic Study of Lynching," *Psychoanalytic Review* 20 (1933): 421—27, esp. 422.

28. For the use of 1886 as a transitional year, see Waldrep, *The Many Faces of Judge Lynch*, p. 113. For the description of the typical lynching victim, see Ayers, *The Promise of the New South*, pp. 156–59; for that of the typical lynch mob, see Philip Dray, *At the Hands of Persons Unknown: The Lynching of Black America* (New York: Random House, 2002), pp. ix–x.

29. Hubert Howe Bancroft, *Popular Tribunals: Volume 1*, in *The Works of Hubert Howe Bancroft*, Volume XXXVI (San Francisco: History Company, 1887), pp. 267–98, esp. p. 282. Patricia Bernstein, *The First Waco Horror: The Lynching of Jesse Washington and the Rise of the NAACP* (Texas Station: Texas A&M University Press, 2005).

30. For a recent example of that kind of discontinuity and the exclusion of Reconstruction from the history of lynching, see Manfred Berg, *Popular Justice: A History of Lynching in America* (Chicago: Ivan R. Dee, 2011), esp. pp. 69–89 and 165–85. Professor Berg's book was published just as I was completing *American Lynching*.

31. The Ohio law is quoted in Cutler, *Lynch-Law*, p. 235.

32. Jessie Daniel Ames, *The Changing Character of Lynching* (Atlanta: Commission on Interracial Cooperation, Inc., 1942), p. 29. Cf. McMurry, *Recorder of the Black Experience*, p. 127; and Waldrep, *The Many Faces of Judge Lynch*, pp. 147–49. This second definition has proven remarkably popular with scholars and has been used in many of the most recent studies of lynching; Waldrep lists the recent historians and sociologists who have used the 1940s summit definition (*The Many Faces of Judge Lynch*, p. 224 n. 140).

33. Ames, *The Changing Character of Lynching*, p. 30. On the NAACP, see Waldrep, *The Many Faces of Judge Lynch*, p. 2.

34. James Harmon Chadbourn, *Lynching and the Law* (Chapel Hill: University of North Carolina Press, 1933), pp. 149–214.

35. Paul A. Gilje, *Rioting in America* (Bloomington and Indianapolis: Indiana University Press, 1996), p. 28. Elliot Jaspin, *Buried in the Bitter Waters: The Hidden History of Racial Cleansing in America* (New York: Basic, 2007), explores a series of episodes where counties had lynchings, riots, and then expulsions of the black population within them. He distinguishes racial cleansings from lynchings and riots (6–7), but he also notes that half of the racial cleansings he studies were precipitated by allegations of black rapists and frequently by their lynching (215).

CHAPTER ONE: THE RISE OF LYNCHING

1. *Proceedings of the National Convention of Colored Men Held in the City of Syracuse, N.Y. Oct. 4, 5, 6 + 7, 1864* (Boston: J. S. Ruck, 1864); reprinted in Howard H. Bell, ed., *Minutes of the Proceedings of the National Negro Conventions 1830–1864* (New York: Arno, 1969), pp. 19–20.

2. Richard Maxwell Brown, *Strain of Violence: Historical Studies of American Violence and Vigilantism* (New York: Oxford University Press, 1975), p. 4.

3. For summaries of these accounts, see: Albert Matthews, "The Term Lynch Law," *Modern Philology* 2.2 (October 1904): 173–95. James Elbert Cutler, *Lynch-Law: An Investigation into the History of Lynching in the United States* (New York: Longmans, Green, 1905), pp. 13–40. Christopher Waldrep, *The Many Faces of Judge Lynch: Extralegal Violence and Punishment in America* (New York: Palgrave Macmillan, 2002), pp. 13–25.

4. Col. William Campbell to Col. Arthur Campbell, July 25, 1780; in Louise Phelps Kellogg, *Frontier Retreat on the Upper Ohio, 1779–1781* (Madison: State Historical Society of Wisconsin, 1917), pp. 236–40; reprinted in Christopher Waldrep, ed., *Lynching in America: A History in Documents* (New York: New York University Press, 2006), pp. 33–34.

5. Thomas Jefferson to Charles Lynch, August 1, 1780; in Julian P. Boyd, ed., *The Papers of Thomas Jefferson* (Princeton, NJ: Princeton University Press, 1951), 3:523; reprinted in Waldrep, *Lynching in America,* p. 34. For a more nuanced account of Jefferson's struggles as a war governor trying to control the militia, see Merrill D. Peterson, *Thomas Jefferson and the New Nation: A Biography* (New York: Oxford University Press, 1970), pp. 166–240, esp. p. 194, on Jefferson's limited role in Charles Lynch's handling of the lead miners and the legislative act of immunity that the militia received for that handling.

6. Col. Charles Lynch to Col. William Preston, August 17, 1780; in Kellogg, *Frontier Retreat,* pp. 250–51; reprinted in Waldrep, *Lynching in America,* p. 36. Col. Charles Lynch to William Hay, May 11, 1782; in Governors' Letters Received, Library of Virginia, Richmond, Virginia; reprinted in Waldrep, *Lynching in America,* pp. 36–37.

7. "A Hint for Attention to Be Paid to Lynch's Law," *Augusta Chronicle* (June 14, 1794).

8. Cutler, *Lynch-Law,* pp. 36, 39. Waldrep, *The Many Faces of Judge Lynch,* p. 25. Some have attempted to recuperate Charles Lynch's reputation; see Thomas Walker Page, "The Real Judge Lynch," *Atlantic Monthly* 88 (December, 1901): 731–43. Page represents Lynch as sentencing the Tories to jail and fining them, not hanging them.

9. Waldrep, *Many Faces of Judge Lynch,* pp. 8, 28.

10. Waldrep, *Lynching in America,* p. 35. Nancy Devereaux to Col. William Preston, August 1780; in Kellogg, *Frontier Retreat,* p. 252; reprinted in Waldrep, *Lynching in America,* p. 35. Charles Lynch to William Hay, May 11, 1782; in Governors' Letters Received, Library of Virginia, Richmond, Virginia; reprinted in Waldrep, *Lynching in America,* p. 36.

11. William Waller Hening, *The Statutes at Large: Being a Collection of All the Laws of Virginia* (Richmond, 1809–1823), Volume 11, pp. 134–35. The Virginia legislature offered similar Acts of Indemnity to other Virginians in 1777, 1779, and 1784. See Matthews, "The Term Lynch Law," pp. 21–22.

12. John Winthrop, "A Declaration in Defense of an Order of Court Made in May, 1637," in Edmund S. Morgan, ed., *Puritan Political Ideas* (Indianapolis, IN: Bobbs-Merrill, 1965), p. 144.

13. Edmund Morgan, *Inventing the People: The Rise of Popular Sovereignty in England and America* (New York: W. W. Norton, 1988), pp. 122–48, 153–73.

14. Waldrep, *Lynching in America*, p. 41.

15. Frank Soule, John H. Gihon, and James Nisbet, *The Annals of San Francisco* (New York: D. Appleton, 1855), p. 315.

16. Tom Watson, "The Voice of the People Is the Voice of God," *Jeffersonian* (August 26, 1915); in Waldrep, *Lynching in America*, p. 195.

17. "The Vicksburg Tragedy," *Vicksburg Register* (July 9, 1835).

18. Ibid. For a fuller account of the Vicksburg lynchings, see Waldrep, *Many Faces of Judge Lynch*, pp. 27–32; and for a shorter one with different numbers of victims, see David Grimsted, *American Mobbing, 1828–1860* (New York: Oxford University Press, 1998), p. 12. Dickson D. Bruce, Jr., *Violence and Culture in the Antebellum South* (Austin: University of Texas Press, 1979), p. 111, discusses the apologists who saw the lynching as a response to the failures of the law.

19. Waldrep, *Lynching in America*, p. 45.

20. "Lynch's Law," *City Gazette and Daily Advertiser* (December 8, 1819). Another article from 1819 also used the same headline but described simply the act of a sheriff and posse arresting a group of thieves and putting them in jail. See "Lynch's Law," *American Beacon and Norfolk & Portsmouth Daily Advertiser* (March 2, 1819). This discrepancy between an earlier and a later, more modern, usage suggests the process by which the term was becoming more fixed in its meaning.

21. "Lynch Law," *New-Hampshire Sentinel* (September 24, 1835).

22. "Frightful Affair," *Portsmouth Journal of Literature and Politics* (August 1, 1835). "Lynch Law—Five Gamblers Hung Without Trial," *Connecticut Courant* (August 3, 1835). "Lynch Law, as It Is Called at the West," *New-Hampshire Sentinel* (July 30, 1835). "Southern Atrocities," *New Bedford Mercury* (August 7, 1835).

23. *Portsmouth Journal of Literature and Politics* (August 22, 1835).

24. "Infamous Outrage Under Lynch Law," *Portsmouth Journal of Literature and Politics* (January 9, 1836).

25. The editor of the *Boston Commercial Gazette* is quoted in "Miscellany. Lynch Law," *New Hampshire Patriot and State Gazette* (August 24, 1835). The *Philadelphia Enquirer* article is reprinted in "Lynch's Law," *Portsmouth Journal of Literature and Politics* (August 8, 1835).

26. "Origin of Lynch's Law," *New Bedford Mercury* (August 7, 1835). "Origin of Lynch Law," *New Bedford Mercury* (July 15, 1836).

27. "Memorial of a number of citizens of the City and County of Philadelphia, praying Congress to adopt the Sub-Treasury system, and to establish an

exclusive metallic currency. December 18, 1837. Referred to the Committee on Finance, and ordered to be printed." Serial Set Vol. No. 314, Session Vol. No. 1, 25th Congress, 2nd Session S. Doc. 22.

28. "Lynch Law," *New Hampshire Patriot and State Gazette* (August 24, 1835). "Lynch Law," *New Bedford Mercury* (September 4, 1835).

29. Grimsted, *American Mobbing*, pp. 4, 13–14, ix.

30. Carl E. Prince, "The Great 'Riot Year': Jacksonian Democracy and Patterns of Violence in 1834," *Journal of the Early Republic* 5.1 (Spring 1985): 1–19.

31. Thomas Brothers, *The United States of North America as They Are; Not as They Are Generally Described: Being a Cure for Radicalism* (London, 1840); qtd. in Sean Wilentz, *The Rise of American Democracy: Jefferson to Lincoln* (New York: W. W. Norton, 2005), p. 402.

32. Richard R. Johns, *Spreading the News: The American Postal Service from Franklin to Morse* (Cambridge, MA: Harvard University Press, 1995), pp. 278–79.

33. Grimsted, *American Mobbing*, pp. 22, 4. For a thorough history of these riots, see Leonard L. Richards, *Gentlemen of Property and Standing: Anti-Abolition Mobs in Jacksonian America* (New York: Oxford University Press, 1970).

34. Grimsted, *American Mobbing*, pp. 22–24. The commentator is Philip Hone, and the comment made in his diary on August 18, 1835. The Kentucky newspaper is the *Lexington Observer*.

35. Ibid., p. 16.

36. Ibid., pp. 11–12. William H. Skaggs, *The Southern Oligarchy: An Appeal in Behalf of the Silent Masses of Our Country Against the Despotic Rule of the Few* (1924; repr., New York: Negro Universities Press, 1969), pp. 314–15.

37. Lawless; qtd. in *Missouri Republican* (May 26, 1836), in Waldrep, *Lynching in America*, pp. 55–57. The Lovejoy episode is widely discussed in many histories; see Richards, *"Gentlemen of Property and Standing,"* pp. 101–11.

38. Abraham Lincoln, "Address Before the Young Men's Lyceum of Springfield, Illinois," January 27, 1838, in Roy P. Basler, ed., *The Collected Works of Abraham Lincoln* (New Brunswick, NJ: Rutgers University Press, 1953–1955), Vol. 1, pp. 108–15.

39. "The Vicksburg Tragedy," *Vicksburg Register* (July 9, 1835).

40. Ibid.

41. Ibid.

42. Richard Slotkin, *The Fatal Environment: The Myth of the Frontier in the Age of Industrialization, 1800–1890* (1985; repr., Norman: University of Oklahoma Press, 1994), pp. 37–38, 211.

43. Richard Maxwell Brown, "Western Violence: Structure, Values, Myth," *The Western Historical Quarterly* 24.1 (February, 1993): 5–20, esp. pp. 5–8.

44. Stephen J. Leonard, *Lynching in Colorado, 1859–1919* (Boulder: University Press of Colorado, 2002), pp. 3, 67, 74, 90.

45. Ibid., pp. 73–87, 123–54, 18–29, 8, 129.

46. Michael J. Pfeifer, *Rough Justice: Lynching and American Society, 1874–1947* (Urbana and Chicago: University of Illinois Press, 2004), p. 29. Mob sign and *Ft. Collins Express,* qtd. in Pfeifer, *Lynching and Criminal Justice in Regional Context: Iowa, Wyoming, and Louisiana, 1878–1946* (Ph.D. diss., University of Iowa, 1998), pp. 130, 108.

47. Pfeifer, *Rough Justice,* p. 30. See Pfeifer, *Lynching and Criminal Justice in a Regional Context,* pp. 174–78, for narratives of the lynchings of African Americans in Wyoming. Pfeifer gives a more detailed list of the phases of Wyoming lynching history, that has five phases (not four) and exposes the debate between rough justice/due process advocates (*Rough Justice,* pp. 29–30).

48. William D. Carrigan, *The Making of a Lynching Culture: Violence and Vigilantism in Central Texas, 1836–1916* (Urbana and Chicago: University of Illinois Press, 2004), pp. 29, 42–43, 21, 48–80.

49. Ibid., p. 32. Slotkin, *The Fatal Environment,* p. 183. Carrigan, *The Making of a Lynching Culture,* pp. 82–83.

50. Ibid., p. [291], Appendix B. Gideon Lincecum, qtd. in Bill Ledbetter, "Slave Unrest and White Panic: The Impact of Black Republicanism in Ante-Bellum Texas," *Texana* 10.4 (1972): 335–50, esp. p. 338. The Denton Central Committee of Slavery, qtd. in William W. White, "The Texas Slave Insurrection of 1860," *Southwestern Historical Quarterly* 52.3 (January, 1949): 259–85, esp. pp. 264–65. For statistics of the number hanged, see Grimsted, *American Mobbing,* p. 175. For Reverend Bewley, see Wesley Norton, "The Methodist Episcopal Church and the Civil Disturbances in North Texas in 1859–1860," *Southwestern Historical Quarterly* 68.3 (1965): 317–41. His name is sometimes recorded as "Buley" in other documents, although that also might be a case of mistaken identity that led to his lynching. For the Gainesville hanging, see James Smallwood, "Disaffection in Confederate Texas: The Great Hanging of Gainesville," *Civil War History* 22 (1976): 349–60; and Richard B. McCaslin, *Tainted Breeze: The Great Hanging at Gainesville, Texas, 1862* (Baton Rouge: Louisiana State University Press, 1994).

51. "Vigilance Committee" is used here exclusively to describe those groups and movements committed to punishing alleged criminals through extra-legal channels. The same term was often used by groups committed to protecting and assisting runaway slaves along the eastern seaboard, as the New York Vigilance Committee did, for instance, and also used as a term to

describe electoral poll watchers, both Whig and Democratic, from the 1830s to the 1860s. For a list of vigilante organizations throughout American history, see "Appendix: The American Vigilante Movements," in Leon Friedman, ed., *Violence in America* (New York: Chelsea House, 1983), Volume 2, pp. 171–80.

52. Owen Wister, *The Virginian*, ed. Robert Shulman (1902; repr., New York: Oxford University Press, 1998), p. 283.

53. Hubert Howe Bancroft, *Popular Tribunals: Volume I*, in *The Works of Hubert Howe Bancroft*, Volume XXXVI (San Francisco: History Company, 1887), pp. 7–8, 12–13, 14, 400. Bancroft, *Popular Tribunals: Volume II*, in *The Works of Hubert Howe Bancroft*, Volume XXXVII (San Francisco: History Company, 1887), pp. 670, 74.

54. Edwin Miles, "Mississippi Slave Insurrection Scare of 1835," *Journal of Negro History* 42 (1957): 48–60. Grimsted, *American Mobbing*, pp. 146, 148.

55. Frederick Allen, *A Decent, Orderly Lynching: The Montana Vigilantes* (Norman: University of Oklahoma Press, 2004), pp. 10–11, 164–66, 226–30, 301–3, 259–60, 294–95, 334–36, 305–7, 230–31. Allen provides a table of the victims of the Montana Vigilantes, including their names and dates of lynchings (pp. 365–66). Bancroft, *Popular Tribunals: Volume II*, p. 166. Allen, *A Decent, Orderly Lynching*, p. 22.

56. Paul Black, "Lynchings in Iowa," *Iowa Journal of History and Politics* 10.2 (1912): 151–254, esp. pp. 242, 174. Genevieve Yost, "History of Lynchings in Kansas," *Kansas Historical Quarterly* 2.2 (1933): 182–219, esp. p. 185. Frank Soule, John H. Gihon, and James Nisbet, *The Annals of San Francisco, Together with the Continuation, Through 1855*, compiled by Dorothy H. Huggins (Palo Alto, CA: Lewis Osborne, 1966), pp. 571, 579.

57. Brown, *Strain of Violence*, p. 97. Ken Gonzales-Day, *Lynching in the West: 1850–1935* (Durham, NC, and London: Duke University Press, 2006), p. 5, also notes the ways "lynch mob" and "vigilance committee" were sometimes indistinguishable in press usage.

58. Waldrep, *The Many Faces of Judge Lynch*, pp. 52–53. Brown, *Strain of Violence*, pp. 136–39. Bancroft, *Popular Tribunals: Volume II*, p. 166. 1851 Committee Constitution, qtd. in Soule, Gihon, and Nisbet, *The Annals of San Francisco, Together with the Continuation, Through 1855*, p. 569. 1856 Committee Constitution, qtd. in Bancroft, *Popular Tribunals: Volume II*, pp. 111–12. Bancroft, *Popular Tribunals: Volume II*, pp. 541, 643–49; and Brown, *Strain of Violence*, p. 139.

59. Bancroft, *Popular Tribunals: Volume I*, p. 261. Bancroft, *Popular Tribunals: Volume II*, 91. Brown, *Stain of Violence*, pp. 134–35. Waldrep, *The Many Faces of Judge Lynch*, p. 66. For the influence of the San Francisco

Committees on other vigilante movements, see Soule, Gihon, and Nisbet, *The Annals of San Francisco, Together with the Continuation, Through 1855*, p. 586; and Bancroft, *Popular Tribunals: Volume I*, pp. 429–729.

60. Bancroft, *Popular Tribunals: Volume II*, pp. 84–85. Brown, *Stain of Violence*, pp. 137–39. Grimsted, *American Mobbing*, p. 240. For the seal and motto, Bancroft, *Popular Tribunals: Volume II*, p. 111. Brown, *Stain of Violence*, pp. 139–41.

61. Pfeifer, *Rough Justice*, pp. 30, 54–55. Slotkin, "Apotheosis of Lynching: The Political Uses of Symbolic Violence," *Western Legal History* 6.1 (Winter/Spring 1993): 1–16, esp. pp. 6–8. Brown, "Western Violence," pp. 18–19. Wister, *The Virginian*, pp. 284, 282. Shulman, "Introduction," in *The Virginian*, p. xix. For contemporary newspaper accounts of the battle between cattle barons and homesteaders in other Wyoming counties, see George W. Hufsmith, *The Wyoming Lynching of Cattle Kate, 1889* (Glendo, Wyoming: High Plains Press, 1993), pp. 209–38.

CHAPTER TWO: THE RACE OF LYNCHING

1. Paul A. Gilje, *Rioting in America* (Bloomington and Indianapolis: Indiana University Press, 1996), p. 179. James Weldon Johnson, "Lynching: America's National Disgrace," *Current History* 19.4 (January 1924): 596–601, esp. p. 597.

2. Theodore Roosevelt, "Lynching and the Miscarriage of Justice," *The Outlook* 99 (November 25, 1911): 706.

3. W. J. Cash, *The Mind of the South* (1941; repr., New York: Random House, 1991), p. 43. Cash offers no source for his statistics. They are reported uncritically by Eugene Genovese, *Roll, Jordan, Roll: The World the Slaves Made* (1974; repr., New York: Random House, 1976), p. 32. William Lloyd Garrison suggested in 1856 that over three hundred white men had been lynched in the past twenty years; quoted in Frank Shay, *Judge Lynch: His First Hundred Years* (New York: Ives Washburn, 1938), p. 63. Shay speculates that while it would be "difficult to estimate the number of Negroes lynched in the same twenty years," he believes the "number was considerably less than for whites." Garrison, in the remainder of the paragraph Shay does not quote from *The Liberator* editorial of December 19, 1856, goes on to say that he believes "a considerably larger number of Negroes met with summary capital punishment during the various insurrection excitements which occurred." Quoted in William H. Skaggs, *The Southern Oligarchy* (New York: Devin-Adair, 1924), p. 317.

4. Shay, *Judge Lynch*, p. 97. "The Sentence Was Immediately Put into Execution," *Norfolk Herald and Public Advertiser* (February 24, 1797);

NOTES TO PAGES 53–54 168

reprinted in Waldrep, *Lynching in America,* p. 62. "Murder and Lynch Law. Baltimore, Feb. 2," *Pittsfield Sun* (February 5, 1852).

5. Clarence L. Mohr, *On the Threshold of Freedom: Masters and Slaves in Civil War Georgia* (1986; repr., Baton Rouge: Louisiana State University Press, 2001), p. 219. Five of the seven were lynched at once, near Columbus, Georgia.

6. Before he raided Harpers Ferry, John Brown raided Missouri, going into Vernon County, killing a farmer and freeing eleven slaves in December 1858. Six weeks later, three abolitionists replicated this feat by going into Clay County, Missouri, and taking fourteen slaves to freedom in Kansas (these slaves were eventually recaptured). Free-soil Kansans had made at least nine such raids into Missouri, creating a climate of fear that led to the lynching of four slaves in the course of three days in the summer of 1859. See Stephen B. Oates, *To Purge This Land with Blood: A Biography of John Brown,* 2d ed. (Amherst: University of Massachusetts Press, 1984), pp. 261–62; and Thomas G. Dyer, "'A Most Unexampled Exhibition of Madness and Brutality': Judge Lynch in Saline County, Missouri, 1859, Part 1," *Missouri Historical Review* 89.3 (1995): 269–89; and Dyer, "'A Most Unexampled Exhibition of Madness and Brutality': Judge Lynch in Saline County, Missouri, 1859, Part 2," *Missouri Historical Review* 89.4 (1995): 367–83.

7. Mohr, *On the Threshold of Freedom,* p. 21. "Panics in Texas and Kansas," *Farmers' Cabinet* (September 5, 1860).

8. See Richard B. McCaslin, *Tainted Breeze: The Great Hanging at Gainesville, Texas, 1862* (Baton Rouge: Louisiana State University Press, 1994). The estimate of two hundred lynchings of Unionists in Texas during the first two years of the Civil War comes from Texas Unionist Andrew J. Hamilton (p. 153). Also see J. Terrell, "Lynch Law in Texas in the Sixties," *Green Bag* 14.8 (1902): 382–83, for an account of two of the Unionists who received reprieves. For a fine fictional treatment of this event by the great-grandson of one the men hanged by the Citizens Court, see L. D. Clark, *A Bright, Tragic Thing: A Tale of Civil War Texas* (El Paso, Texas: Cinco Puntos, 1992).

9. The report from the *Clinton Gazette* of Mississippi is reprinted in "Horrible Conspiracy," *Salem Gazette* (August 7, 1835). The report by an apologist for the Committee of Safety, Frank Shackelford's *Proceedings of the Citizens of Madison County, Mississippi at Livingston, in July 1835, in Relation to the Trial and Punishment of Several Individuals Implicated in a Contemplated Insurrection in This State* (Jackson, Mayson, and Smoot, 1836) is reprinted in Waldrep, *Lynching in America,* pp. 63–67.

10. Douglas R. Egerton, *Gabriel's Rebellion: The Virginia Slave Conspiracies of 1800 and 1802* (Chapel Hill: University of North Carolina Press, 1993), esp. pp. 186–88.

11. Stephen B. Oates, *The Fires of Jubilee: Nat Turner's Fierce Rebellion* (1975; New York: Harper & Row, 1990), pp. 125–26, 99. John W. Cromwell, "The Aftermath of Nat Turner's Insurrection," *Journal of Negro History* 5.2 (April 1920): 208–34, esp. p. 212, notes that in a "little more than one day 120 Negroes were killed."

12. The contemporary is quoted in the *Boston Weekly News-Letter* (November 8, 1739); qtd. in Peter H. Wood, *Black Majority: Negroes in Colonial South Carolina from 1670 Through the Stono Rebellion* (New York: W. W. Norton, 1974), p. 318.

13. Bertram Wyatt-Brown, *Southern Honor: Ethics and Behavior in the Old South* (New York: Oxford University Press, 1982), p. 389.

14. Shay, *Judge Lynch*, pp. 97, 53, 54–55. Mohr, *On the Threshold of Freedom*, pp. 219, 10–11, 22–23, 58.

15. Wyatt-Brown, *Southern Honor*, pp. 388–89.

16. *Waverly and St. Thomas Saturday Morning Visitor* (May 28, 1859); qtd. in Dyer, "'A Most Unexampled Exhibition of Madness and Brutality,'" p. 277. Three months later, this same newspaper argued that hanging and burning are "too good in cases of rape," advocating castration as a fit punishment instead (p. 281).

17. Clarksville *Jeffersonian* (December 13, 1856); qtd. in Charles B. Dew, *Bond of Iron: Master and Slave at Buffalo Forge* (New York: W. W. Norton, 1994), p. 267.

18. Armstead L. Robinson, "In the Shadow of Old John Brown: Insurrection Anxiety and Confederate Mobilization, 1861–1863," *Journal of Negro History* 65.4 (Autumn 1980): 279–97, esp. 279.

19. Genovese, *Roll, Jordan, Roll*, p. 617.

20. Robert Edgar Conrad, *Children of God's Fire: A Documentary History of Black Slavery in Brazil* (Princeton, NJ: Princeton University Press, 1983), pp. 251, 254.

21. A. Leon Higginbotham, *In the Matter of Color: Race and the American Legal Process: The Colonial Period* (New York: Oxford University Press, 1978), p. 179.

22. The preceding two paragraphs were taken from my *Neo-Slave Narratives: Studies in the Social Logic of a Literary Form* (New York: Oxford University Press, 1999), p. 111.

23. Henry Cleveland, *Alexander H. Stephens, in Public and Private, with Letters and Speeches, Before, During, and Since the War* (Philadelphia, 1866), pp. 721–23; qtd. in Mohr, *On the Threshold of Freedom*, p. 50.

24. Wyatt-Brown, *Southern Honor*, p. 453.
25. Herbert Aptheker, *American Negro Slave Revolts* (1943; repr., New York: International, 1987), esp. Chapter Two: "The Fear of Rebellion."
26. Winthrop Jordan, *White Over Black: American Attitudes Toward the Negro, 1550–1812* (1968; repr., New York: W. W. Norton, 1977), pp. 114–15.
27. Edmund S. Morgan, *American Slavery, American Freedom: The Ordeal of Colonial Virginia* (New York: W. W. Norton, 1975), esp. p. 376.
28. The quotation in the subtitle is taken from *Report of the Joint Select Committee to Inquire into the Condition of Affairs in the Late Insurrectionary States*, 13 vols. (Washington, DC: Government Printing Office, 1872), House Reports, 42d Congress, 2d sess., volume 1, p. 1. It will be cited hereafter as *Report of the Committee* and, where applicable, by state and volume number.
29. Mohr, *On the Threshold of Freedom*, p. 52.
30. Eric Foner, *Reconstruction: America's Unfinished Revolution, 1863–1877* (1988; repr., New York: Harper & Row, 1989), pp. 198–209.
31. *Macon Telegraph and Confederate* (April 17, 1865); qtd. in Mohr, *On the Threshold of Freedom*, p. 280.
32. Allen W. Trelease, *White Terror: The Ku Klux Klan Conspiracy and Southern Reconstruction* (1971; repr., Baton Rouge: Louisiana State University Press, 1995), pp. 3–17. For a debate about the Reconstruction Klan as a terrorist organization or a more spontaneous one, see Paul D. Escott, "White Republicanism and Ku Klux Klan Terror: The North Carolina Piedmont During Reconstruction," in *Race, Class, and Politics in Southern History: Essays in Honor of Robert F. Durden*, ed. Jeffrey J. Crow, Paul D. Escott, and Charles L. Flynn, Jr. (Baton Rouge: Louisiana State University Press, 1989), pp. 3–34; and Michael Perman, "Counter Reconstruction: The Role of Violence in Southern Redemption," in *The Facts of Reconstruction: Essays in Honor of John Hope Franklin*, ed. Eric Anderson and Alfred A. Moss, Jr. (Baton Rouge: Louisiana State University Press, 1991), pp. 121–40.
33. Foner, *Reconstruction*, pp. 342–43. Trelease, *White Terror*, p. 154. Richard Maxwell Brown, *Strain of Violence: Historical Studies of American Violence and Vigilantism* (New York: Oxford University Press, 1975), p. 214; cf. Appendix 4, p. 323. Joe Gray Taylor, *Louisiana Reconstructed 1863–1877* (Baton Rouge: Louisiana State University Press, 1974), pp. 168–69.
34. George C. Rable, *But There Was No Peace: The Role of Violence in the Politics of Reconstruction* (Athens: University of Georgia Press, 1984), pp. 145–49. Foner, *Reconstruction*, p. 558.
35. Leon Litwack, *Been in the Storm So Long: The Aftermath of Slavery* (1979: New York: Random House, 1980), pp. 280–81.

36. For the Memphis riot, see James Gilbert Ryan, "The Memphis Riot of 1866: Terror in a Black Community During Reconstruction," *Journal of Negro History* 62.3 (1977): 243–57; and Rable, *But There Was No Peace,* pp. 33–42, who notes that the Memphis riot "became the prototype for twentieth-century race riots" (p. 33).

37. Ibid., p. 54. James G. Hollandsworth, Jr., *An Absolute Massacre: The New Orleans Race Riot of July 30, 1866* (Baton Rouge: Louisiana University Press, 2001). Trelease, *White Terror,* pp. xliii, 135. *Report of the Committee,* pp. 250–52. Foner, *Reconstruction,* pp. 342–43. Trelease, *White Terror,* p. 130. Cf. Skaggs, *Southern Oligarchy,* pp. 322–23.

38. Gilles Vandal, "'Bloody Caddo': White Violence Against Blacks in a Louisiana Parish, 1865–1876," *Journal of Social History* 25.2 (Winter 1991): pp. 376, 378. Black people represented 71 percent of all homicide victims, while white people represented 80 percent of the presumed perpetrators.

39. John Edward Bruce, *The Blood Red Record. A Review of the Horrible Lynchings and Burning of Negroes by Civilized White Men in the United States, As Taken from the Records* (Albany: Argus, 1901), p. 20. Henry Adams, a black Louisiana native, gave various estimates of the number of victims of Reconstruction, ranging from 1,645 in Louisiana alone to half a million, presumably throughout the South. See William Cohen, *At Freedom's Edge: Black Mobility and the Southern White Quest for Racial Control, 1861–1915* (Baton Rouge: Louisiana State University Press, 1991), pp. 165, 167.

40. Saidiya V. Hartman, *Scenes of Subjection: Terror, Slavery, and Self-Making in Nineteenth-Century America* (New York: Oxford University Press, 1997), pp. 125–63, has shown how the freedman's handbooks, guides produced to aid the formerly enslaved in the mores of freedom and "proper conduct" after emancipation, also aimed at controlling the public presentation of the freed people and engendered a new kind of subjection for those emancipated. In this way, they also aimed at a particular kind of social control.

41. Rable, *But There Was No Peace,* p. 25.

42. Albert Bushnell Hart, "Lynching," in *Cyclopedia of American Government,* ed. Andrew C. McLaughlin and Albert Bushnell Hart (1914; 2d ed., New York: D. Appleton, 1930), vol. 2, p. 381.

43. "Petition from Kentucky Negroes," [March 25, 1871], in *A Documentary History of the Negro People in the United States,* ed. Herbert Aptheker (New York: Citadel, 1951), vol. 2, pp. 594–99. The petition states that this list of 116 acts of violence constitutes about half of the total acts of violence.

44. Robert Smalls, *Congressional Record,* 44th Cong., 1st sess., vol. 4, pt. 5, pp. 4041–42; in Aptheker, *Documentary History of the Negro People in the*

United States, vol. 2, pp. 610–14. Foner, *Reconstruction*, pp. 570–72. Also see Otis A. Singletary, *Negro Militia and Reconstruction* (Austin: University of Texas Press, 1957), esp. pp. 139–41.

45. Thomas Nelson Page, "The Lynching of Negroes—Its Causes and Its Prevention," *North American Review* 173.566 (January 1904): 33–48, esp. pp. 36–37.

46. Myrta Lockett Avary, *Dixie After the War: An Exposition of Social Conditions Existing in the South, During the Twelve Years Succeeding the Fall of Richmond* (n.p., n.d. [1906]), p. 377.

47. New Orleans *Daily Picayune* (October 6, 1868); cited in Taylor, *Louisiana Reconstructed*, p. 169. Cash, *The Mind of the South*. The New Orleans *Daily Picayune* (July 4, 1874) would resort to the same rhetoric in offering an account of an armed black militia that, the newspaper claimed, were out to kill white men and enslave white women; cited in Rable, *But There Was No Peace*, p. 131.

48. *Report of the Committee*, Georgia, Vol. 1, pp. 356, 359, 360, 363, 363. For more on the case of Henry Lowther, see Martha Hodes, *White Women, Black Men: Illicit Sex in the 19th-Century South* (New Haven: Yale University Press, 1997), pp. 154–58, and Hannah Rosen, *Terror in the Heart of Freedom: Citizenship, Sexual Violence, and the Meaning of Race in the Postemancipation South* (Chapel Hill: University of North Carolina Press, 2009), pp. 198–99, 343, note 71.

49. Jordan, *White Over Black*, p. 121.

50. Cohen, *At Freedom's Edge*, pp. 211–12.

51. The story of James Costello's lynching is in Iver Bernstein, *The New York City Draft Riots: Their Significance for American Society and Politics in the Age of the Civil War* (New York: Oxford University Press, 1990), pp. 28–29; and Barnet Schecter, *The Devil's Own Work: The Civil War Draft Riots and the Fight to Reconstruct America* (New York: Walker, 2005), pp. 204–5.

CHAPTER THREE: THE AGE OF LYNCHING

1. Royal Daniel, "While Hose Is Tortured the Multitude Applauds," *Atlanta Journal* (April 24, 1899).

2. "Griggs Defends South for Lynching of Negroes," *Atlanta Journal* (February 5, 1900). "The Georgia Exhibition," *Springfield Weekly Republican* (April 28, 1899); qtd. in Ralph Ginzburg, ed., *100 Years of Lynching* (1962; repr., Baltimore: Black Classic, 1988), pp. 19–21.

3. Edwin T. Arnold, *"What Virtue There Is in Fire": Cultural Memory and the Lynching of Sam Hose* (Athens and London: University of Georgia Press, 2009), pp. 112, 150, 135. Arnold has written the most thorough study of the Hose lynching and its aftermath. I have relied extensively on his work.

4. W.E.B. DuBois, *A Pageant in Seven Decades, 1868–1938* (Atlanta, 1938), p. 254; qtd. in Arnold, *"What Virtue There Is in Fire,"* p. 171. Ida B. Wells-Barnett, *Lynch-Law in Georgia* (Chicago: Chicago Colored Citizens, 1899), p. 1.

5. Arnold, *"What Virtue There Is in Fire,"* pp. 177–78, makes the argument about *The Leopard's Spots.* Tom Dixon, *The Flaming Sword* (1939; repr., Lexington: University Press of Kentucky, 2005), pp. 126–39, 137, [xiii].

6. The newspaper coverage of lynchings was extensive—and profitable, as at least some newspapers sold more issues when they reported stories of lynchings. For instance, the "extras" issued by both the *San Francisco Examiner* and the *San Francisco Chronicle* detailing the lynching of Harold Thurman and Jack Holmes, two white men accused of kidnapping and murdering department store heir Brooke Hart, were spectacularly successful. The *Examiner* sold 150,000 copies above its circulation, and the *Chronicle* sold more of that issue than it had of any newspaper in its history to that date (1933). Brian McGinty, "Shadows in St. James Park," *California History* 57.4 (1978): 291–307, esp. p. 301.

7. For the full story of the *Chicago Tribune's* publishing lynching records, see Christopher Waldrep, *The Many Faces of Judge Lynch: Extralegal Violence and Punishment in America* (New York: Palgrave Macmillan, 2002), pp. 112–14.

8. Linda O. McMurry, *Recorder of the Black Experience: A Biography of Monroe Nathan Work* (Baton Rouge: Louisiana State University Press, 1985), pp. 120–21.

9. For the Anti-Lynching Crusaders, see "The Anti-Lynching Crusaders," *Crisis* 25.1 (November 1922): 8; and "The Ninth Crusade," *Crisis* 25.5 (March 1923): 213–17. For more on the NAACP's rocky and exploitative relationship with the women who led the Anti-Lynching Crusaders, and for Ida B. Wells's critique of the political agenda of the Crusaders, see Paula J. Giddings, *Ida, A Sword Among Lions: Ida B. Wells and the Campaign Against Lynching* (New York: HarperCollins, 2008), pp. 628–31.

10. Robert L. Zangrando, *The NAACP Crusade Against Lynching, 1909–1950* (Philadelphia: Temple University Press, 1980), p. 13. George C. Wright, *Racial Violence in Kentucky, 1865–1940: Lynchings, Mob Rule, and "Legal Lynchings"* (Baton Rouge: Louisiana University Press, 1990), p. 180. James Harmon Chadbourn, *Lynching and the Law* (Chapel Hill: University of North Carolina Press, 1933), p. 29. Zangrando, *The NAACP Crusade Against Lynching,* p. 165.

11. "Lynching: An American Kultur?" *New Republic* 14 (April 13, 1918): pp. 311–12, esp. p. 311.

12. Stewart E. Tolnay and E. M. Beck, *A Festival of Violence: An Analysis of Southern Lynchings, 1882–1930* (Urbana: University of Illinois Press, 1995), p. ix. The data compiled by Tolnay and Beck do not include victims of race riots. The NAACP started flying the banner on September 8, 1936, and stopped flying it after 1938, when its lease was threatened. See "The Cover," *Crisis* 43.10 (October, 1936): 293.

13. Jacquelyn Dowd Hall, *Revolt Against Chivalry: Jessie Daniel Ames and the Women's Campaign Against Lynching*, rev. ed. (New York: Columbia University Press, 1993), p. 150. Charles Chesnutt, "A Deep Sleeper," in *The Conjure Woman and Other Conjure Tales*, ed. Richard H. Brodhead (Durham: Duke University Press, 1993), p. 141. John Edgar Wideman, "Charles Chesnutt and the WPA Narratives: The Oral and Literate Roots of Afro-American Literature," in *The Slave's Narrative*, ed. Charles T. Davis and Henry Louis Gates, Jr. (New York: Oxford University Press, 1985), pp. 59–78, esp. p. 78, first made this insightful point about Chesnutt's pun.

14. James Weldon Johnson, *Lynching: America's National Disgrace* (New York: NAACP, 1924), p. 2. Walter White, *Rope and Faggot: A Biography of Judge Lynch* (1929; repr., Notre Dame, IN: University of Notre Dame Press, 2001), p. 82.

15. *New Orleans Times-Democrat* (August 12, 1893); qtd. in William F. Holmes, "Whitecapping: Agrarian Violence in Mississippi, 1902–1906," *Journal of Southern History* 35 (May 1969): 165–85, esp. pp. 137–38.

16. John Ross, *At the Bar of Judge Lynch: Lynching and Lynch Mobs in America* (Ph.D. diss., Texas Tech University, 1983), pp. 172–73, 209, 210–11. W. Fitzhugh Brundage, *Lynching in the New South: Georgia and Virginia, 1880–1930* (Urbana: University of Illinois Press, 1993), pp. 19–20. The primary differences between these two classificatory schemes is that Brundage merges the terrorist and vigilante mobs, does not recognize the organized mob, adds posses as a type of mob, gives private mobs more latitude in terms of size—for Ross, their upper limit is fifteen, for Brundage fifty—and does not distinguish private mobs from secret mobs, which Ross does by noting that the former did not, and the latter did, wear masks and otherwise hide their identities.

17. Brundage, *Lynching in the New South*, pp. 28–29, 33–35, 36–43. Ross, *At the Bar of Judge Lynch*, pp. 172–236. See Philip Dray, *At the Hands of Persons Unknown: The Lynching of Black America* (New York: Random House, 2002), p. ix–x, for the structure of a typical mass mob.

18. I have come up with these figures based on Brundage's statistics of mob victims, 1880–1930, based on type of mob (*Lynching in the New South*, p. 262). I have not included cases where the type of mob is unknown.

Again, I am aware of, and caution others of, the fact that these statistics are flawed to the extent that they do not include victims of race riots.

19. The editor of the *Vicksburg Evening Post;* qtd. in Christopher Waldrep and Michael Bellesiles, eds., *Documenting American Violence: A Sourcebook* (New York: Oxford University Press, 2006), p. 162.

20. Ida B. Wells, *A Red Record* [1895] in *Southern Horror and Other Writings: The Anti-Lynching Campaign of Ida B. Wells, 1892–1900,* ed. Jacqueline Jones Royster (Boston: St. Martin's, 1997), pp. 91–96. Wells also mentions the lynching of Edward Coy as one of the first of these spectacle lynchings. Coy was burned to death at the stake three miles east of Texarkana, Arkansas, in 1892 in front of a mob of six thousand. See "Burned at the Stake: An Arkansas Colored Man's Punishment," *Baltimore Sun* (February 22, 1892).

21. James R. McGovern, *Anatomy of a Lynching: The Killing of Claude Neal* (Baton Rouge: Louisiana State University Press, 1982), pp. 77–82.

22. Wells, *A Red Record,* p. 93.

23. Grace Elizabeth Hale, *Making Whiteness: The Culture of Segregation in the South, 1890–1940* (New York: Random House, 1998), pp. 207, 222, 201. The statistics of lynchings from 1893 to 1934 are taken from Tolnay and Beck, *A Festival of Violence,* pp. 271–72, ix. Cf. Joel Williamson, *The Crucible of Race: Black-White Relations in the American South Since Emancipation* (New York: Oxford University Press, 1984), pp. 117–18.

24. Gail Bederman, *Manliness and Civilization: A Cultural History of Gender and Race in the United States, 1880–1917* (Chicago: University of Chicago Press, 1995), p. 97. James M. Inverarity, "Populism and Lynching in Louisiana, 1889–1896: A Test of Erikson's Theory of the Relationship Between Boundary Crises and Repressive Justice," *American Sociological Review* 41 (April 1976): 262–80. Hall, *Revolt Against Chivalry,* p. 137. Tolnay and Beck, *A Festival of Violence,* p. 251. Nell Irvin Painter, "'Social Equality,' Miscegenation, Labor, and Power," in *The Evolution of Southern Culture,* ed. Numan V. Bartley (Athens: University of Georgia Press, 1988), pp. 47–67. Orlando Patterson, *Rituals of Blood: Consequences of Slavery in Two American Centuries* (Washington, DC: Civitas, 1998), pp. 179, 210. Hale, *Making Whiteness,* pp. 203, 229, 205–6, 236. Hall, *Revolt Against Chivalry,* pp. 141, 152–53.

25. Antonio Gramsci, *Selections from the Prison Notebooks,* ed. and trans. Quentin Hoare and Geoffrey Nowell Smith (New York: International, 1971), pp. 208–9. Jürgen Habermas, *The Structural Transformation of the Public Sphere: An Inquiry into a Category of Bourgeois Society,* trans. Thomas Burger with the assistance of Frederick Lawrence (1962; repr.,

Cambridge, MA: MIT Press, 1991), p. 27. Nancy Fraser, "Rethinking the Public Sphere: A Contribution to the Critique of Actually Existing Democracy," in *Habermas and the Public Sphere,* ed. Craig Calhoun (Cambridge, MA: MIT Press, 1992), p. 133. Habermas, "Further Reflections on the Public Sphere," trans. Thomas Burger, in *Habermas and the Public Sphere,* pp. 453–54.

26. Habermas, *Structural Transformation of the Public Sphere,* pp. 32–33, 36–37. Habermas, "Further Reflections on the Public Sphere," p. 454.

27. Hall, *Revolt Against Chivalry,* p. 194.

28. Rebecca Lattimer Felton, in *Atlanta Journal* (August 12, 1897); quoted in Brundage, *Lynching in the New South,* p. 198. "Only One Sixth of Lynchings for Rape," *Crisis* 42 (January 1935): 14. Zangrando, *The NAACP Crusade Against Lynching,* p. 11.

29. Jessie Daniel Ames; qtd. in Oliver Cromwell Cox, *Caste, Class and Race: A Study in Social Dynamics* (1948; repr., New York: Monthly Review, 1970), pp. 558. Arthur F. Raper, *The Tragedy of Lynching* (1933; repr., Montclair, NJ: Patterson Smith, 1969), p. 47.

30. Williamson, *The Crucible of Race,* p. 185. Wells, *A Red Record,* p. 100. McGovern, *Anatomy of a Lynching,* pp. 85, 88.

31. *The Facts in the Case of the Horrible Murder of Little Myrtle Vance and Its Fearful Expiation at Paris, Texas, February 1st, 1893, with Photographic Illustrations* (Paris, Texas: P. L. James, 1893), pp. 7, 98, 111.

32. Wells, *A Red Record,* p. 91. Wells, *Mob Rule in New Orleans* [1900], in *Southern Horror and Other Writings,* pp. 202–3. Wells, *A Red Record,* p. 93. It should be noted that another treatise written by a Paris, Texas, lyncher also contests the idea that those who lynched Henry Smith were a "mob." See J. M. Early, *"An Eye for an Eye"; Or the Fiend and the Fagot. An Unvarnished Account of the Burning of Henry Smith at Paris, Texas, February 1, 1893, and the Reason He Was Tortured* (Paris, Texas: Junius Early, n.d.), pp. 38, 48: "it was no mob."

33. Cox, *Caste, Class and Race,* pp. 555, 549, 554, 549.

34. Fraser, "Rethinking the Public Sphere," pp. 8, 13–14, 24, 26.

35. As I noted above, I am not claiming that the lynch mob of the age of lynching constitutes the first appearance of the coercive public. Rather, the lynch mob of this era, which frequently gets treated as an ephemeral agent without institutional life, constitutes the continuation of those earlier coercive publics that had a more traditional institutional existence (vigilante organizations and white supremacist groups).

36. David M. Oshinsky, *"Worse Than Slavery": Parchman Farm and the Ordeal of Jim Crow Justice* (New York: Free Press, 1996), pp. 211–12.

37. Raper, *The Tragedy of Lynching*, p. 19 on "legal lynchings."

38. Hale, *Making Whiteness*, p. 207. Cf. Ross, *At the Bar of Judge Lynch*, p. 28: "perhaps the most detailed account of a lynching ever written from the lyncher's point of view."

39. Early, *"An Eye for an Eye,"* advertisements following title page and page 70. The governor's message is quoted on pages 50–55.

40. Elliot Jaspin, *Buried in the Bitter Waters: The Hidden History of Racial Cleansing in America* (New York: Basic, 2007), p. 48.

41. Jessie Daniel Ames, *The Changing Character of Lynching: Review of Lynching, 1931–1941* (Atlanta: Commission on Interracial Cooperation, 1942), pp. 2, 5, 8–9.

42. "Maryland Witnesses Wildest Lynching Orgy in History," *New York Times* (October 19, 1933); reprinted in Ralph Ginzburg, ed., *100 Years of Lynching*, (1962; repr., Baltimore: Black Classic Press, 1988), pp. 200–2. "Heart and Genitals Carved from Lynched Negro's Corpse," *New York World-Telegram* (December 8, 1933); reprinted in Ginzburg, *100 Years of Lynching*, pp. 211–12. "Girls in Teens Take Part in Raid on Funeral Home," *New York Post* (May 25, 1937); reprinted in Ginzburg, *100 Years of Lynching*, pp. 231–32. Dray, *At the Hands of Persons Unknown*, pp. 359–60. Julius E. Thompson, *Lynchings in Mississippi: A History, 1865–1965* (Jefferson, NC: McFarland, 2007), p. 105.

43. Historians debate which lynching constituted the "last" spectacle lynching and, implicitly, when to date the end of the age of lynching. John Ross argues that the "last large mob" appeared on October 17, 1942, when a "hundred men" took Howard Wash from jail and hanged him from a bridge. James A. Burran identifies the "1942 Texarkana, Texas, mob that tortured to death William Vinson for rape as the last open mob." Dominic J. Capeci argues that the 1942 immolation of Cleo Wright in Sikeston, Missouri, "signaled the beginning of the end" of that kind of racial lynching. Laura Wexler refers to the 1946 mob murder of two African American couples as the "last mass lynching in America" (but here "mass" likely refers more to the number of victims than the size of the mob). See Ross, *At the Bar of Judge Lynch*, p. 140. Burran, cited in Ross, *At the Bar of Judge Lynch*, p. 151. Dominic J. Capeci, Jr., *The Lynching of Cleo Wright* (Lexington: University Press of Kentucky, 1998), p. 193. Laura Wexler, *Fire in a Canebrake: The Last Mass Lynching in America* (New York: Scribner, 2003).

44. "Tuskegee Omits 'Lynching Letter,'" *New York Times* (December 31, 1953). For an example of hopeful media coverage of Tuskegee's report, see "End of Lynching," *Washington Post* (January 2, 1954). The *Crisis* responded to

the announcement by Tuskegee that 1952 was a lynch-free year by noting that the Tuskegee definition of "lynching" was "too technical and doctrinaire," and that the claim of the "end of lynching" would actually weaken the cause of those who hoped to end "lynching, less technically defined." Marguerite Cartwright, "The Mob Still Rides—Tuskegee Notwithstanding," *Crisis* 60 (April 1953): 222.

CHAPTER FOUR: THE DISCOURSE OF LYNCHING

1. "Interview with Shawn Berry," *60 Minutes II*, CBS News. Shawn Berry was one of the three who lynched James Byrd.

2. I have defined in more detail elsewhere something like what I am here calling "discourse." See Ashraf H. A. Rushdy, *Neo-slave Narratives: Studies in the Logic of a Literary Form* (New York: Oxford University Press, 1999). I have also greatly profited from Richard Slotkin's illuminating discussions of the ways "myths" operate in a similar fashion in American history; see, especially, Slotkin, *Regeneration Through Violence: The Mythology of the American Frontier, 1600–1860* (1973; repr., Norman: University of Oklahoma Press, 2000), and Slotkin, *The Fatal Environment: The Myth of the Frontier in the Age of Industrialization, 1800–1890* (1985; repr., Norman: University of Oklahoma Press, 1998).

3. *South Carolina News and Courier* (Charleston) (March 5, 1880); reprinted in Christopher Waldrep, ed., *Lynching in America: A History in Documents* (New York: New York University Press, 2006), p. 113. *Mississippi Free Trader* (March 8, 1854), in Waldrep, *Lynching in America*, pp. 77–78.

4. For the Seminole War cases, see Waldrep, *Lynching in America*, pp. 42–45. For Fort Pillow, see James M. McPherson, *The Negro's Civil War: How American Blacks Felt and Acted During the War for the Union* (1965; repr., New York: Ballantine, 1991), pp. 220–26. Dudley Taylor Cornish, *The Sable Arm: Black Troops in the Union Army, 1861–1865* (1956; repr., Lawrence: University of Kansas Press, 1987), pp. 173–77; William Wells Brown, *The Negro in the American Rebellion* (Boston: A. G. Brown, 1880), pp. 235–47; Albert Castel, "The Fort Pillow Massacre: An Examination of the Evidence," in *Black Flag over Dixie: Racial Atrocities and Reprisals in the Civil War*, ed. Gregory J. W. Urwin (Carbondale: Southern Illinois University Press, 2004), pp. 89–103; and Derek W. Frisby, "'Remember Fort Pillow!': Politics, Atrocity Propaganda, and the Evolution of Hard War," in *Black Flag over Dixie: Racial Atrocities and Reprisals in the Civil War*, ed. Gregory J. W. Urwin (Carbondale: Southern Illinois University Press, 2004), pp. 104–31.

5. "The Vicksburg Tragedy," *Vicksburg Register* (July 9, 1835).

6. Sir Matthew Hale, *The History of the Pleas of the Crown. Now First Published from his Lordship's Original Manuscript, and the Several References to the Records Examined by the Originals, with Large Notes by Sollom Emlyn* (London, 1736), vol. 1, p. 635.

7. *Mississippi Free Trader* (March 8, 1854), in Waldrep, *Lynching in America*, p. 77.

8. James M. Shackleford, *Marshall Democrat* (July 22, 1859); this letter, the first of the five Shackleford wrote for this newspaper, is reprinted in Waldrep, *Lynching in America*, pp. 78–79. On the effect of the escaped slaves and John Brown's raid, see Thomas G. Dyer, "'A Most Unexampled Exhibition of Madness and Brutality': Judge Lynch in Saline County, Missouri, 1859: Part One," *Missouri Historical Review* 89.3 (1995): 269–89, esp. pp. 272, 274.

9. For the *Lexington Express* and subsequent debate, see Dyer, "'A Most Unexampled Exhibition of Madness and Brutality': Judge Lynch in Saline County, Missouri, 1859: Part Two," *Missouri Historical Review* 89.4 (1995): 367–83, esp. pp. 370–71.

10. Ida B. Wells, *A Red Record* (Chicago: Donohue & Henneberry, 1895), p. 8.

11. Frederick Douglass, "Why Is the Negro Lynched?" (1894), in *The Life and Writings of Frederick Douglass,* ed. Philip S. Foner (New York: International, 1955), vol. 4, p. 501. Wells, *A Red Record,* pp. 8–9. Irenas J. Palmer, *The Black Man's Burden, Or, The Horrors of Southern Lynchings* (Olean, NY: Olean Evening Herald Print, 1902), p. 33, also liberally borrows from Douglass in his discussion of the rise and evolution of the intellectual justifications for lynching.

12. Douglass, "Why Is the Negro Lynched?," p. 501. Wells, *A Red Record,* pp. 9–10.

13. Wells, *A Red Record,* p. 10. Douglass, "Why Is the Negro Lynched?," pp. 502, 503. Wells, *A Red Record,* pp. 11, 10.

14. Douglass, "Why Is the Negro Lynched?," pp. 517, 515.

15. Joel Williamson, *The Crucible of Race: Black-White Relations in the American South Since Emancipation* (New York: Oxford University Press, 1984), p. 178.

16. Williamson, *Crucible of Race,* p. 320, argues that the racists who rose to political and intellectual power in the 1880s until about 1915 were not demagogues, dishonest, or dissembling. In my reading of those racists who contributed to the discourse of lynching, they appear to be demagogic, dishonest, and dissembling. Some labor under a conviction that will not allow them to hear alternative or contradictory accounts, but others, who may well be sincere in their beliefs, are nonetheless deceptive in their rhetorical strategies for defending those beliefs.

17. Thomas Nelson Page, *The Negro: The Southerner's Problem* (New York: Charles Scribner's Sons, 1904), pp. 84, 9, 111, 99, 88.

18. Page, *The Negro*, p. 84. Douglass, "Why Is the Negro Lynched?," p. 499. Page, *The Negro*, pp. 21, 84, 95, 96, 112.

19. Ibid., pp. 171, 177, 96.

20. Ibid., pp. 95, 93, 116, 101, 100.

21. Ibid., pp. 98, 99.

22. Ibid., p. 99. Jacquelyn Dowd Hall, *Revolt Against Chivalry: Jessie Daniel Ames and the Women's Campaign Against Lynching*, rev. ed. (New York: Columbia University Press, 1993), p. xx. Page, *The Negro*, pp. xi, 87, 111, 113, 98, 115. R. W. Shufeldt, *The Negro: A Menace to American Civilization* (Boston: Gorham, 1907), pp. 150, 13. Cf. Philip A. Bruce, *The Plantation Negro as Freeman: Observations on His Character, Condition, and Prospects in Virginia* (New York: G. P. Putnam's Sons, 1889), p. 99: "The religion of the plantation negro is a code of belief, and not a code of morals, having no real connection with the practical side of his existence, and slight bearing on the common motives of his conduct."

23. Williamson, *The Crucible of Race*, pp. 117, 460. Williamson does not provide any specific text or set of events to substantiate why 1889 is the originating date; he suggests that the death of the black rapist/beast motif is connected to the death of radicalism, which, in Williamson's account, represents the most racist mentality of Southern intellectuals about the ultimate fate of African Americans (on radicalism, see Williamson, *Crucible of Race*, pp. 5–7, 492). Williamson also suggests that the anti-lynching refutation of the charge of lynching for rape with statistical evidence would not appear until 1905 (pp. 117, 529 n. 11). Ida B. Wells had already challenged the statistical evidence by 1892 and 1893. See Wells, *Southern Horrors: Lynch Law in All Its Phases* (New York: New York Age Print, 1892), p. 14; and Wells, *The Reason Why the Colored American Is Not in the World's Columbian Exposition* (1893), in Wells, *Selected Works of Ida B. Wells* (New York: Oxford University Press, 1991), pp. 76–77.

24. David W. Blight, *Race and Reunion: The Civil War in American Memory* (Cambridge, MA: Harvard University Press, 2001), p. 282. Page, *The Negro*, pp. 207–8.

25. Myrta Lockett Avary, *Dixie After the War: An Exposition of Social Conditions Existing in the South, During the Twelve Years Succeeding the Fall of Richmond* (n.p., [1906]), pp. 58, 377, 381.

26. Douglass, "Why Is The Negro Lynched?," pp. 496, 504, 505. Pauline E. Hopkins, *Contending Forces: A Romance Illustrative of Negro Life North and South* (Boston: Colored Cooperative, 1900), pp. 14–15.

27. Avary, *Dixie After the War*, p. 401.

28. Jacquelyn Dowd Hall has superbly delineated the ways that the threat of rape and lynching worked intimately together to dramatize "hierarchical power relationships based both on gender and on race." See Hall, *Revolt Against Chivalry*, pp. 129–57, esp. pp. 149–56; and Hall, "'The Mind That Burns in Each Body': Women, Rape, and Racial Violence," in *Powers of Desire: The Politics of Sexuality*, ed. Ann Snitow, Christine Stansell, and Sharon Thompson (New York: Monthly Review Press, 1983), pp. 328–49.

29. Page, *The Negro*, p. 112. Bruce, *The Plantation Negro as Freeman*, pp. 53, 26, 84, 19. Avary, *Dixie After the War*, p. 395. Cf. Hall, *Revolt Against Chivalry*, pp. xxvi–xxvii. Angela Davis, *Women, Race, and Class* (New York: Random House, 1981), pp. 172–201, was one of the first modern scholars to analyze the myth of the black rapist, which she does with exquisite insights, and among the first to demonstrate how the "fictional image of the Black man as rapist" has as its "inseparable companion" the "image of the Black woman as chronically promiscuous" (p. 182).

30. *Lynchings and What They Mean: General Findings of the Southern Commission on the Study of Lynching* (Atlanta: The Commission, [1931]), p. 5.

31. Maurice Thompson, "The Court of Judge Lynch," *Lippincott's Monthly Magazine* 64.380 (August 1899): 254–62, esp. p. 256.

32. "Original Communications: Sexual Crimes Among Southern Negroes— Scientifically Considered—An Open Correspondence," *Virginia Medical Monthly* 20.2 (May 1893): 105–25, esp. pp. 106, 107–8, 122, 116, 110–11.

33. Ben Tillman, in *Charleston News and Courier* (July 7, 1892). Cole Blease, qtd. in Bryant Simon, *A Fabric of Defeat: The Politics of South Carolina Millhands, 1910–1948* (Chapel Hill: University of North Carolina Press, 1998), pp. 32, 33. Cf. Waldrep, *The Many Faces of Judge Lynch*, p. 121.

34. "Governor Davis's Speech at Eureka Springs," in *Jeff Davis, Governor and United States Senator: His Life and Speeches*, ed. L. S. Dunaway (Little Rock, 1913), p. 78. *Little Rock Arkansas Gazette* (October 26, 1905).

35. *Sparta Ishmaelite*, qtd. in *Newnan Herald and Advertiser* (May 8, 1899); qtd. in Mary Louise Ellis, *"Rain Down fire": The Lynching of Sam Hose* (Ph.D. diss., Florida State University, 1992), p. 148.

36. Ben Tillman, in *Congressional Record*, 59th Cong., 2d sess. (January 21, 1907), p. 1441. For a discussion of Tillman's political conversion from a more moderate to a more racist position, and his concomitant shifting opinions and actions on lynching, see Williamson, *Crucible of Race*, p. 133.

37. Rebecca Latimer Felton, in *Atlanta Journal* (August 12, 1897). Felton became the first female U.S. senator when she was appointed to complete

the term of Tom Watson after his death in 1922. On the disenfranchisement of black Americans in Georgia, see John Dittmer, *Black Georgia in the Progressive Era, 1900–1920* (Urbana: University of Illinois Press, 1977), pp. 100–4.

38. Andrew H. Sledd, "The Negro: Another View," *Atlantic Monthly* 90 (July 1902): 65–73. I have drawn on several accounts of this and the Bassett case. See, especially, Bruce Clayton, *The Savage Ideal: Intolerance and Intellectual Leadership in the South, 1890–1914* (Baltimore: Johns Hopkins University Press, 1977), pp. 77–81, 89–101; Ayers, *The Promise of the New South*, pp. 424–26; and Williamson, *Crucible of Race*, pp. 259–67.

39. John Spencer Bassett, "Stirring Up the Fires of Race Antipathy," *South Atlantic Quarterly* 2 (1903): 297–305. Josephus Daniels, in *Raleigh News and Observer* (November 1, 1903). For Daniels's defense of Sledd's rights, see Williamson, *Crucible of Race*, p. 266. The Smithfield Methodist Church letter and John Bruton's letter are both quoted in Williamson, *Crucible of Race*, p. 264.

40. John Carlisle Kilgo, "An Inquiry Concerning Lynchings," *South Atlantic Quarterly* 1 (January 1902): 4–9.

41. For the Jessie Duke episode, see H. Leon Prather, Sr., *We Have Taken a City: Wilmington Racial Massacre and Coup of 1898* (Plainsboro, NJ: Associated University Presses, 1984), pp. 78–79. Wells, *Southern Horrors*, pp. 4, [iii], 4–5. Alexander Manly, "Mrs. Fellows's Speech," *Wilmington Record* (August 18, 1898); qtd. in H. Leon Prather, Sr., "We Have Taken a City: A Centennial Essay," in *Democracy Betrayed: The Wilmington Race Riot of 1898 and Its Legacy* (Chapel Hill: University of North Carolina Press, 1998), p. 23. E. Franklin Frazier, "The Pathology of Race Prejudice," *Forum* 70 (June 1927): 856–62, esp. pp. 859, 861. For the threats on Frazier's life, see Anthony M. Platt, *E. Franklin Frazier Reconsidered* (New Brunswick, NJ: Rutgers University Press, 1991), pp. 159–60; and Jonathan Scott Holloway, *Confronting the Veil: Abram Harris, Jr., E. Franklin Frazier, and Ralph Bunche, 1919–1941* (Chapel Hill: University of North Carolina Press, 2002), pp. 144–45.

42. Wells, *Southern Horrors*, p. 30.

43. Booker T. Washington, "Lynching in the South," *The Southern Workman and Hampton School Record* 28.10 (1899): 373–76, esp. p. 373. In October of 1899, Washington published *The Future of the American Negro* (Boston: Small, Maynard, 1899), in which he contested (with statistics) that black men were lynched for rape.

44. Thomas E. Miller, *Congressional Record*, 51st Cong., 1st sess. (1891): 707–8; qtd. in Prather, *We Have Taken a City*, pp. 74–75.

45. Lillian Smith, *Killers of the Dream* (1949; repr., New York: W. W. Norton, 1994), p. 145.

CONCLUSION: THE MEANINGS OF LYNCHING

1. D. W. Griffith, *Birth of a Nation* (1915). Oscar Micheaux, *Within Our Gates* (1919). Toni Cade Bambara; qtd. in Jonathan Markovitz, *Legacies of Lynching: Racial Violence and Memory* (Minneapolis: University of Minnesota Press, 2004), p. 40.

2. I draw on Kenneth Burke's terms of dramatism. See Kenneth Burke, *A Grammar of Motives* (1945; repr., Berkeley: University of California Press, 1969), pp. xv–xxiii, for the five key terms of dramatism (act, scene, agent, agency, and purpose—explaining what was done, when and where, by whom, through what means, and to what end).

3. Jacquelyn Dowd Hall, *Revolt Against Chivalry: Jessie Daniel Ames and the Women's Campaign Against Lynching*, rev. ed. (New York: Columbia University Press, 1993), p. xx. Also see Hall, "'The Mind That Burns in Each Body': Women, Rape, and Racial Violence," in *Powers of Desire: The Politics of Sexuality*, ed. Ann Snitow, Christine Stansell, and Sharon Thompson (New York: Monthly Review, 1983), pp. 328–49.

4. Hall, *Revolt Against Chivalry*, p. xxi.

5. Hall, it should be noted, was among the first of the modern scholars who saw lynching as a changing ritual in postbellum America. She deftly describes the functions lynching assumed during three key moments in its evolution. She noted that, first, during Reconstruction, the lynching of black men and the rape of black women "became the most spectacular emblems of counterrevolution" in Southern communities. Then, at the height of the Populist era, a quarter-century later, lynching was employed as a "mode of political repression," a "diffuse reassertion of white solidarity," a "general warning to blacks of the danger of political assertiveness," and "a means of uniting whites across class lines in the face of a common enemy." Finally, with the end of World War I and the onset of modernity, a quarter-century later, lynching became effectively a communal ritual used by inhabitants of small towns and rural areas in resisting the modern nation-state, especially the modernization of law enforcement and a penal system that the nation-state came to monopolize. In other words, lynching became a way of asserting old communal values—including the value of "private violence" in the pursuit of "repressive justice"—against an emerging social order in which the modern nation-state was able to "monopolize the use of physical force within its territory." See Hall, *Revolt Against Chivalry*, pp. 131, 132, 144.

6. Ibid., p. 149.

7. Ibid., pp. 153, 156.

8. For other studies of gender and lynching, see Hazel V. Carby, "'On the Threshold of Woman's Era': Lynching, Empire, and Sexuality in Black Feminist Theory," *Critical Inquiry* 12 (Autumn 1985): 262–77; Robyn Wiegman, "The Anatomy of Lynching," *Journal of the History of Sexuality* 3.3 (1993): 445–67; Elsa Barkley Brown, "Imaging Lynching: African American Women, Communities of Struggle, and Collective Memory," in *African American Women Speak Out on Anita Hill-Clarence Thomas*, ed. Geneva Smitherman (Detroit: Wayne State University Press, 1995), pp. 100–24. Gail Bederman, *Manliness and Civilization: A Cultural History of Gender and Race in the United States, 1880–1917* (Chicago: University of Chicago Press, 1995); Barbara Holden-Smith, "Lynching, Federalism, and the Intersection of Race and Gender in the Progressive Era," *Yale Journal of Law and Feminism* 8.1 (1996): 31–78; Crystal N. Feimster, "'Ladies and Lynching': The Gendered Discourse of Mob Violence in the New South, 1880–1930" (Ph.D. diss., Princeton University, 2000); Feimster, *Southern Horrors, Women and the Politics of Rape and Lynching* (Cambridge, Mass: Harvard University Press, 2009); and Hannah Rosen, *Terror in the Heart of Freedom: Citizenship, Sexual Violence, and the Meaning of Race in the Postemancipation South* (Chapel Hill: University of North Carolina Press, 2009).

9. Walter White, *Rope and Faggot: A Biography of Judge Lynch* (New York: Alfred A. Knopf, 1929), pp. 76, 82.

10. Stewart E. Tolnay and E. M. Beck, *Festival of Violence: An Analysis of Southern Lynchings, 1882–1930* (Urbana and Chicago: University of Illinois Press, 1995), pp. 18–19, 198–99, 159, 215. For other studies emphasizing the economics of lynching, with differing emphases, see James M. Inverarity, "Populism and Lynching in Louisiana, 1889–1896: A Test of Erikson's Theory of the Relationship Between Boundary Crises and Repressive Justice," *American Sociological Review* 41 (April 1976): 262–80; and Nell Irvin Painter, "'Social Equality,' Miscegenation, Labor, and Power," in *The Evolution of Southern Culture*, ed. Numan V. Bartley (Athens: University of Georgia Press, 1988), pp. 47–67.

11. Grace Elizabeth Hale, *Making Whiteness: The Culture of Segregation in the South, 1890–1940* (New York: Pantheon, 1998), p. 125.

12. Ibid., pp. 200–1, 203, 205–6.

13. Ibid., pp. 228–29.

14. Ibid., pp. 233, 236, 238.

15. White, *Rope and Faggot*, pp. 40, 43.

16. Both Patterson and Matthews want to show that the religious interpretation provides something that the earlier models focusing on gender, race, and economics lacked. As Matthews puts it, "It is clear that something more than mere punishment, sexual and gendered anxiety, and the logic of power was inherent in lynching." That is not to say either Patterson or Matthews was dismissing those earlier models. They were intent on showing how the South's religious imperatives can help us better understand some of the leaps of logic that led to lynching. For instance, Matthews comments on the economic interpretation in the following way: "If the logic of market relations and the consumption of commodities by different races could ironically destabilize segregation in certain restricted ways, *true believers* of the segregationist faith could nonetheless regain stability by affirming racial orthodoxy in the face of such materialistic dissent." He did not want to displace the economic interpretation, but to show alternative models for explaining the motives of lynchers. See Donald G. Matthews, "Lynching Religion: Why the Old Man Shouted 'Glory!'," in *Southern Crossroads: Perspectives on Religion and Culture,* ed. Walter H. Conser, Jr., and Rodger M. Payne (Lexington: University Press of Kentucky, 2008), pp. 315–53, esp. pp. 345, 342.

17. Patterson draws on the classical anthropological writings of Henri Hubert and Marcel Mauss to develop the tableau of sacrifice—the setting and dynamics that change what might otherwise be a simply brutal act of violence into a ritual. Hubert and Mauss focus on those strategies that people develop for consecrating the act of sacrifice itself and the physical place where the act was performed. They also attend to the ritual beliefs that these groups develop about the victim of the sacrifice, as well as the two forms of sacrificing that victim (the use of fire as a divine agent of cleansing, and ritual cannibalism, either actual or symbolic, as a final way of consuming the sacrificed victim). Orlando Patterson, *Rituals of Blood: Consequences of Slavery in Two American Centuries* (Washington: Civitas, 1998), pp. 175, 182–83, 179, 192, 173.

18. Ibid., p. 210.

19. Ibid., pp. 210–12.

20. Ibid., pp. 212, 213, 215.

21. Ibid., pp. 191, 196, 198. "The cooked Negro, properly roasted, has been tamed and culturally transformed and can now be eaten, communally, in imitation of the Euro-Americans' own God savoring his burnt offering" (200). To understand how communities in the South could rationalize and understand these kinds of actions, Patterson turns to an analysis of what others have called the South's "culture of honor," and what Patterson

calls "the culture of honor and violence in the South." Patterson identifies four factors that promoted that culture: 1) "the honorific traditions brought over by Scotch-Irish immigrants who arrived in the South between the late seventeenth and early nineteenth centuries"; 2) "the frontier environment of the South"; 3) the institution of slavery; and 4) the "secular religion of racism." He argues that the first two initiated, and the last two institutionalized, the culture of honor and violence in the South. See ibid., pp. 190–91. Patterson draws on the insights of social psychologists who study that culture of honor, especially Richard E. Nisbet and D. V. Cohen.

22. Ibid., pp. 208, 218.

23. Ibid., p. 222.

24. Donald G. Matthews, "The Southern Rite of Human Sacrifice," *Journal of Southern Religion* (2000), http://jsr.fsu.edu/matthews.htm.

25. Donald G. Matthews, "Lynching Is Part of the Religion of Our People: Faith in the Christian South," in *Religion in the American South: Protestants and Others in History and Culture,* ed. Beth Barton Schweiger and Donald G. Matthews (Chapel Hill: University of North Carolina Press, 2004), pp. 153–94, esp. pp. 155, 163, 181. Matthews substantiates his argument about segregation as religion by drawing on anthropologist Mary Douglas's comment that holiness "means keeping distinct the categories of creation." Matthews discusses how segregation worked in particular to marginalize black people, and thereby render them a "class of people to be punished as payment for the failures of white people in the complex transition to modernity."

26. Matthews, "The Southern Rite of Human Sacrifice." That distinction between a people who could not "understand" but could "sense" the logic that drove them to perform ritual acts of human sacrifice is important for Matthews's larger argument, which is that throughout the South there existed what Raymond Williams called "structures of feeling" that permitted those acts that otherwise would have been seen as clearly transgressions. He is careful to note that he is not saying "that evangelical religion and segregation, linked as they were in the emotional life of white southerners, *caused* lynching." What he is saying instead is that "they together did create ways of thinking that could justify" lynching. Thus does he trace what he calls the "violent logic" of white Southerners who were "crazed by a fascination with purity and profanation that cloaked political designs" and made sacred their "aspiration to supremacy." See Matthews, "Lynching Is Part of the Religion of Our People," p. 157.

27. Matthews, "The Southern Rite of Human Sacrifice."

28. Matthews, "Lynching Religion: Why the Old Man Shouted 'Glory!'," pp. 346, 326.

29. Matthews, "The Southern Rite of Human Sacrifice." Drawing on a 1905 book written by the pastor of the First Presbyterian Church of Newport News, Virginia, Edwin Talliaferro Wellford, tellingly titled *The Lynching of Jesus,* Matthews shows how Wellford challenged the unspoken assumptions about lynching victims, who became martyrs and saviors.

30. Matthews, "Lynching Is Part of the Religion of Our People," pp. 166, 183.

31. Ibid., p. 156.

32. While it is somewhat played down in Hall, who sees lynching as a strategy to deny or resist the implications of modernity, segregation plays a crucial role in Patterson's and Matthews's analyses, as well as in Hale's. For all of them, segregation provides both the grounds of their analyses (as in Matthews's comment on "segregation *as* religion"), and also the background setting that they believe lynchings arose to address.

33. Elliot Jaspin, *Buried in the Bitter Waters: The Hidden History of Racial Cleansing in America* (New York: Basic, 2007).

34. *To Secure These Rights: Report of the President's Committee on Civil Rights* (New York: Simon & Schuster, 1947), p. 6.

35. Maurice Thompson, "The Court of Judge Lynch," *Lippincott's Monthly Magazine* 64.380 (August 1899): 254–62, esp. p. 258. The president of Trinity College in Durham, North Carolina (now Duke University), proposed the same argument; see John Carlisle Kilgo, "An Inquiry Concerning Lynchings," *South Atlantic Quarterly* 1 (January 1902): 4–9.

36. Both the *Jacksonville Florida Times-Union and Citizen* (August 8, 1901) and the unnamed New York newspaper are quoted in Robert P. Ingalls, *Urban Vigilantes in the New South: Tampa, 1882–1936* (1988; repr., Gainesville: University Press of Florida, 1993), pp. 77, 86.

37. Richard Maxwell Brown, *No Duty to Retreat: Violence and Values in American History and Society* (New York: Oxford University Press, 1991), pp. 17, 20.

38. *Wesleyan Christian Advocate* (April 5, 1899); qtd. in Mary Louise Ellis, "'Rain Down Fire': The Lynching of Sam Hose" (Ph.D. diss., Florida State University, 1992), p. 180.

39. Ida B. Wells, "Lynch Law in All Its Phases," in Mildred I. Thompson, *Ida B. Wells-Barnett: An Exploratory Study of an American Black Woman, 1893–1930* (Brooklyn: Carlson, 1990), pp. 171–87, esp. p. 184. The essay was first published in *Our Day* (May 1893): 333–37. Pauline E. Hopkins, *Contending Forces: A Romance Illustrative of Negro Life North and South* (Boston: Colored Cooperative, 1900), pp. 14–15.

40. Edmund Morgan, *American Slavery, American Freedom: The Ordeal of Colonial Virginia* (New York: W. W. Norton, 1975), p. 376. Vincent Harding, "Beyond Chaos: Black History and the Search for the New Land," in *Amistad 1: Writings on Black History and Culture,* ed. John A. Williams and Charles F. Harris (New York: Random House, 1970), pp. 267–92, esp. p. 280.

41. William W. Hening, *Statutes at Large: Being a Collection of All the Laws of Virginia from the First Session of the Legislature in the Year 1619* (Richmond, VA: Franklin Press, 1809–1823), vol. 1, p. 226.

42. Hening, *Statutes at Large,* vol. 2, p. 270. Even laws that attempted to be more generous in their apportioning of humanity to slaves, such as a 1799 Georgia law making it illegal to maim or kill a slave, made exceptions in "cases of insurrection by such a slave" or in case it "should happen by accident, in giving such slave moderate correction." The Georgia law is cited in Herbert Aptheker, *American Negro Slave Revolts* (1943; repr., New York: International, 1987), p. 75.

43. Hening, *Statutes at Large,* vol. 3, pp. 460–61.

44. Later, slave owners could dispense with even this meager state involvement (two justices of the peace and a sheriff) and simply "outlaw" a slave, a legal act that placed the slave beyond law and his killers beyond prosecution. Indeed, as historian Gerald Mullins points out, the slave's killers were rewarded from both the public treasury and the slave's owner, who sometimes advertised a higher reward for the return of a dead slave than for a live one. See Gerald W. Mullin, *Flight and Rebellion: Slave Resistance in Eighteenth-Century Virginia* (New York: Oxford University Press, 1972), pp. 56–57.

45. Bertram Wyatt-Brown, *Southern Honor: Ethics and Behavior in the Old South* (New York: Oxford University Press, 1982), pp. 460, 401.

46. "Tom, A Negro Slave Man," *Boston Gazette* (December 5, 1763); reprinted in Christopher Waldrep, ed., *Lynching in America: A History in Documents* (New York: New York University Press, 2006), pp. 61–62.

47. Michel Foucault, *Discipline and Punish: The Birth of the Prison,* trans. Alain Sheridan (New York: Penguin, 1977), pp. 32–69. I am not trying to do justice to the nuances of Foucault's argument about spectacle here; I am merely noting how lynchings could, with modifications, fit into his description of penal practice.

48. I should also emphasize that I am not making a case for a causal connection between these early slave laws and later lynch mobs. Lynchers would not later triumphantly cite these laws, in the ways that Americans refer to the Declaration of Independence or the Bill of Rights as the origins of a particular set of practices that they deemed originally theirs. For the role

that vigilantes played in controlling and oppressing free blacks, see Ira Berlin, *Slaves Without Masters: The Free Negro in the Antebellum South* (New York: Oxford University Press, 1974), esp. pp. 316–40.

49. Daniel Jonah Goldhagen, *Hitler's Willing Executioners: Ordinary Germans and the Holocaust* (New York: Alfred A. Knopf, 1996), pp. 174–75.

50. Hening, *The Statutes at Large,* vol. 3, p. 459.

EPILOGUE: AMERICAN LYNCHING

1. Angela Y. Davis, *Women, Race, and Class* (1981; repr., New York: Random House, 1983), p. 196. See Susan Brownmiller, *Against Our Will: Men, Women and Rape* (New York: Simon and Schuster, 1975), pp. 210–55; and Davis's critique in *Women, Race, and Class,* pp. 172–201.

BIBLIOGRAPHY

Allen, Frederick. *A Decent, Orderly Lynching: The Montana Vigilantes*. Norman: University of Oklahoma Press, 2004.

Allen, James. "Notes on the Plates." In *Without Sanctuary: Lynching Photography in America*. n.p.: Twin Palms, 2000.

Ames, Jessie Daniel. *The Changing Character of Lynching*. Atlanta: Commission on Interracial Cooperation, Inc., 1942.

Amstutz, Mark R. *The Healing of Nations: The Promise and Limits of Political Forgiveness*. Lanham: Rowman & Littlefield, 2005.

"The Anti-Lynching Crusaders," *Crisis* 25.1 (November 1922): 8.

Apel, Dora. *Imagery of Lynching: Black Men, White Women, and the Mob*. New Brunswick, NJ: Rutgers University Press, 2004.

Apel, Dora, and Shawn Michelle Smith. *Lynching Photographs*. Berkeley: University of California Press, 2007.

"Appendix: The American Vigilante Movements." In *Violence in America*, edited by Leon Friedman. New York: Chelsea House, 1983. Volume 2, pp. 171–80.

Aptheker, Herbert. *American Negro Slave Revolts*. 1943; repr. New York: International, 1987.

———, ed. *A Documentary History of the Negro People in the United States, 1945–1951: Volume 5: From the End of World War II to the Korean War*. New York: Caroll, 1993.

Arnold, Edwin T. *"What Virtue There Is in Fire": Cultural Memory and the Lynching of Sam Hose*. Athens: University of Georgia Press, 2009.

"An Art Exhibit Against Lynching," *Crisis* 42.4 (April, 1935): 106.

Avary, Myrta Lockett. *Dixie After the War: An Exposition of Social Conditions Existing in the South, During the Twelve Years Succeeding the Fall of Richmond*. n.p.: n.d. [1906].

Ayers, Edward L. *The Promise of the New South: Life After Reconstruction*. New York: Oxford University Press, 1992.

———. *Vengeance and Justice: Crime and Punishment in the 19th Century American South*. New York: Oxford University Press, 1984.

Bancroft, Hubert Howe. *Popular Tribunals: Volume I*. In *The Works of Hubert Howe Bancroft*, Volume XXXVI. San Francisco: History Company, 1887.

———. *Popular Tribunals: Volume II*. In *The Works of Hubert Howe Bancroft*, Volume XXXVII. San Francisco: History Company, 1887.

Barkan, Elazar. *The Guilt of Nations: Restitution and Negotiating Historical Injustice.* New York: W. W. Norton, 2000.

Barzun, Jacques. "Introduction." In *The Selected Writings of John Jay Chapman,* edited by Jacques Barzun. New York: Farrar, Straus and Cudahy, 1957.

Bassett, John Spencer. "Stirring Up the Fires of Race Antipathy," *South Atlantic Quarterly* 2 (1903): 297–305.

Beaulieu, Lovell. "No Longer Surprised by Racial Hate Crimes," *Des Moines Register* (June 20, 1998).

Bederman, Gail. *Manliness and Civilization: A Cultural History of Gender and Race in the United States, 1880–1917.* Chicago: University of Chicago Press, 1995.

Berg, Manfred. *Popular Justice: A History of Lynching in America.* Chicago: Ivan R. Dee, 2011.

Berlin, Ira. *Slaves Without Masters: The Free Negro in the Antebellum South.* New York: Oxford University Press, 1974.

Bernstein, Iver. *The New York City Draft Riots: Their Significance for American Society and Politics in the Age of the Civil War.* New York: Oxford University Press, 1990.

Bernstein, Patricia. *The First Waco Horror: The Lynching of Jesse Washington and the Rise of the NAACP.* College Station: Texas A&M University Press, 2005.

Black, Paul. "Lynchings in Iowa," *Iowa Journal of History and Politics* 10.2 (1912): 151–254.

Blair, Lewis. "Lynching as Fine Art," *Our Day* 13.76 (1894): 307–14.

Blight, David W. *Race and Reunion: The Civil War in American Memory.* Cambridge, MA: Harvard University Press, 2001.

Bradley, David. "Commentary: Perspective on the Texas Murder/100 Years of 'Isolated Incidents'/Society Must Respond to a Black Man's Lynching with the Same Self-Examination as a Schoolyard Shooting," *Los Angeles Times* (June 11, 1998).

Brothers, Thomas. *The United States of North America as They Are; Not as They Are Generally Described: Being a Cure for Radicalism.* London, 1840.

Brown, Joseph H. "All Murders Merit Similar Outrage," *Tampa Tribune* (June 28, 1998).

Brown, Richard Maxwell. *No Duty to Retreat: Violence and Values in American History and Society.* New York: Oxford University Press, 1991.

———. *Strain of Violence: Historical Studies of American Violence and Vigilantism.* New York: Oxford University Press, 1975.

————. "Western Violence: Structure, Values, Myth," *Western Historical Quarterly* 24.1 (February 1993): 5–20.

Brown, William Wells. *The Negro in the American Rebellion.* Boston: A. G. Brown, 1880.

Brownmiller, Susan. *Against Our Will: Men, Women and Rape.* New York: Simon and Schuster, 1975.

Bruce, Dickson D., Jr. *Violence and Culture in the Antebellum South.* Austin: University of Texas Press, 1979.

Bruce, Dorothy. "A Time to Kill: When a Black Man Was Brutally Lynched in Texas This Week, African Americans Were Enraged at the Prospect of the White Suspects Escaping the Death Penalty," *The Journal* (June 12, 1998).

Bruce, John Edward. *The Blood Red Record. A Review of the Horrible Lynchings and Burning of Negroes by Civilized White Men in the United States, As Taken from the Records.* Albany: Argus, 1901.

Bruce, Philip A. *The Plantation Negro as Freeman: Observations on His Character, Condition, and Prospects in Virginia.* New York: G. P. Putnam's Sons, 1889.

Brundage, W. Fitzhugh. *Lynching in the New South: Georgia and Virginia, 1880–1930.* Urbana: University of Illinois Press, 1993.

"Burned at the Stake: An Arkansas Colored Man's Punishment," *Baltimore Sun* (February 22, 1892).

Burke, Kenneth. *A Grammar of Motives.* 1945; repr. Berkeley: University of California Press, 1969.

Cameron, James. *A Time of Terror: A Survivor's Story.* 1982; repr. Baltimore: Black Classic, 1994.

Capeci, Dominic J., Jr. *The Lynching of Cleo Wright.* Lexington: University Press of Kentucky, 1998.

Carby, Hazel V. *Reconstructing Womanhood: The Emergence of the Afro-American Woman Novelist.* New York: Oxford University Press, 1987.

Carr, Cynthia. *Our Town: A Heartland Lynching, a Haunted Town, and the Hidden History of White America.* New York: Crown, 2006.

Carrigan, William D. *The Making of a Lynching Culture: Violence and Vigilantism in Central Texas, 1836–1916.* Urbana: University of Illinois Press, 2004.

Cartwright, Marguerite. "The Mob Still Rides—Tuskegee Notwithstanding," *Crisis* 60 (April 1953): 222.

Cash, W. J. *The Mind of the South.* 1941; repr. New York: Random House, 1991.

Castel, Albert. "The Fort Pillow Massacre: An Examination of the Evidence." In *Black Flag Over Dixie: Racial Atrocities and Reprisals in the Civil War,* edited by Gregory J. W. Urwin. Carbondale: Southern Illinois University Press, 2004.

Chadbourn, James Harmon. *Lynching and the Law.* Chapel Hill: University of North Carolina Press, 1933.

Chapman, John Jay. "Coatesville." In *Unbought Spirit: A John Jay Chapman Reader,* edited by Richard Stone. Urbana: University of Illinois Press, 1998.

Chesnutt, Charles. "A Deep Sleeper." In *The Conjure Woman and Other Conjure Tales,* edited by Richard H. Brodhead. Durham: Duke University Press, 1993.

Clark, L. D. *A Bright, Tragic Thing: A Tale of Civil War Texas.* El Paso, Texas: Cinco Puntos, 1992.

Clayton, Bruce. *The Savage Ideal: Intolerance and Intellectual Leadership in the South, 1890–1914.* Baltimore: Johns Hopkins University Press, 1977.

Cohen, William. *At Freedom's Edge: Black Mobility and the Southern White Quest for Racial Control, 1861–1915.* Baton Rouge: Louisiana State University Press, 1991.

Cole, J. Timothy. *The Forest City Lynching of 1900: Populism, Racism, and White Supremacy in Rutherford County, North Carolina.* Jefferson, NC: McFarland, 2003.

Conrad, Robert Edgar. *Children of God's Fire: A Documentary History of Black Slavery in Brazil.* Princeton, NJ: Princeton University Press, 1983.

Cornish, Dudley Taylor. *The Sable Arm: Black Troops in the Union Army, 1861–1865.* 1956; repr. Lawrence: University of Kansas Press, 1987.

"The Cover," *Crisis* 43.10 (October 1936): 293.

Cox, Oliver Cromwell. *Caste, Class and Race: A Study in Social Dynamics.* 1948; repr. New York: Monthly Review, 1970.

Cromwell, John W. "The Aftermath of Nat Turner's Insurrection," *Journal of Negro History* 5.2 (April 1920): 208–34.

Cutler, James Elbert. *Lynch-Law: An Investigation into the History of Lynching in the United States.* Longman, Green, 1905.

Davis, Angela. *Women, Race, and Class.* New York: Random House, 1981.

Dawson, John. *Healing America's Wounds.* Ventura, CA: Regal, 1994.

Dew, Charles B. *Bond of Iron: Master and Slave at Buffalo Forge.* New York: W. W. Norton, 1994.

Dittmer, John. *Black Georgia in the Progressive Era, 1900–1920* (Urbana: University of Illinois Press, 1977.

Dodson, Bernhardt, Jr. "Miami Vigil Pays Its Respect to James Byrd," *Miami Times* (June 25, 1998).

Douglass, Frederick. *Why Is the Negro Lynched?* (1894). In *The Life and Writings of Frederick Douglass*, edited by Philip S. Foner. New York: International, 1955.

Downey, Dennis B., and Raymond M. Hyser. *No Crooked Death: Coatesville, Pennsylvania, and the Lynching of Zachariah Walker.* Urbana: University of Illinois Press, 1991.

Dray, Philip. *At the Hands of Persons Unknown: The Lynching of Black America.* New York: Random House, 2002.

Dyer, Thomas G. "'A Most Unexampled Exhibition of Madness and Brutality': Judge Lynch in Saline County, Missouri, 1859, Part 1," *Missouri Historical Review* 89.3 (1995): 269–89.

———. "'A Most Unexampled Exhibition of Madness and Brutality': Judge Lynch in Saline County, Missouri, 1859, Part 2," *Missouri Historical Review* 89.4 (1995): 367–83.

Early, J. M. *"An Eye for an Eye"; Or the Fiend and the Fagot. An Unvarnished Account of the Burning of Henry Smith at Paris, Texas, February 1, 1893, and the Reason He Was Tortured.* Paris, Texas: Junius Early, n.d.

Egerton, Douglas R. *Gabriel's Rebellion: The Virginia Slave Conspiracies of 1800 and 1802.* Chapel Hill: University of North Carolina Press, 1993.

Ellis, Mary Louise. "'Rain Down Fire': The Lynching of Sam Hose." Ph.D. diss., Florida State University, 1992.

Escott, Paul D. "White Republicanism and Ku Klux Klan Terror: The North Carolina Piedmont During Reconstruction." In *Race, Class, and Politics in Southern History: Essays in Honor of Robert F. Durden*, edited by Jeffrey J. Crow, Paul D. Escott, and Charles L. Flynn, Jr. Baton Rouge: Louisiana State University Press, 1989. 3–34.

Feimster, Crystal. "'Ladies and Lynching': The Gendered Discourse of Mob Violence in the New South, 1880–1930." Ph.D. diss., Princeton University, 2000.

———. *Southern Horrors: Women and the Politics of Rape and Lynching.* Cambridge, MA: Harvard University Press, 2009.

Finnegan, Terence. "Lynching and Political Power in Mississippi and South Carolina." In *Under Sentence of Death: Lynching in the South*, edited by W. Fitzhugh Brundage. Chapel Hill: University of North Carolina Press, 1997. 189–218.

Flowers, B. O. "The Rise of Anarchy in the United States," *Arena* 30.3 (September, 1903): 305.

Foner, Eric. *Reconstruction: America's Unfinished Revolution, 1863–1877.* 1988; repr. New York: Harpers & Row, 1989.

Foote, Kenneth E. *Shadowed Ground: America's Landscape of Violence and Tragedy.* 1997; rev. ed., Austin: University of Texas Press, 2003.

Foucault, Michel. *Discipline and Punish: The Birth of the Prison,* translated by Alain Sheridan. New York: Penguin, 1977.

Fraser, Nancy. "Rethinking the Public Sphere: A Contribution to the Critique of Actually Existing Democracy." In *Habermas and the Public Sphere,* edited by Craig Calhoun. Cambridge, MA: MIT Press, 1992.

Frazier, E. Franklin. "The Pathology of Race Prejudice," *Forum* 70 (June 1927): 856–62.

"Frightful Affair," *Portsmouth Journal of Literature and Politics* (August 1, 1835).

Frisby, Derek W. "'Remember Fort Pillow!': Politics, Atrocity Propaganda, and the Evolution of Hard War." In *Black Flag over Dixie: Racial Atrocities and Reprisals in the Civil War,* edited by Gregory J. W. Urwin. Carbondale: Southern Illinois University Press, 2004.

Genovese, Eugene. *Roll, Jordan, Roll: The World the Slaves Made.* 1974; repr. New York: Random House, 1976.

Giddings, Paula J. *Ida, A Sword Among Lions: Ida B. Wells and the Campaign Against Lynching.* New York: HarperCollins, 2008.

Gilje, Paul A. *Rioting in America.* Bloomington: Indiana University Press, 1996.

Ginzburg, Ralph, ed. *100 Years of Lynching.* 1962; repr. Baltimore: Black Classic, 1988.

Godshalk, David Fort. *Veiled Visions: The 1906 Atlanta Riot and the Reshaping of American Race Relations.* Chapel Hill: University of North Carolina Press, 2005.

Goldsby, Jacqueline. *A Spectacular Secret: Lynching in American Life and Literature.* Chicago: University of Chicago Press, 2006.

Gonzales-Day, Ken. *Lynching in the West: 1850–1935.* Durham, NC: Duke University Press, 2006.

"Governor Davis's Speech at Eureka Springs." In *Jeff Davis, Governor and United States Senator: His Life and Speeches,* edited by L. S. Dunaway. Little Rock, AK, 1913.

Gramsci, Antonio. *Selections from the Prison Notebooks,* edited and translated by Quentin Hoare and Geoffrey Nowell Smith. New York: International, 1971.

Gravely, Will. "Race, Truth, and Reconciliation in the United States: Reflections on Desmond Tutu's Proposal," *Journal of Religion and Society* 3 (2001).

"The Great American Specialty," *Crisis* 27.4 (February 1924): 168.

Griffith, D. W. *Birth of a Nation* (1915).

Grimké, Angelina Weld. "Rachel." In *Strange Fruit: Plays on Lynching by American Women*, edited by Kathy A. Perkins and Judith L. Stephens. Bloomington: Indiana University Press, 1998.

Grimsted, David. *American Mobbing, 1828–1860*. New York: Oxford University Press, 1998.

"The Gruesome Texas Killing," *Baltimore Afro-American* (June 19, 1998).

Habermas, Jürgen. "Further Reflections on the Public Sphere." In *Habermas and the Public Sphere*, edited by Craig Calhoun, translated by Thomas Burger. Cambridge, MA: MIT Press, 1992. 453–54.

———. *The Structural Transformation of the Public Sphere: An Inquiry into a Category of Bourgeois Society*, translated by Thomas Burger with the assistance of Frederick Lawrence. 1962; repr. Cambridge, MA: MIT Press, 1991.

Hale, Grace Elizabeth. *Making Whiteness: The Culture of Segregation in the South, 1890–1940*. New York: Random House, 1998.

Hale, Sir Matthew. *The History of the Pleas of the Crown. Now first published from his Lordship's Original Manuscript, and the Several References to the Records Examined by the Originals, with Large Notes by Sollom Emlyn*. London, 1736.

Hall, Jacquelyn Dowd. "'The Mind That Burns in Each Body': Women, Rape, and Racial Violence." In *Powers of Desire: The Politics of Sexuality*, edited by Ann Snitow, Christine Stansell, and Sharon Thompson. New York: Monthly Review, 1983. 328–49.

———. *Revolt Against Chivalry: Jessie Daniel Ames and the Women's Campaign Against Lynching*, rev. ed. New York: Columbia University Press, 1993.

Hart, Albert Bushnell. "Lynching." In *Cyclopedia of American Government*, edited by Andrew C. McLaughlin and Albert Bushnell Hart. 1914; 2d ed. New York: D. Appleton, 1930.

Hartman, Saidiya V. *Scenes of Subjection: Terror, Slavery, and Self-Making in Nineteenth-Century America*. New York: Oxford University Press, 1997.

"Hatred and the James Byrd Murder," *Caribbean Today* (June 30, 1998).

Hening, William W. *Statutes at Large: Being a Collection of All the Laws of Virginia from the First Session of the Legislature in the Year 1619*. Richmond, VA: Franklin Press, 1809–1823.

Higginbotham, A. Leon. *In the Matter of Color: Race and the American Legal Process: The Colonial Period*. New York: Oxford University Press, 1978.

Hine, Darlene Clark, and Kathleen Thompson. *A Shining Thread of Hope: The History of Black Women in America.* New York: Broadway, 1998.

Hodes, Martha. *White Women, Black Men: Illicit Sex in the 19th-Century South.* New Haven: Yale University Press, 1997.

Hollandsworth, James G., Jr. *An Absolute Massacre: The New Orleans Race Riot of July 30, 1866.* Baton Rouge: Louisiana University Press, 2001.

Holloway, Jonathan Scott. *Confronting the Veil: Abram Harris, Jr., E. Franklin Frazier, and Ralph Bunche, 1919–1941.* Chapel Hill: University of North Carolina Press, 2002.

Holmes, William F. "Whitecapping: Agrarian Violence in Mississippi, 1902–1906," *Journal of Southern History* 35 (May 1969): 165–85.

Holness, Karen A. "Byrd Slaying Symbolic of Ongoing Racism," *Miami Times* (June 25, 1998).

Hopkins, Pauline E. *Contending Forces: A Romance Illustrative of Negro Life North and South.* Boston: Colored Cooperative, 1900.

"Horrible Conspiracy," *Salem Gazette* (August 7, 1835).

Hovey, Richard B. *John Jay Chapman: An American Mind.* New York: Columbia University Press, 1959.

Howe, M. A. DeWolfe. *John Jay Chapman and His Letters.* Boston: Houghton Mifflin, 1937.

Hufsmith, George W. *The Wyoming Lynching of Cattle Kate, 1889.* Glendo, WY: High Plains, 1993.

Ignatieff, Michael. *The Warrior's Honor: Ethnic Wars and the Modern Conscience.* New York: Henry Holt, 1997.

"Infamous Outrage Under Lynch Law," *Portsmouth Journal of Literature and Politics* (January 9, 1836).

Ingalls, Robert P. *Urban Vigilantes in the New South: Tampa, 1882–1936.* 1988; repr. Gainesville: University Press of Florida, 1993.

"Interview with Shawn Berry," *60 Minutes II.* CBS News. 1999.

Inverarity, James M. "Populism and Lynching in Louisiana, 1889–1896: A Test of Erikson's Theory of the Relationship Between Boundary Crises and Repressive Justice," *American Sociological Review* 41 (April 1976): 262–80.

"The Issue of Race in America," *Washington Informer* (June 24, 1998).

Jaspin, Elliot. *Buried in the Bitter Waters: The Hidden History of Racial Cleansing in America.* New York: Basic, 2007.

Johns, Richard R. *Spreading the News: The American Postal Service from Franklin to Morse.* Cambridge, MA: Harvard University Press, 1995.

Johnson, James Weldon. "Lynching: America's National Disgrace," *Current History* 19.4 (January 1924): 596–601.

———. *Lynching: America's National Disgrace* New York: NAACP, 1924.

Jordan, Winthrop. *White over Black: American Attitudes Toward the Negro, 1550–1812.* 1968; repr. New York: W. W. Norton, 1977.

Kilgo, John Carlisle. "An Inquiry Concerning Lynchings," *South Atlantic Quarterly* 1 (January 1902): 4–9.

Ledbetter, Bill. "Slave Unrest and White Panic: The Impact of Black Republicanism in Ante-Bellum Texas," *Texana* 10.4 (1972): 335–50.

Leonard, Stephen J. *Lynching in Colorado, 1859–1919.* Boulder: University Press of Colorado, 2002.

Lincoln, Abraham. "Address Before the Young Men's Lyceum of Springfield, Illinois" (January 27, 1838). In *The Collected Works of Abraham Lincoln,* edited by Roy P. Basler. New Brunswick, NJ: Rutgers University Press, 1953–1955. Volume 1, pp. 108–15.

Litwack, Leon. *Been in the Storm So Long: The Aftermath of Slavery.* 1979; repr. New York: Random House, 1980.

———. *Trouble in Mind: Black Southerners in the Age of Jim Crow.* 1998; repr. New York: Random House, 1999.

"Lynch Law," *New Bedford Mercury* (September 4, 1835).

"Lynch Law," *New Hampshire Patriot and State Gazette* (August 24, 1835).

"Lynch Law," *New-Hampshire Sentinel* (September 24, 1835).

"Lynch Law—Five Gamblers Hung Without Trial," *Connecticut Courant* (August 3, 1835).

"Lynch Law, as It Is Called at the West," *New-Hampshire Sentinel* (July 30, 1835).

"Lynching," *Crisis* 10 (June 1915): 71.

"Lynching: An American Kultur?" *New Republic* 14 (April 13, 1918): 311–12.

"Lynching as a Japanese Sculptor Sees It," *Christian Century* 52.7 (February 13, 1935): 196–97.

"Lynching Resolution Rejected in Waco," *New York Times* (May 17, 2006).

Lynchings and What They Mean: General Findings of the Southern Commission on the Study of Lynching. Atlanta: The Commission, [1931].

"Lynch's Law," *American Beacon and Norfolk & Portsmouth Daily Advertiser* (March 2, 1819).

"Lynch's Law," *City Gazette and Daily Advertiser* (December 8, 1819).

"Lynch's Law," *Portsmouth Journal of Literature and Politics* (August 8, 1835).

Madison, James H. *A Lynching in the Heartland: Race and Memory in America.* New York: Palgrave, 2001.

Manly, Alexander. "Mrs. Fellows's Speech," *Wilmington Record* (August 18, 1898).

Margolick, David. *Strange Fruit: The Biography of a Song.* New York: HarperCollins, 2001.

Markovitz, Jonathan. *Legacies of Lynching: Racial Violence and Memory.* Minneapolis: University of Minnesota Press, 2004.

Matthews, Albert. "The Term Lynch Law," *Modern Philology* 2.2 (October, 1904): 173–95.

McCarthy, Sheryl. "Racism Bubbles Up in Large and Small Ways," *Newsday* (June 15, 1998).

McCaslin, Richard B. *Tainted Breeze: The Great Hanging at Gainesville, Texas, 1862.* Baton Rouge: Louisiana State University Press, 1994.

McFeely, William S. "Afterword." In *Under Sentence of Death: Lynching in the South,* edited by W. Fitzhugh Brundage. Chapel Hill: University of North Carolina Press, 1997.

McGinty, Brian. "Shadows in St. James Park," *California History* 57.4 (1978): 291–307.

McGovern, James R. *Anatomy of a Lynching: The Killing of Claude Neal.* Baton Rouge: Louisiana State University Press, 1982.

McMurry, Linda O. *Recorder of the Black Experience: A Biography of Monroe Nathan Work.* Baton Rouge: Louisiana State University Press, 1985.

McPherson, James M. *The Negro's Civil War: How American Blacks Felt and Acted During the War for the Union.* 1965; repr. New York: Ballantine, 1991.

"Memorial of a Number of Citizens of the City and County of Philadelphia, Praying Congress to Adopt the Sub-Treasury System, and to Establish an Exclusive Metallic Currency," December 18, 1837. Referred to the Committee on Finance, and ordered to be printed. Serial Set Volume No. 314, Session Volume No. 1, 25th Cong., 2d sess., S. Doc. 22.

Micheaux, Oscar. *Within Our Gates* (1919).

Miles, Edwin. "Mississippi Slave Insurrection Scare of 1835," *Journal of Negro History* 42 (1957): 48–60.

Miller, Kelly. "Art as Cure for Lynching," *Christian Century* 52.16 (April 17, 1935): 516–17.

Miller, Thomas E. *Congressional Record,* 51st Cong., 1st sess. (1891): 707–8.

"Miscellany. Lynch Law," *New Hampshire Patriot and State Gazette* (August 24, 1835).

Mohr, Clarence L. *On the Threshold of Freedom: Masters and Slaves in Civil War Georgia.* 1986; repr. Baton Rouge: Louisiana State University Press, 2001.

Morgan, Edmund S. *American Slavery, American Freedom: The Ordeal of Colonial Virginia.* New York: W. W. Norton, 1975.

———. *Inventing the People: The Rise of Popular Sovereignty in England and America.* 1988; repr. New York: W. W. Norton, 1989.

Mullin, Gerald W. *Flight and Rebellion: Slave Resistance in Eighteenth-Century Virginia* New York: Oxford University Press, 1972.

"Murder and Lynch Law. Baltimore, Feb. 2," *Pittsfield Sun* (February 5, 1852).

"My Country, 'Tis of Thee," *Crisis* 41.11 (November 1934): 342.

Myers, Steven Lee. "Bush, at Commemoration, Says Nooses Are Symbol of 'Gross Injustice,'" *New York Times* (February 13, 2008).

National Association For the Advancement of Colored People, *Thirty Years of Lynching in the United States, 1889–1918.* New York: NAACP, 1919.

"The Ninth Crusade," *Crisis* 25.5 (March, 1923): 213–17.

Norton, Wesley. "The Methodist Episcopal Church and the Civil Disturbances in North Texas in 1859–1860," *Southwestern Historical Quarterly* 68.3 (1965): 317–41.

Novel, Thomas. "Still Lynching After All These Years," *Community Contact* (June 24, 1998).

Oates, Stephen B. *The Fires of Jubilee: Nat Turner's Fierce Rebellion.* 1975; repr. New York: Harper & Row, 1990.

———. *To Purge This Land with Blood: A Biography of John Brown,* 2d ed. Amherst: University of Massachusetts Press, 1984.

Oggel, L. Terry. "Speaking Out About Race: 'The United States of Lyncherdom' Clemens Really Wrote." In *Prospects: An Annual of American Cultural Studies.* Volume 25. New York: Cambridge University Press, 2000.

"Only One Sixth of Lynchings for Rape," *Crisis* 42 (January 1935): 14.

"Origin of Lynch Law," *New Bedford Mercury* (July 15, 1836).

"Origin of Lynch's Law," *New Bedford Mercury* (August 7, 1835).

"Original Communications: Sexual Crimes Among Southern Negroes— Scientifically Considered—An Open Correspondence," *Virginia Medical Monthly* 20.2 (May 1893): 105–25.

Oshinksy, David M. *"Worse Than Slavery": Parchman Farm and the Ordeal of Jim Crow Justice.* New York: Free Press, 1996.

Page, Clarence. "Sadly, There's Still Plenty of Hate to Go Around," *Chicago Tribune* (June 14, 1998).

Page, Thomas Nelson. "The Lynching of Negroes—Its Causes and Its Prevention," *North American Review* 173.566 (January 1904): 33–48.

———. *The Negro: The Southerner's Problem.* New York: Charles Scribner's Sons, 1904.

Page, Thomas Walker. "The Real Judge Lynch," *Atlantic Monthly* 88 (December 1901): 731–43.

Painter, Nell Irvin. "'Social Equality,' Miscegenation, Labor, and Power." In *The Evolution of Southern Culture,* edited by Numan V. Bartley. Athens: University of Georgia Press, 1988. 47–67.

Palmer, Irenas J. *The Black Man's Burden, Or, The Horrors of Southern Lynchings.* Olean, NY: Olean Evening Herald Print, 1902.

"Panics in Texas and Kansas," *Farmers' Cabinet* (September 5, 1860).

Patterson, Orlando. *Rituals of Blood: Consequences of Slavery in Two American Centuries.* Washington, DC: Civitas, 1998.

Perkins, Kathy A. "The Impact of Lynching on the Art of African American Women." In *Strange Fruit: Plays on Lynching by American Women,* edited by Kathy A. Perkins and Judith L. Stephens. Bloomington: Indiana University Press, 1998.

Perman, Michael. "Counter Reconstruction: The Role of Violence in Southern Redemption." In *The Facts of Reconstruction: Essays in Honor of John Hope Franklin,* edited by Eric Anderson and Alfred A. Moss, Jr. Baton Rouge: Louisiana State University Press, 1991. 121–40.

Peterson, Merrill D. *Thomas Jefferson and the New Nation: A Biography.* New York: Oxford University Press, 1970.

"Petition from Kentucky Negroes," [March 25, 1871]. In *A Documentary History of the Negro People in the United States,* edited by Herbert Aptheker. New York: Citadel, 1951. Volume 2, pp. 594–99.

Pfeifer, Michael J. "Lynching and Criminal Justice in Regional Context: Iowa, Wyoming, and Louisiana, 1878–1946." Ph.D. diss., University of Iowa, 1998.

———. *Rough Justice: Lynching and American Society, 1874–1947.* Urbana: University of Illinois Press, 2004.

Platt, Anthony M. *E. Franklin Frazier Reconsidered.* New Brunswick, NJ: Rutgers University Press, 1991.

Portsmouth Journal of Literature and Politics (August 22, 1835).

Prather, H. Leon, Sr. "We Have Taken a City: A Centennial Essay," in *Democracy Betrayed: The Wilmington Race Riot of 1898 and Its Legacy.* Chapel Hill: University of North Carolina Press, 1998.

———. *We Have Taken a City: Wilmington Racial Massacre and Coup of 1898.* Rutherford, NJ: Associated University Presses, 1984.

Prince, Carl E. "The Great 'Riot Year': Jacksonian Democracy and Patterns of Violence in 1834," *Journal of the Early Republic* 5.1 (Spring 1985): 1–19.

Proceedings of the National Convention of Colored Men Held in the City of Syracuse, N.Y. Oct. 4, 5, 6 + 7, 1864. Boston: J. S. Ruck, 1864; reprinted in *Minutes of the Proceedings of the National Negro Conventions 1830–1864,* edited by Howard H. Bell. New York: Arno, 1969.

Rable, George C. *But There Was No Peace: The Role of Violence in the Politics of Reconstruction.* Athens: University of Georgia Press, 1984.

"Race Hate in Texas," *Irish Times* (June 12, 1998).

Raiford, Leigh. "The Consumption of Lynching Images." In *Only Skin Deep: Changing Visions of the American Self,* edited by Coco Fusco and Brian Wallis. New York: International Center for Photography and Harry N. Abrams, 2003. 266–73.

Raper, Arthur F. *The Tragedy of Lynching.* 1933; repr. Montclair, NJ: Patterson Smith, 1969.

Raspberry, William. "Redemption in East Texas," *Washington Post* (June 19, 1998).

Report of the Joint Select Committee to Inquire into the Condition of Affairs in the Late Insurrectionary States. 13 volumes. Washington, DC: Government Printing Office, 1872.

Resnikoff, Philip. "A Psychoanalytic Study of Lynching," *Psychoanalytic Review* 20 (1933): 421—27.

Richards, L. *Gentlemen of Property and Standing: Anti-abolition Mobs in Jacksonian America.* New York: Oxford University Press, 1970.

Robeson, Paul. *Paul Robeson Speaks,* edited by Philip S. Foner. New York: Carol, 1978.

Robinson, Armstead L. "In the Shadow of Old John Brown: Insurrection Anxiety and Confederate Mobilization, 1861–1863," *Journal of Negro History* 65.4 (Autumn 1980): 279–97.

Roosevelt, Theodore. "Lynching and the Miscarriage of Justice," *Outlook* 99 (November 25, 1911): 706.

Rosen, Hannah. *Terror in the Heart of Freedom: Citizenship, Sexual Violence, and the Meaning of Race in the Postemancipation South.* Chapel Hill: University of North Carolina Press, 2009.

Ross, John. "At the Bar of Judge Lynch: Lynching and Lynch Mobs in America." Ph.D. diss., Texas Tech University, 1983.

Rowan, Carl. "What Jasper Murder Tells Us About America," *Houston Chronicle* (June 13, 1998).

Rubenstein, Richard E. *When Jesus Became God: The Struggle to Define Christianity During the Last Days of Rome.* Orlando, FL: Harcourt, 1999.

Rushdy, Ashraf H. A. *Neo-Slave Narratives: Studies in the Social Logic of a Literary Form.* New York: Oxford University Press, 1999.

Ryan, James Gilbert. "The Memphis Riot of 1866: Terror in a Black Community During Reconstruction," *Journal of Negro History* 62.3 (1977): 243–57.

Schecter, Barnet. *The Devil's Own Work: The Civil War Draft Riots and the Fight to Reconstruct America.* New York: Walker, 2005.

Schuyler, George. *Black No More.* 1931; repr. Boston: Northeastern University Press, 1989.

"Second Annual Report, NAACP." In *A Documentary History of the Negro People in the United States,* edited by Herbert Aptheker. 1973; repr. New York: Citadel, 1990. Volume 3, 38–39.

To Secure These Rights: Report of the President's Committee on Civil Rights. New York: Simon & Schuster, 1947.

Shay, Frank. *Judge Lynch: His First Hundred Years.* New York: Ives Washburn, 1938.

Singletary, Otis A. *Negro Militia and Reconstruction.* Austin: University of Texas Press, 1957.

"Shocking to the Soul," *Miami Times* (June 18, 1998).

Shufeldt, R. W. *The Negro: A Menace to American Civilization.* Boston: Gorham, 1907.

Simmons, Enoch Spencer. *A Solution of the Race Problem in the South.* Raleigh, NC: Edwards and Broughton, 1898.

Simon, Bryant. *A Fabric of Defeat: The Politics of South Carolina Millhands, 1910–1948.* Chapel Hill: University of North Carolina Press, 1998.

Skaggs, William H. *The Southern Oligarchy: An Appeal in Behalf of the Silent Masses of Our Country Against the Despotic Rule of the Few.* 1924; repr. New York: Negro Universities Press, 1969.

Sledd, Andrew H. "The Negro: Another View," *Atlantic Monthly* 90 (July 1902): 65–73.

Slotkin, Richard. "Apotheosis of Lynching: The Political Uses of Symbolic Violence," *Western Legal History* 6.1 (Winter/Spring 1993): 1–16.

———. *The Fatal Environment: The Myth of the Frontier in the Age of Industrialization, 1800–1890.* 1985; repr. Norman: University of Oklahoma Press, 1994.

———. *Regeneration Through Violence: The Mythology of the American Frontier, 1600–1860.* 1973; repr. Norman: University of Oklahoma Press, 2000.

Smalls, Robert. *Congressional Record*, 44th Cong., 1st sess., Volume IV, pt. 5, pp. 4041–42. In *Documentary History of the Negro People in the United States*, edited by Herbert Aptheker. New York: Citadel, 1951. Volume 2, pp. 610–14.

Smallwood, James. "Disaffection in Confederate Texas: The Great Hanging of Gainesville," *Civil War History* 22 (1976): 349–60.

Smead, Howard. *Blood Justice: The Lynching of Mack Charles Parker.* New York: Oxford University Press, 1986.

Smith, J. B., and Tommy Witherspoon. "Race Coalition Seeks Apology, Though Most City, County Leaders Express Reluctance," *Waco Tribune-Herald* (May 16, 2006).

Smith, Lillian. *Killers of the Dream.* 1949; rep. New York: W. W. Norton, 1994.

Soule, Frank, John H. Gihon, and James Nisbet. *The Annals of San Francisco.* New York: D. Appleton, 1855.

———. *The Annals of San Francisco, Together with the Continuation, Through 1855,* compiled by Dorothy H. Huggins. Palo Alto, CA: Lewis Osborne, 1966.

"Southern Atrocities," *New Bedford Mercury* (August 7, 1835).

Taylor, Joe Gray. *Louisiana Reconstructed 1863–1877.* Baton Rouge: Louisiana State University Press, 1974.

Terrell, J. "Lynch Law in Texas in the Sixties," *Green Bag* 14.8 (1902): 382–83.

Thomas-Lester, Avis. "A Senate Apology for History on Lynching," *Washington Post* (June 14, 2005).

Thompson, Julius E. *Lynchings in Mississippi: A History, 1865–1965.* Jefferson, NC: McFarland, 2007.

Thompson, Maurice. "The Court of Judge Lynch," *Lippincott's Monthly Magazine* 64.380 (August, 1899): 254–62.

Tillman, Ben. *Congressional Record,* United States Senate, 59th Cong., 2d sess., 1441 (January 12, 1907).

Tolnay, Stewart E., and E. M. Beck. *A Festival of Violence: An Analysis of Southern Lynchings, 1882–1930.* Urbana: University of Illinois Press, 1995.

Tourgée, Albion W. *A Fool's Errand,* edited by John Hope Franklin. 1879; repr. Cambridge, MA; Harvard University Press, 1961.

Trelease, Allen W. *White Terror: The Ku Klux Klan Conspiracy and Southern Reconstruction.* 1971; repr. Baton Rouge: Louisiana State University Press, 1995.

Trout, Maybelle. "The Last Mob Lynching/Central Texas Town Recalls 'Santa Claus' Case 65 Years Ago," *Houston Chronicle* (October 16, 1994).

"Tuskegee Omits 'Lynching Letter,'" *New York Times* (December 31, 1953).

Twain, Mark. "The United States of Lyncherdom," in *Mark Twain: Collected Tales, Sketches, Speeches, and Essays, 1901–1910*. New York: Library of America, 1992.

Vandal, Gilles. "'Bloody Caddo': White Violence Against Blacks in a Louisiana Parish, 1865–1876," *Journal of Social History* 25.2 (Winter 1991): 376, 378.

"The Vicksburg Tragedy," *Vicksburg Register* (July 9, 1835).

Vidal, Gore. "Lincoln, Lincoln and the Priests of Academe," *United States: Essays, 1952–1992*. New York: Random House, 1993. 669–700.

"Waco City Council Apologizes for Lynching 100 Years Ago," *Daily Texan* (June 22, 2006).

"A Wake-up Call," *Bay State Banner* (June 18, 1998).

Waldrep, Christopher, ed. *Lynching in America: A History in Documents*. New York: New York University Press, 2006.

———. *The Many Faces of Judge Lynch: Extralegal Violence and Punishment in America*. New York: Macmillan, 2002.

Waldrep, Christopher, and Michael Bellesiles, eds. *Documenting American Violence: A Sourcebook*. New York: Oxford University Press, 2006.

Washington, Booker T. *The Future of the American Negro*. Boston: Small, Maynard, 1899.

———. "Lynching in the South," *The Southern Workman and Hampton School Record* 28.10 (1899): 373–76.

Wells, Ida B. "Lynch Law in All Its Phases." In Mildred I. Thompson, *Ida B. Wells-Barnett: An Exploratory Study of an American Black Woman, 1893–1930*. Brooklyn: Carlson, 1990. 171–87.

———. *Mob Rule in New Orleans* [1900]. In *Southern Horror and Other Writings: The Anti-Lynching Campaign of Ida B. Wells, 1892–1900*, edited by Jacqueline Jones Royster. Boston: St. Martin's, 1997. 202–3.

———. "The Reason Why the Colored American Is Not in the World's Columbian Exposition" (1893). In *Selected Works of Ida B. Wells*. New York: Oxford University Press, 1991.

———. *A Red Record*. Chicago: Donohue & Henneberry, 1895.

———. *A Red Record* [1895]. In *Southern Horror and Other Writings: The Anti-Lynching Campaign of Ida B. Wells, 1892–1900*, edited by Jacqueline Jones Royster. Boston: St. Martin's, 1997.

———. *Southern Horrors: Lynch Law in All Its Phases*. New York: New York Age Print, 1892.

Wexler, Laura. *Fire in a Canebrake: The Last Mass Lynching in America*. New York: Scribner, 2003.

White, Tony. "Chance for Death Penalty Bleak," *Baltimore Afro-American* (June 19, 1998).

White, Walter. *Rope and Faggot: A Biography of Judge Lynch.* 1929; repr. Notre Dame, IN: University of Notre Dame Press, 2001.

White, William W. "The Texas Slave Insurrection of 1860," *Southwestern Historical Quarterly* 52.3 (January 1949): 259–85.

Whitfield, Stephen J. *A Death in the Delta: The Story of Emmett Till.* Baltimore: Johns Hopkins University Press, 1988.

Wideman, John Edgar. "Charles Chesnutt and the WPA Narratives: The Oral and Literate Roots of Afro-American Literature." In *The Slave's Narrative,* edited by Charles T. Davis and Henry Louis Gates, Jr. New York: Oxford University Press, 1985. 59–78.

Wilentz, Sean. *The Rise of American Democracy: Jefferson to Lincoln.* New York: W. W. Norton, 2005.

Williamson, Joel. *The Crucible of Race: Black-White Relations in the American South Since Emancipation.* New York: Oxford University Press, 1984.

Winthrop, John. "A Declaration in Defense of an Order of Court Made in May, 1637." In *Puritan Political Ideas,* edited by Edmund S. Morgan. Indianapolis, IN: Bobbs-Merrill, 1965.

Wister, Owen. *The Virginian,* edited by Robert Shulman. 1902; repr. New York: Oxford University Press, 1998.

Wood, Peter H. *Black Majority: Negroes in Colonial South Carolina from 1670 Through the Stono Rebellion.* New York: W. W. Norton, 1974.

Worth, Robert F. "The Legacy of a Lynching," *American Scholar* 67.2 (Spring 1998): 65–66, 74–77.

Wright, George C. *Racial Violence in Kentucky, 1865–1940: Lynchings, Mob Rule, and "Legal Lynchings."* Baton Rouge: Louisiana University Press, 1990.

Wyatt-Brown, Bertram. *Southern Honor: Ethics and Behavior in the Old South.* New York: Oxford University Press, 1982.

Yost, Genevieve. "History of Lynchings in Kansas," *Kansas Historical Quarterly* 2.2 (1933): 182–219.

Zangrando, Robert L. *The NAACP Crusade Against Lynching, 1909–1950.* Philadelphia: Temple University Press, 1980.

INDEX

Age of Lynching, 72–78, 132, 137, 155; distinctive developments in, 75–76; spectacle lynching in, 78–80

American Negro Slave Revolts (Aptheker), 58

Ames, Jessie Daniel, 83, 125

Anti-Lynching Crusaders, 74, 91, 125

Aptheker, Herbert, 58

Armwood, George, 91

Association of Southern Women for the Prevention of Lynching (ASWPL), 7, 19–20, 74, 82–83, 90–91, 113–14, 125

Atlanta Constitution, 71

Atlanta Journal, 70

Atlanta University, 71

Atlantic Monthly, 118

Austin, Stephen F., 41

Avary, Myra Lockett, 66, 110–11, 113

Baltimore Sun, 11

Bancroft, Hubert Howe, 2–4, 6, 17, 43, 46–47

Barrow, Bennet, 55

Bassett, John Spencer, 118–19

Bedford County, Virginia, militia, 23, 25–26, 28, 35, 36, 37, 97

Berryman, Jacob, 11

Bewley, Anthony, 42

Birth of a Nation (Griffiths), ix, 123–24

Black Codes, 59–60

Blair, Lewis, x

Blease, Governor Cole, 7, 115

Booker, Sancho, 54

Boone, Daniel, 31

Boston Commercial Gazette, 31

Boston Gazette, 148

Broderick, David C., 48

Brothers, Thomas, 32

Brown, Charles, 11

Brown, John, 53, 101

Bruce, Philip A., 112–13

Bruton, John F., 119

Buren, Martin Van, 33

Bush, George W., xiv, 6, 51

Campbell, William, 23, 26

Cannidy, Lola, 79

Cash, Wilbur, 52, 53, 55, 66

Chamberlain, Eliza, 11

Chesnutt, Charles, 75

Chicago Tribune, 15, 16, 73, 76

Cincinnati Daily Enquirer, 11

Civil society, 81–88; coercive public in, 86–88, 92–93, 153

Clansman (Dixon), ix

Cleveland Plain-Dealer, 11

Clinton Gazette, 54, 58

Commission on Interracial Cooperation (CIC), 74, 82, 83

Connecticut Courant, 30

Constitutional and Union Guards, 61

Costello, James, 68

Cox, Oliver Cromwell, 85, 137

Crisis (NAACP), 87

Culture of vigilantism, 143, 148–51

Cutler, James, x–xi, 8–13

Daniels, Josephus, 118

Davis, Governor Jeff, 116

Discourse of lynching, xiii, 50, 67–68, 76, 95, 102–3, 126–27, 154; formation of lynching for rape discourse, 96–102; politicians' contributions to, 115–18; Reconstruction as a trope in, 66; work of lynching for rape discourse, 112–14

Dixie After the War (Avary), 110

Dixon, Thomas, Jr., ix, 2, 71

Douglass, Frederick, 73, 102–3, 105, 110–11, 139

DuBois, W. E. B., 71, 142

Duke, Jessie C., 120

Dukes, John, 91

"Eye for an Eye"; or The Fiend and the Fagot, 88

Facts in the Case of the Horrible Murder of Little Myrtle Vance, 84, 88

Felton, Rebecca Lattimer, 7, 82, 117–18, 120

Flaming Sword (Dixon), 71

Forrest, Nathan Bedford, 97

Forsyth, John, 33

Ft. Collins Express, 40, 49

Frank, Leo, 27, 78

Frazier, E. Franklin, 120

Freedman's Bureau, 62, 64

Frontier justice rationale, 25–26, 27–28, 35, 37, 64–65, 97, 100–101, 140, 152

Frontier pattern of collective violence, 38–42

Garnet, H. H., 22, 50

George of Cappadocia, x

Gregory, David, 91

Griffiths, D. W., ix, 123–24

Hale, Matthew, 100

Hammond, James Henry, 33

Harper's Ferry, 53, 54

Hart, Albert Bushnell, 65

Holliday, Billie, 6

Hopkins, Pauline, 111, 144

Hose, Sam, 69–72

House of Burgesses (Virginia), xi–xii, 144, 155

Indianapolis Sentinel, 11

Jackson, Andrew, 29, 33, 36, 97, 101

Jackson, George, 11

Jasper, Texas, 94, 122, 154

Jefferson, Thomas, 23, 25, 44

Jena 6, xiv

Johnson, Andrew, 60

Johnson, James Weldon, 51, 71, 76

Johnson County War, 48–49

Kendall, Amos, 33

Kilgo, John Carlisle, 119

Kilpatrick, Kwame, xiii

Kinston, North Carolina, 10–11

Knights of the White Camelia, 61, 66

Ku Klux Klan, 11–14, 60–61, 63, 67, 77, 81, 98, 102, 123

Ku Klux Klan Act of 1871, 60

Lawless, Judge Luke, 34, 50

Leopard's Spots (Dixon), ix, 71

Lexington Express, 101

Lincecum, Gideon, 42

Lincoln, Abraham, 35

Lippincott's Monthly Magazine, 141

Lost Cause myth, 109–10, 113, 121, 132, 134, 154

Louisiana Advertiser, 30

Lovejoy, Elijah, 34

Lowther, Henry, 67

Lynch, Charles, 23–25, 29, 32, 36, 49, 139

Lynch, John, 31

Lynch Club of Charleston, South
Carolina, 30

Lynch mobs; as agent of civil society,
81–89, 92–93, 153; logic of the mob's
possessing an augmented and
constituted self, 142–43; types of
distinguished, 77

Lynching; capacious and specific
definitions of, 5–6, 18–21, 77;
interpretations of meaning of, 80,
124–36; relationship to state apparatus,
63–66; six different forms of lynching,
138–40; slave laws and, 146–53; slavery
and, 52–58, 138–53; two kinds of
problems in defining, 4–21; working
capacious definition, 20–21

Lynching of Claude Neal (NAACP), 79

Manly, Alexander, 120

McGehee, Tom, 91

McIntosh, Francis, 34

Medill, Joseph, 73

Micheaux, Oscar, 123–24

Miller, Thomas E., 121

Montana Vigilantes, 44–45, 81

Montgomery Herald, 120

Moore, Isaac, 11

Murrell, John, 33

Najibullah, Muhammad, x

National Association for the
Advancement of Colored People
(NAACP), x–xi, 7, 16, 19–20, 74–75,
79, 82, 84, 88, 90–91, 140

National Convention of Colored Men, 22

Neal, Claude, 79–80, 84, 86, 89

New Bedford Mercury, 30–32

*New-Hampshire Patriot and State
Gazette*, 12–13

New-Hampshire Sentinel, 30

New Orleans Daily Picayune, 66

New Public Opinion on Lynching
(ASWPL), 82

New Republic, 75

New York City draft riots, 22, 68

New York Herald, 10, 11, 13

Page, Thomas Nelson, 66, 104–13

Pale Faces, 61

Paris, Texas, 78, 79, 88–89, 107

Parker, John Mack, 92

Philadelphia Enquirer, 31

Pizanthia, José, 44

Plummer, Henry, 44

Popular sovereignty, 1–2, 4, 7, 9, 26–28,
36–37, 44, 49, 59, 63, 89, 97–101, 110,
113, 140–44, 148–49, 152

Popular Tribunals (Bancroft), 2, 43

*Portsmouth Journal of Literature and
Politics*, 30–31

Prosser, Gabriel, 54

Raleigh News and Observer, 119

Raper, Arthur, 83, 86

Reconstruction, 9, 12–17, 19, 36, 51–52,
58–68, 72, 93, 96, 101–2, 105–6, 109,
126, 131, 136, 143, 151, 155

Red Record (Wells), 79

Resistance to lynching, xii

Revolutionary War, 23–28

Roosevelt, Franklin Delano, xiii

Roosevelt, Theodore, 52, 116

St. Louis Observer, 34

San Francisco Vigilance Committees
(1851, 1856), 2, 18, 27, 43–48, 81, 139

Shackleford, James M., 101

Shufeldt, R. W., 108

Slave laws, xi–xii

Sledd, Andrew H., 118–19
Smith, Henry, 71, 78–80, 84–85, 87–88, 107
Smith, Lillian, 121
South Atlantic Quarterly, 118–19
Southern Commission on the Study of Lynching, 74
Southern Literary Messenger, 32
Spanish-American War, 70
Stephens, Alexander H., 57
Stewart, Virgil, 33–34
Stono Rebellion, 55
Stuart, James, 18

Terrell, Mary Church, 73
Terry, Alfred H., 60
Thomas, Clarence, xiii
Thompson, Alice, 11
Thompson, Maurice, 141
Till, Emmett, 7, 92
Tillman, Senator Ben, 7, 115–16
Tourgée, Albion, 10, 14
Truman, Harry, 140
Turner, Nat, 54
Tuskegee Institute, 7, 15, 16, 19, 73, 76, 90–92
Twain, Mark, ix, 14–15

Urban race riots, 61–62

Vicksburg, Mississippi, 28–38, 61, 98, 139
Vicksburg Evening Post, 78
Vicksburg Register, 28–29, 35–36, 98
Vigilance Committee of Thirteen, 44
Vigilante Movements, 42–49
Virginia Medical Monthly, 114
Virginia Slave Statutes, 145–46, 153
Virginian (Wister), 1, 42

Washington, Booker T., 121
Washington, Jesse, 18
Watson, Tom, 27, 101
We Charge Genocide, 140
Wells, Ida B., x–xi, 71, 73, 79, 82, 84, 87, 89, 91, 102–3, 120–21, 126, 137, 139, 144
Wesleyan Christian Advocate, 143
White, Walter, 76, 127, 131
White Brotherhood, 61
White League, 61
Whitecaps of Lawrence County, Mississippi, 76
Wilson, Woodrow, ix
Winthrop, John, 26
Wister, Owen, 1–4, 6, 17, 42, 48–49
Within Our Gates (Micheaux), 123–24
Work, Nathan Monroe, 7, 73
World Almanac, 73